THE GOD OF LOVE'S LETTER *AND* THE TALE OF THE ROSE

The Other Voice in Early Modern Europe:
The Toronto Series, 79

In memory of Albert Rabil, Jr. (1934–2021)

CHRISTINE DE PIZAN

The God of Love's Letter *and* The Tale of the Rose: *A Bilingual Edition*

Edited and translated by
THELMA S. FENSTER *and* CHRISTINE RENO

With
JEAN GERSON
A Poem on Man and Woman
Translated from the Latin by
THOMAS O'DONNELL

Foreword by
JOCELYN WOGAN-BROWNE

Iter Press
NEW YORK | TORONTO

2021

New York and Toronto
IterPress.org

Printed in the United States of America

ISBN 978-1-64959-006-0 (paper)
ISBN 978-1-64959-007-7 (ebook)

Library of Congress Cataloging-in-Publication Data

Names: Christine, de Pisan, approximately 1364–approximately 1431, author. | Fenster, Thelma S., editor, translator. | Reno, Christine, 1944– editor, translator. | O'Donnell, Thomas (Medievalist), translator. | Wogan-Browne, Jocelyn, writer of foreword. | Christine, de Pisan, approximately 1364–approximately 1431. Works. Selections. French (Fenster; Reno) | Christine, de Pisan, approximately 1364–approximately 1431. Works. Selections. English (Fenster; Reno) | Christine, de Pisan, approximately 1364–approximately 1431. Epistre au dieu d'amours. French (Fenster; Reno) | Christine, de Pisan, approximately 1364–approximately 1431. Epistre au dieu d'amours. English (Fenster; Reno) | Christine, de Pisan, approximately 1364–approximately 1431. Dit de la rose. French (Fenster; Reno) | Christine, de Pisan, approximately 1364–approximately 1431. Dit de la rose. English (Fenster; Reno) | Gerson, Jean, 1363–1429. Carmen de viro et muliere. English (O'Donnell)

Title: Christine de Pizan : The god of love's letter and The tale of the rose : a bilingual edition / edited and translated by Thelma S. Fenster, Christine Reno ; with Jean Gerson, A poem on man and woman ; translated by Thomas O'Donnell ; foreword by Jocelyn Wogan-Browne. Other titles: God of love's letter and The tale of the rose : a bilingual edition | Other voice in early modern Europe. Toronto series ; 79.

Description: Bilingual edition. | New York : Iter Press, 2021. | Series: The other voice in early modern Europe : the Toronto series ; 79 | Includes bibliographical references and index. | Poems in Middle French and facing English translation, with introduction and notes in English. | Summary: "Critical editions and translations of two early works by the French proto-feminist author Christine de Pizan addressing the misogynist ideology of the Roman de la Rose and other writings, with a translation of a related Latin work by the contemporary theologian Jean Gerson"-- Provided by publisher.

Identifiers: LCCN 2020009002 (print) | LCCN 2020009003 (ebook) | ISBN 9781649590060 (paperback) | ISBN 9781649590077 (ebook)

Subjects: LCSH: Cupid (Roman deity)--Poetry. | Women--Poetry. | LCGFT: Poetry.

Classification: LCC PQ1575 .A2 2021 (print) | LCC PQ1575 (ebook) | DDC 841/.2--dc23

LC record available at https://lccn.loc.gov/2020009002

LC ebook record available at https://lccn.loc.gov/2020009003

Cover Illustration

Harley MS 4431, fol. 51r. British Library, London.

Cover Design

Maureen Morin, Library Communications, University of Toronto Libraries.

We dedicate this volume

To

Angus J. Kennedy

superb bibliographer, editor, translator, and reader

of Christine de Pizan,

generous scholar and exemplar:

in recognition of Christine Studies' great debt to him

de souverain sens et bon conseil

...et vrai ami

Contents

Acknowledgments

For feminist academics, it is a tenet that scholarship is rarely accomplished by just one, two, or three researchers, and this is especially true in Christine Studies. Without the many modern editions completed and annotated by superb scholars, our tools would have been far fewer and more difficult of access, even with the increasing availability of digitized manuscripts. Without translations into other languages, Christine de Pizan's works would perhaps be unknown to all but a small audience of cognoscenti, the conversation about her the poorer for being excluded from a rich multicultural and multilingual group of admirers and enthusiasts. We are grateful to all those both named and unnamed in this volume for their hard work and many insights.

We were extremely fortunate to have had Angus J. Kennedy as our reader for the press. Our debt to him is enormous, thanks to the corrections and improvements he offered us through his conscientiousness, his great gifts as a Christine reader, and the wealth of knowledge and experience he brought to the task.

We have benefitted from the explanations and insights of Fr. Brian Davies, O.P., and Rev. Robert Imbelli, as we have from the observations of James Laidlaw. William Kibler kindly read an earlier draft of the translations. E. Jeffrey Richards gave us invaluable access to his searchable database of many of Christine's works. Anne Paupert shared key vocabulary with us from the edition of the *Livre de la cité des dames* that she and Claire Le Ninan will soon publish. Barbara Blair helped Thelma Fenster read an article in Dutch. Brigitte Bedos Rezak and Inès Villela-Petit generously provided essential historical and art historical information. We thank Karen Fresco for sharing her unpublished analysis of Westminster manuscript 21. We are especially honored that Jocelyn Wogan-Browne has supplied a Foreword, which so cogently explains why Christine de Pizan remains a crucial voice for our time. We have been deeply grateful for the advice, encouragement, and gracious professionalism of Margaret King, editor for the Other Voice series, and Margaret English-Haskin, Project Manager for Iter. We thank copyeditor Cheryl Lemmens for her thorough review of the typescript, helpful suggestions, and patient willingness to answer our many questions. We warmly thank Anne DeCorte for the critical technical help she gave us.

Abbreviations

Album	Gilbert Ouy, Christine Reno, and Inès Villela-Petit, with Olivier Delsaux and Tania van Hemelryck, eds. and collaborators, and with the advice of James Laidlaw and Marie-Thérèse Gousset. *Album Christine de Pizan.* Turnhout: Brepols, 2012.
BL	British Library
BnF	Bibliothèque nationale de France
Città	*La Città delle dame*, ed. Earl Jeffrey Richards, trans. [into Italian] Patrizia Caraffi, 2nd ed. Milan: Luni, 1998.
CNRS	Centre nationale de la recherche scientifique
DR ed. Hicks	*Le Débat sur Le Roman de la Rose.* Edited by Eric Hicks. Paris: Honoré Champion, 1977.
DR ed. and trans. Hult	*Debate of the "Romance of the Rose."* Edited and translated by David F. Hult. Chicago and London: University of Chicago Press, 2010.
DMF	*Dictionnaire du Moyen Français (1330–1500).* Accessible online at <http://www.atilf.fr/dmf/>.
fol., fols.	folio, folios
Mutacion	*Le Livre de la Mutacion de Fortune.* Edited by Suzanne Solente. 4 vols. Paris: Picard, 1959–66.
Œuvres poétiques	*Œuvres poétiques de Christine de Pisan.* Edited by Maurice Roy. 3 vols. Paris: Firmin Didot, 1886–96.
om.	omitted
RR ed. Lecoy	Guillaume de Lorris and Jean de Meun, *Le Roman de la Rose.* Edited by Félix Lecoy. 3 vols. Paris: Honoré Champion, 1965–70.
RR trans. Horgan	Guillaume de Lorris and Jean de Meun, *The Romance of the Rose.* Translated by Frances Horgan. Oxford: Oxford University Press, 1994.
ST	Thomas Aquinas, *Summa Theologica.* Translated by the Fathers of the English Dominican Province. 3 vols. Latin and English. New York: Benziger Bros., 1947–48.

Foreword

In this book, two highly respected Christine de Pizan scholars bring their literary, linguistic, textual, and codicological expertise to two early works by Christine championing women. The meticulous editions and translations presented here are based on the earliest extant manuscripts of *The God of Love's Letter* and *The Tale of the Rose*, and they are welcome for making it possible to see how Christine subsequently revised the texts. And they are especially welcome, too, for what Fenster and Reno reveal about Christine's early thought. The substantial introduction and textual annotations show that Christine had already absorbed neo-Aristotelian thinking and used it to equip herself with an intellectual paradigm for defending women in unprecedented and systematic terms derived from natural philosophy. The book's new insights increase our understanding of Christine as an intellectual and writer of extraordinary creativity in her rebuttal and replacement of gender models. Fenster and Reno's book makes it clear that Christine's voice is more than ever one we should hear.

The precise timbre of that voice has been a matter of debate since at least the 1970s (a debate that had been part, too, of the nineteenth-century reception of Christine): much thought has been expended on the issue of whether Christine's is a feminist voice. To say that it is can incur the reproach of anachronism, of creating an unhistorical proto-feminism valued because it prefigures later ideologies. But in the face of our own persisting gender inequalities, giving attention—attention of a properly contextualized kind—to the history of women's calling-out of inequity is important. Women, after all, remain one of the largest minoritized groups: that there is historical evidence for their resistance to injustice and prejudice suggests that women have not simply permitted or colluded in their minority status, but that much effort has been put into disabling and confining them. Moreover, amidst the contemporary heterogeneity of feminisms and their complex intersectionalities with issues of race, class, and justice as currently understood, there seems little point in defining Christine in or out of particular models of feminism, although there is every point in understanding as carefully as possible what she is doing.

Both works presented here, *The God of Love's Letter* and *The Tale of the Rose*, are marked by Christine's principled, political, and very well-informed attention to *la cause des femmes*. In one of their most striking contributions, Fenster and Reno focus on how Christine's systematic use of the language of natural law was directed to the defense of women in *The God of Love's Letter*. They pay close, transformative attention to Christine's neo-Aristotelian lexis and show how she repositioned Aristotelian categories of nature, inclination, and habit to create an intellectually authoritative discourse on women's nature that could address academic theory as well as social practice. Christine's *Letter* draws on some of the aristocratic discourse of *courtoisie*, but it is no courtly game. Rather, it depends on an understanding of divine, natural, and human law, in which Cupid's letter is nothing less than the letter of the law. The *Letter* is thus a hitherto overlooked early instance of Christine's capacity to take on and redeploy for her own purposes entire edifices of thought, and also, importantly, the first clue to her interest in developing a virtue ethics applying to women. In this text, as in Christine's later work, scholasticism is alive—and newly salient and newly open to examination—in the vernacular.

The Tale of the Rose, on the other hand, is an experiment in imagining women's autonomous sociopolitical capacity: in the visionary setting up of an Order of the Rose organized and controlled by women for the defense of women, Christine moves beyond similar orders run, with however benevolent intentions, by men in the service of women. She scripts her own legitimate and independent advocacy in the beautiful gold and blue document Loyalty delivers to her by dream-vision as a mandate for disseminating her ideas. Whether the Order was ever set up, how far the poem is a record or not, is in a sense beside the point: the poem, in all its graciousness and aspiration, does its own political work.

As presented and elucidated here, these texts have obvious importance both in themselves and in creating a new account of Christine's canon and its development. And they have contributions to make to many European literatures, Christine de Pizan's works having had such wide dissemination and influence in medieval France, Flanders, Italy, Spain, Portugal, and England. I can, for instance, now put these works before my students of medieval English literature as part of a transregional culture in which Christine's works circulated in French and English amidst the multilingualisms of late medieval England (where Christine's son Jean was sent by her to the Earl of Salisbury, and where he joined Henry IV's court after Salisbury's murder in 1400). The poet Hoccleve's *Lepistre de Cupide*, a medieval English-language adaptation of *The God of Love's Letter*, was first presented together with Christine's *Letter* in a collaboration by Fenster with her colleague Mary Erler some thirty years ago.[1] But Fenster and Reno's new edition and revised translation is needed, excitingly enough, because of the exponential growth in knowledge about Christine and her works: the present volume is both the outcome of and a contribution to new ways of seeing Christine de Pizan. Christine's *Letter* repays comparison with, for example, Chaucer's *Legend of Good Women* (which draws, as Carolyn Collette has shown, on humanist and Aristotelian

1. Thelma S. Fenster and Mary Carpenter Erler, ed. and trans., *Poems of Cupid, God of Love: Christine de Pizan's* Epistre au dieu d'Amours *and* Dit de la Rose; *Thomas Hoccleve's* The Letter of Cupid; *with George Sewell's* The Proclamation of Cupid (Leiden and New York: Brill, 1990).

discourses[2]) and its deployment of Cupid's court. So too, *The Tale of the Rose* is a thought-experiment and a program to conjure with alongside Chaucer's *Wife of Bath's Tale.* Both these latter works consider questions of delegated sovereignty in various ways: in *The Wife of Bath's Tale*, a judicial (not only social) court of women decide a rapist's sentence in a process for which Arthur has transferred oversight to Guenevere. In *The Tale of the Rose,* the genesis of a female order for the protection of women, governed by women themselves, is initially laid out within the social space afforded by one of the Duke of Orléans's Parisian residences, but emerges without the baggage entailed in a male-governed order's service of women. In the Wife's *Tale*, Guenevere's judgment that the rapist-knight may have a year in which he either finds a satisfactory answer to what women want or faces execution is used by Chaucer as a space in which the question of women's rights to any kind of autonomy is opened up and re-entangled with their relations to their husbands (in the rapist-knight's compulsory marriage to his rescuer). The fitness of aristocratic rule and chivalric ideology is dissected both by the authoritative, artisanal, much-married female teller of the Wife's *Tale* and by its principal internal speaker, the powerful self-governing old faery-woman who chooses to marry and to reconstruct the rapist-knight. For Christine, it seems, such questions have already been thought through: the postulate of an order serving women, in however courtly and chivalric a setting, should not depend on an ideology of male chivalric service but on female autonomy for its participants. Like the authoritatively Dantean argument of Chaucer's faery-woman, *The Tale of the Rose* demands a new model in which ethics rather than lineage determines nobility. Launched amidst the proliferation of chivalric orders committed to the defense of women and/but run by men at the turn of the fifteenth century, the *Tale* is a challenging work of experimental social imagination.

In our world's contemporary war on women (nowadays often spearheaded or licensed by various levels of government in the United States of America), medievalist feminist scholars have a signal contribution to make. They can dislodge the routine equation of the Middle Ages with some dark era of misogyny from which we have escaped and progressed. This self-flattering assumption licenses many present abuses, but is historically unverifiable. On an almost weekly basis new studies appear of women's rulership, political influence, sociocultural patronage, and numerous other activities in medieval Europe. Nevertheless, no one would deny that there were structural and influential misogynist constructs in the Middle Ages, and Fenster and Reno sagely include an example here in the shape of Chancellor Jean Gerson's *Poem on Man and Woman* (lucidly translated by Thomas O'Donnell). It is a splendid way of illuminating the complexity of what Christine was up against. For all that Gerson gave considerable thought to pastoral writing

2. Carolyn P. Collette, *Rethinking Chaucer's* Legend of Good Women (York: York Medieval Press, 2014).

for women in his letters to his sisters, anyone who has ever been "mansplained" will immediately see in his *Poem* how apparent reasonableness and logic rest on a reflex structural misogyny that perceives no need to examine its own premises. Readers will feel, too, the frustrating intricacy with which unconscious privilege and unexamined "authoritative" pronouncements are intertwined. The difficulties Christine takes on in dis-articulating all this and finding a basis on which rational and equitable discussion can proceed is vivid in Fenster and Reno's juxtaposition of her *Letter*'s early defense of women with Gerson's.

It would be foolhardy to think that these difficulties have been left behind in our world, or that Christine no longer provides illuminating models. Current structural misogynies may be differently inflected, but are no less crippling and dangerous. It ill beseems any modern society or state that grudges or attacks full autonomy for its female citizens to plume itself as against the Middle Ages, let alone to appropriate the Middle Ages as a licensing origin point for its own barbaric practices. In spite of legal and customary conceptions of rule as male and men as the governing class, medieval Europe was a domain in which women ruled principalities, realms, and counties, and where, as the remarkable works made freshly available here show, they could rule in matters of intellect, vision, and creativity.

JOCELYN WOGAN-BROWNE*

* Jocelyn Wogan-Browne is Thomas F. X. and Theresa Mullarkey Emerita Chair in Literature at Fordham University, New York. Most recently, she has co-edited and co-translated, with Thelma Fenster and Delbert Russell, *Vernacular Literary Theory from the French of Medieval England: Texts and Translations, c. 1120–c. 1450* (Woodbridge, UK, and Rochester, NY: D. S. Brewer, 2016). Her current book project focuses on women and multilingualism in late medieval England.

Introduction

Christine de Pizan and the Other Voice

Christine de Pizan (ca. 1365–ca. 1430) was born in Italy but moved to the court of King Charles V of France at the age of about four, after her father, Tommaso da Pizzano, became the king's astrologer and physician. She married at fifteen (and happily), but was a widow by the age of twenty-five; in addition, her father had died a year or so before her husband. Christine turned to writing to support herself and her family, now consisting of a son, daughter, mother, and niece.[1] She wrote the major portion of her work between 1399 and 1410, although certain of her lyric poems date from before that period; it is remarkable that a good part of her output was completed in the first five or six years of the fifteenth century. The following (partial) list gives a sense of Christine's extraordinary accomplishment. In addition to hundreds of short poems, there were five long "courtly" poems: the *Dit de Poissy* (*Tale of Poissy*), 1400; *Debat de deux amans* (*Debate of Two Lovers*), 1400; the *Trois Jugemens* (*Three Judgments*), 1400;[2] the *Dit de la pastoure* (*Tale of the Shepherdess*), 1403; and the *Duc des vrais amans* (*Duke of True Lovers*), possibly 1405.[3] Other works addressed various subjects in verse or prose, or sometimes in mixed verse and prose. These included her letters in the Debate of the *Rose* (see pp. 10–11); several lengthy, learned works such as the *Epistre Othea* (*Epistle of Othea*), 1400–1401; *Chemin de longue etude* (*Path of Long Learning*), 1402–1403; *Mutacion de Fortune* (*Mutability of Fortune*), 1403; *Fais et bonnes meurs du sage roy Charles V* (*Deeds and Good Practices of the Wise King Charles V*), 1404; *Cité des dames* (*City of Ladies*), ca. 1405; *l'Advision Cristine* (*Christine's Vision*), 1405–1406; *Prodhommie de l'homme / Prudence* (*Man's Integrity / Prudence*), 1405–1406;[4] and *Corps de Policie* (*Body Politic*), 1407;[5] a book on warfare, the *Fais d'armes et de chevalerie* (*Feats of Arms and of Chivalry*), 1410, as well as the *Enseignemens moraulx* (*Moral Teachings*), 1399–1402, and *Cent Ballades d'amant*

1. A second son died some time before October 2, 1402, the date of a letter Christine wrote in the Debate of the *Rose* in which she states that "je ay ung seul filz" (I have only one son). See *Le Débat sur le Roman de la Rose*, ed. Eric Hicks (Paris: Honoré Champion, 1977; rpt. Geneva: Slatkine, 1996), 128.

2. The most recent editions of these three poems are in *The Love Debate Poems of Christine de Pizan: Le Livre du Debat de deux amans, Le Livre des Trois Jugemens, Le Livre du Dit de Poissy*, ed. Barbara K. Altmann (Gainesville: University Press of Florida, 1998).

3. We have only a relative date for this work: it preceded the *Trois Vertus*, traditionally dated 1405; in this latter work (Bk. 1, ch. 26) Christine writes that she had already included the dame de la Tour's letter against wifely adultery in the *Duc des vrais amans*.

4. Neither one of these two nearly identical works has been edited.

5. A new English translation of the *Corps de Policie*, by Angus J. Kennedy, is forthcoming in The Other Voice series.

et de dame (*Hundred Ballades of a Lover and Lady*), possibly 1407–1410.[6] Three devotional works were written between 1402 and 1403: *Oraison Nostre Dame* (*Prayer on Our Lady*); *Quinze Joyes de Nostre Dame rimees* (*Fifteen Joys of Our Lady in Rhyme*); and *Oroison de la vie et passion de Nostre Seigneur* (*Prayer on Our Lord's Life and Passion*). The number and variety of Christine's compositions over such a short period indicate the depth of her learning before and after her husband's death. She herself observed that between 1399 and 1405 she wrote fifteen major volumes, not counting specific shorter narratives, and that together they made up seventy substantial quires.[7] Her need for financial support was pressing, but she also possessed an intellectual drive that required expression.

Among Christine's early writings were six works about "woman." The *Epistre au dieu d'Amours* (*The God of Love's Letter*), 1399, introduces issues to be pursued at greater length later, in the much longer *Cité des dames*. The *Dit de la Rose* (*Tale of the Rose*), 1402, complements the *Epistre*, since both rebuke, in their separate ways, the misogyny of the influential thirteenth-century vernacular poem, the *Roman de la Rose* (*Romance of the Rose*), which itself dealt ironically with some principal tenets of contemporary natural law. Her censure of the *Roman* became even more pointed during the epistolary exchange known as the Debate of the *Rose*, which began before 1402; Christine's letters in the Debate further emphasize many points in her defense of women. The *Livre des Trois Vertus* (*Book of the Three Virtues*), ca. 1405, also known as the *Trésor de la cité des dames* (*Treasury of the City of Ladies*), is an advice manual for women of all stations in society, including poor women. In her final work, the *Ditié de Jehanne d'Arc* (*Poem about Joan of Arc*), 1429, a jubilant Christine celebrates Joan's deeds.

When Christine wrote the *Epistre*, her first narrative poem, she was already known in court circles for her lyric poems.[8] In some of them she had touched on themes that would reappear in the *Epistre*, such as pretense and betrayal in love, but those were motifs made familiar in courtly literature. Not until she wrote the *Epistre* could readers begin to see the larger, political resonance of Christine's campaign for women's dignity. Contemporary theology held that, at the level of

6. The *Fais d'armes* was translated into English by William Caxton in 1489; the French text, however, has not been published since 1527 (misleadingly titled *L'Arbre de batailles et fleur de chevalerie* [Paris: Philippe Le Noir]). See *The Book of Fayttes of Armes and of Chyualrye*, translated and printed by William Caxton from the French original by Christine de Pisan (London: Published for the Early English Text Society by Humphrey Milford, Oxford University Press, 1932; reissued with corrections, 1937).

7. *Le Livre de l'Advision Cristine*, ed. Christine Reno and Liliane Dulac (Paris: Honoré Champion, 2001), Bk. 3, ch. 10.

8. Note on the translation of the title: in medieval French the preposition *a* (*à*) was often used to indicate possession, and the construction still exists in modern French in such expressions as "à moi" ("mine") or "la femme aux cheveux blonds" ("the blond-haired woman"). The *Epistre au dieu d'Amours* meant a letter "belonging to," thus by, the God of Love.

the soul, all humans were equal, but once incarnate, men were leaders and women their helpmeets. Christine never openly contested that hierarchy, but she certainly objected to its abuses: men could vilify women with impunity, for in practice women had little redress against an entrenched system of male hegemony. She argued for women's ability to understand subtle thinking, which provided the capacity for ethical behavior. Her own experience—her desire for knowledge, and the education to which it led her—was probative, but it also revealed to her a long history of men's writing against women, and it gave her the tools with which to contest the misuse of masculine privilege. The two poems presented here in new editions and translations, the *Epistre* and *Dit*, take their place as her first public challenge to misogynous discourse and to the slighting behavior men could practice toward women.

Modern facing-page editions and translations of both poems first appeared in 1990, in *Poems of Cupid*.[9] In undertaking these second modern editions and translations, we have hoped to offer work that benefits from the great strides that have been made in Christine Studies since that time. *Poems of Cupid* featured the latest manuscript witnesses for each poem, but we have chosen here to produce the earliest texts of the two poems in order to offer a "genetic" edition of each—that is, an edition that traces the evolution of the poems written by the author as they were worked upon and recopied. We believe it is crucial to understand Christine's uniquely comprehensive approach to her writing, and to see her at work adjusting her text, making corrections or stylistic improvements (evidence of her own correcting hand appears in all fifty-four of the extant manuscripts now recognized as having been produced under her supervision); sometimes, too, she added or removed items in the interests of political judiciousness.[10] Her involvement with every aspect of a text's or manuscript's production invites us to see the person Christine, an engaged thinker and writer, but also a uniquely self-sufficient businesswoman and publicist for her ideas.

While nearly all her writing deserves a place in the Other Voice series, her defenses of "woman" especially, because they speak in the exceptional voice of a woman publicly defending women against the excesses of fifteenth-century androcentric culture, bring us a special, lone Other Voice speaking up against a vast chorus that might well have preferred her to remain silent about women's rights.

9. *Poems of Cupid, God of Love: Christine de Pizan's* Epistre au dieu d'Amours *and* Dit de la Rose; *Thomas Hoccleve's* The Letter of Cupid; *with George Sewell's* The Proclamation of Cupid, ed. and trans. Thelma Fenster and Mary Carpenter Erler (Leiden: Brill, 1990).

10. See in particular James C. Laidlaw, "Christine de Pizan: An Author's Progress," *Modern Language Review* 78 (1983): 532–50; Laidlaw, "Christine de Pizan: A Publisher's Progress," *Modern Language Review* 82 (1987): 35–75; and Gilbert Ouy, Christine Reno, and Inès Villela-Petit, with Olivier Delsaux and Tania van Hemelryck, eds. and collaborators, and with the advice of James Laidlaw and Marie-Thérèse Gousset, *Album Christine de Pizan* (Turnhout: Brepols, 2012).

Background: The Roman de la Rose

The years between 1399 and 1402 were an important moment in French literary history and in the reception history of a celebrated thirteenth-century poem, the *Roman de la Rose*, whose reach extended far beyond its time and place. Its misogynist tenor dismayed and angered Christine, and although she was not the first or the only French intellectual to find fault with the work, she was the first to record objections from a woman's point of view to its deeply degrading view of women. In between writing the *Epistre* and the *Dit*, in a period of a little over a year from June–July 1401 to October 1402,[11] Christine participated in the Debat du *Roman de la Rose* (Debate of the *Romance of the Rose*), an exchange of letters in prose in which she explained to a group of her humanist contemporaries why she found the *Roman* objectionable. She met with their condemnation for her views, but she never changed her opinion, moving on to significantly expand her ideas about women and the need for their defense.

The *Roman* was begun ca. 1230 by Guillaume de Lorris, who wrote the first approximately 4,000 verses, and it was continued and terminated in the 1270s by Jean de Meun, who added nearly 18,000 verses.[12] Together the two sections recount, in allegorized terms, the steps in the conquest of a rose. The two parts vary in character, with modern criticism sometimes referring to Lorris's portion

11. See the list of Debate documents and their dates in *Le Débat sur le Roman de la Rose*, ed. Hicks (cited in note 1 above), lii–liv; all citations here are taken from this edition. A newer edition by Andrea Valentini provides the Debate letters in the format Christine herself chose for presentation to the Queen and to the Provost of Paris—that is, in a dossier prominently featuring her own letters. See *Le Livre des Epistres du debat sus le* Rommant de la Rose (Paris: Classiques Garnier, 2014; rpt. 2016). An English translation based on the Hicks edition is the *Debate of the "Romance of the Rose,"* ed. and trans. David F. Hult (Chicago and London: University of Chicago Press, 2010). A modern French translation is that of *Le Débat sur le Roman de la Rose*, trans. Virginie Greene (Paris: Honoré Champion, 2006). On Christine's feelings and stance in the Debate and elsewhere in her writing, see the perceptive comments of Jean-Claude Mühlethaler, "Désir et étonnement: de l'auteur au lecteur. Emotion, écriture et lecture au temps de Christine de Pizan," *Le Moyen français* 75 (2014): 19–42.

12. All citations here are taken from Guillaume de Lorris and Jean de Meun, *Le Roman de la Rose*, ed. Félix Lecoy. 3 vols. (Paris: Honoré Champion, 1965–70). Citations in English are from *The Romance of the Rose*, trans. Frances Horgan (Oxford: Oxford University Press, 1994) The *Roman* has garnered a considerable modern body of criticism which is dealt with to 2017 in these bibliographies: Heather M. Arden, ed., *The Roman de la Rose: An Annotated Bibliography* (New York and London: Garland, 1993); Herman Braet, *Nouvelle bibliographie du* Roman de la Rose (Louvain, Paris, and Bristol, CT: Peeters, 2017); and Catherine Bel and Herman Braet, eds., *De la Rose: Texte, image, fortune* (Louvain, Paris, and Dudley, MA: Peeters, 2006). See also the *Roman de la Rose* Digital Library (a joint project of Johns Hopkins University Sheridan Libraries and the Bibliothèque nationale de France) at the Digital Library of Medieval Manuscripts: <http://dlmm.library.jhu.edu/en/romandelarose/>. A brief review of recent trends in *Rose* scholarship is provided by Jonathan Morton in "Etat présent: *Le Roman de la Rose*," *French Studies* 69 (2015): 79–86.

as "courtly" and to Meun's as "scholastic." In Lorris's opening section, a young nobleman, called Lover, falls asleep and dreams that he has set out walking one May morning and has arrived at the Garden of Pleasure. Its exterior wall features portraits of figures such as Avarice, Hatred, Old Age, Poverty, Sorrow, and the like, all personifications of qualities or traits antithetical to love and positioned to face away from the garden. Once the dreamer has been received into the garden by its gatekeeper, Idleness, he meets the personifications Love, Courtesy, Joy, Pleasant Looks, and others. Strolling about, the dreamer reaches the fountain of Narcissus, named for the handsome young man of myth who fell in love with his own reflection in a pool, not realizing that it was only an image: fixated by the sight, and the victim of a love that can never be returned, Narcissus loses the will to live. In the *Roman*, however, the dreamer gazes into the fountain and sees one special rosebud reflected in a pair of crystals at the fountain floor. Wounded by Love's arrows, he falls in love with the rosebud and accepts Love's commandments. The stages in his courtship of the rose are then told through the activities of allegories such as Fair Welcome and Friend, on the one hand, and Jealous Husband, Shame, and *Dangier*, or Resistance/Rebuff, on the other. Reason warns against love's follies, but Lover is unpersuaded. He is prevented from reaching the rose by Jealousy, who builds a castle around the garden and sets Old Woman to guard the door—but at that, Lorris's poem stops.

When Jean de Meun continues the narrative, he adds lengthy speeches by various personifications. Reason counsels Lover to abandon his pursuit of the rose, but Lover rejects her advice. Friend counsels on ways to seduce the rose, and the Jealous Husband, commenting on marriage, lambastes wives for being faithless and meretricious. Old Woman recommends that women take many lovers, and fleece them while they can. Further escapades and speeches follow. Eventually, Love's army, abetted by Venus, comes to Lover's aid. They pledge to defeat Chastity, which pleases Nature, for she confesses to her priest Genius her regret at having created man, who can be mulishly reluctant to perpetuate the species. Genius utters a sermon condemning those who fail to use the organs given by Nature to further the human species. Lover finally succeeds in entering the castle and taking the rose.

Christine's displeasure with the *Roman* stemmed in part from Jean de Meun's failure to provide clear and straightforward moral instruction, as was expected of medieval works. She argued instead that it did just the opposite, teaching readers improper behavior. Today, the *Roman* has many admirers, but their appreciation of the poem is not always without reservation. The poem's conclusion still gives pause: there, Lover achieves sexual union with the silent rose, for whom refusal has never seemed an option. It is therefore not surprising that many see in this a depiction of rape.[13] Further, we should understand that for another group, such

13. For Rosalind Brown-Grant this is a depiction of "allegorical rape." See *Christine de Pizan and the Moral Defence of Women: Reading Beyond Gender* (Cambridge: Cambridge University Press, 1999), 35.

a resolution would have been titillating and thus unacceptable in a work of this kind. Christine herself points out that upon hearing the conclusion of the *Roman*, women would blush to hear the "horrible things included in the ending."[14]

Christine further objected to perceived obscenities in the *Roman*, such as references to genitalia. This earned her the accusation of prudishness. As a writer cognizant of contemporary literary aesthetics, however, she objected not to sexually explicit language per se, but rather to its jarring use, as she saw it, in the mouths of Reason and Genius in particular. Medieval literary theory called for figures to speak in character, a point that would become key in the Debate of the *Rose*. Equally, she singled out the ending of the poem as especially heinous, for she believed a text should conclude explicitly upon a summing-up, "in the juridical sense," as Rosalind Brown-Grant has observed. She deemed the final chapter of the *Roman* to be "particularly pernicious" because the rape "is the final impression that the reader will take away from the text."[15]

In an otherwise impressively talky work, the silent rose is the only figure never to speak. (Had the rose been endowed with a voice, what might she have said? Given Lover's strenuous efforts to reach her, the *Roman* suggests that she repeatedly rebuffed him, but the medieval reader is expected to accept that men play the dominant role in species preservation, and if a woman must be forced, so be it.) To the extent that the rose can be said to exist at all, it is in the dreamer's imaginary, where "woman" is not really "a woman" at all; as a rose, she is a traditional, colloquial symbol for the vagina, woman synecdochally reduced to her genitalia. A vagina that spoke could of course undermine the portrait Jean de Meun wanted to provide of an acquiescing figure who is an unprotesting means of gratification and insemination. But the *Roman* is after all a dream, and those who wish to excuse the depiction of forcible sex upon which it ends sometimes invoke the dream framework, in which there can be no true or false. The rose's fate is driven by Lover's aspirations, but it should be noted that he too seems impelled by textual forces beyond his power to resist.

In the end, the plethora of voices in the *Roman* debating and contradicting one another results in a critical stalemate: just what is the *Roman* teaching? A precise answer remains elusive to this day, although it has been much discussed in the scholarly literature. Perhaps, as Noah Guynn suggests, the poem's popularity

---

See also Noah D. Guynn, "Authorship and Sexual/Allegorical Violence in Jean de Meun's *Roman de la Rose*," in *Allegory and Sexual Ethics in the High Middle Ages* (New York: Palgrave Macmillan, 2007), 137–70. For a succinct, fuller synopsis of the *Roman*, see Sarah Kay, *The Romance of the Rose* (London: Grant and Cutler, 1995), 117–19.

14. *DR* ed. and trans. Hult, 179.

15. Brown-Grant further suggests that Christine may be echoing Dante's advice that what the speaker most hopes to convey should be placed at the end of a talk; for discussion of these points, see Brown-Grant, *Moral Defence of Women*, 30–43.

(there are nearly three hundred surviving manuscripts) can be explained by its "encyclopaedic range of themes and styles and its openness to diverse interpretive approaches."[16]

Pushing Back 1: The Epistre au dieu d'Amours

The God of Love's "excommunication" of men who deceive women, a document with elements of a diplomatic act,[17] puts the reader in a royal court at a key moment. In the illustration in one of the manuscripts in which the *Epistre* appears, BnF fr. 835, an image at fol. 45r shows the god seated outdoors handing a piece of folded parchment to a young nobleman kneeling at his side. In British Library manuscript Harley 4431, known as the Queen's Manuscript, Cupid is presented at fol. 51r seated in a garden, surrounded by trees; again, a young nobleman kneels to his right and receives the letter. This imaginary *locus amoenus* presents a kindly but authoritative god who has presumably descended to an earthly location in order to hand the letter over to a human messenger, who will then disseminate its contents.[18] Both illustrations feature birds flying overhead.[19] Each illustrator interprets this pleasant scene differently, however. In the Paris manuscript the

16. Noah D. Guynn, "*Le Roman de la Rose*," in *The Cambridge Companion to Medieval French Literature*, ed. Simon Gaunt and Sarah Kay (Cambridge: Cambridge University Press, 2008), 48–62, at 48.

17. Tania van Hemelryck notes that the *Epistre*'s format resembles the parts of a diplomatic act: the *suscription*, which names the author of the act (Cupid), vv. 1–2; the *adresse*, which names those for whom the letter is intended (all Cupid's loyal subjects), v. 6, and is followed by the *salut*, or greeting, v. 7; the *notification* ("We make it publicly known"), v. 8; the *exposé*, or detailing of the reason(s) that led to the decision to prepare the *Letter* (we have received complaints from injured ladies), vv. 9ff; the *dispositif*, or details of the final judgment, the juridical decision, vv. 775–95; the statement of time and place (*date*), vv. 796–800; the final signature (*salut final*), vv. 825–26; the list of witnesses (*signes de validation*), vv. 801ff.; and finally the formulas of authentification (*formules d'authentification*), including, in one manuscript text of the poem (BnF, fr. 835), the anagram Christine creates for her own name, *Creintis*, "Fearful." See "*L'Epistre au dieu d'amours* ou 'l'origine du monde' auctorial de Christine de Pizan," *Le Moyen français* 78–79 (2016): 241–54. See also Earl Jeffrey Richards, "'*Seulette a part*'—The 'Little Woman on the Sidelines' Takes Up Her Pen: The Letters of Christine de Pizan," in *Dear Sister: Medieval Women and the Epistolary Genre*, ed. Karen Cherewatuk and Ulrike Wiethaus (Philadelphia: University of Pennsylvania Press, 1993), 139–70. For a bibliography of medieval treatises including those on letter-writing, see James J. Murphy, *Medieval Rhetoric: A Select Bibliography*, 2nd ed. (Toronto: University of Toronto Press, 1989).

18. At the conclusion of the *Livre des Trois Vertus* (Bk. 3, ch. [14]) a manual of advice for women, Christine sends her work out to be disseminated in all countries.

19. In a recent personal communication, Inès Villela-Petit associates the bird motif with the renewal of spring (*reverdie*), a theme integral to courtly lyric poems of that genre and consonant with the *Epistre*'s setting in the month of May. Both miniatures feature three white birds; the Queen's Manuscript shows a fourth, a green ring-necked parakeet, which expresses contemporary aristocratic interest in exotic fauna.

colors are soft, light greens and pinks, evoking love's sweetness. In the British Library manuscript, colors are strong: Cupid's vermilion mantle rather brings to mind burning passion.

The *Epistre* centers on a number of seemingly unrelated themes whose common thread is that they respond to prevailing negative generalizations about women. These would have been familiar to the medieval reader but the poem's modern public must often infer what they were from the defenses the God of Love develops. Several items in the defense are not original, having appeared in works by other writers,[20] but Christine breathes life into them through her evocation of lively scenes: overachieving suitors bustling about in their created personas; lazy knights, ensconced before warming fires, boasting about their amorous conquests and slyly bringing the company around to "forcing" the information out of them—these are psychologically resonant "slice of life" portraits designed to be penetrating, mocking, and humorous.

To the reproach that women are faithless and deceitful, the God of Love retorts in several ways.[21] Men are duplicitous (that is, as the word suggests, they practice a form of "doubleness" or two-facedness), whereas women are "simple" (not simple-minded) in that they are not duplicitous and do not think about or practice doubleness.[22] It is women who are thus deceived by men, who instead should be kind to them, for they are their mothers, helpmeets, and nurturers.[23]

20. See Alcuin Blamires, *The Case for Women in Medieval Culture* (Oxford: Clarendon Press; New York: Oxford University Press, 1997), esp. "The Formal Case: The Corpus," 19–49, and "The Formal Case: Origins, Procedures," 50–69.

21. Tracy Adams argues that the *Epistre* in particular depicts the crisis in France in 1399, and that its God of Love is "helpless" and "flummoxed," an implied parallel to the ailing King Charles VI (1368–1422), whose grave mental illness imperiled France. See *The Life and Afterlife of Isabeau of Bavaria* (Baltimore: Johns Hopkins University Press, 2010), 51–52. It is true that in their opening complaint the women stress a decline in chivalry in France especially, but nothing in the god's portrait suggests a feeble or ineffectual king. Indeed, scholars generally agree that Christine intended to rewrite Cupid as an improved version of the *Roman*'s Cupid, in keeping with the remedial tenor of the god's letter as a whole. Comparison with a king of France is not impossible, but if so, this God of Love would seem rather to recall Charles V, the "wise king," whom Christine so admired for "doing the right thing," as Cupid does here when he "excommunicates" false lovers.

22. On simplicity as a "stance" (French *posture*) that Christine adopts, see Claire-Marie Schertz, "Autour de Christine de Pizan: Entre lyrisme courtois et engagement politique," *COnTEXTES* 13 (2013), <https://journals.openedition.org/contextes/5798>. See also Thelma S. Fenster, "Strong Voices, Weak Minds? The Defenses of Eve by Isotta Nogarola and Christine de Pizan, Who Found Themselves in Simone de Beauvoir's Situation," in *Strong Voices, Weak History: Early Women Writers and Canons in England, France and Italy*, ed. Pamela Benson and Victoria Kirkham (Philadelphia: University of Pennsylvania Press, 2005), 58–77; and Fenster, "*Simplece* et sagesse: Christine de Pizan et Isotta Nogarola sur la culpabilité d'Eve," in *Une femme de lettres au Moyen Age: Etudes autour de Christine de Pizan*, ed. Liliane Dulac and Bernard Ribémont (Orléans: Paradigme, 1995), 481–93.

23. See Blamires, "Honoring Mothers," in *The Case for Women*, 70–95.

Women cannot deceive men because they do not do what men do: Jason betrayed Medea (vv. 435–42) and Aeneas abandoned Dido (vv. 443–58), but Penelope remained faithful to Ulysses during his long absence, in spite of being pressed by suitors (vv. 459–64).

The argument against women could swing two ways, however. If women were not clever enough to be duplicitous, then they were too gullible (Eve of Genesis) and gave themselves too readily (but if that is the case, the god asks [vv. 391–404], why must they be pursued so energetically in the *Roman*?). Women may well be trusting—perhaps too trusting—but they were created by God without the aggressive traits that cause war and destruction, with the result that they don't bring grievous harm to people or nations (vv. 643–50). Turning the tables against the commonplace medieval accusation that women gossip, the God of Love shows that men also gossip, and their gossip does more harm: because of men's greater influence and the sexual nature of their talk, women become the victims of men's boastful indiscretions or downright fabrications, sacrificed in what is fundamentally a contest between men.

Clerical culture is also to blame. The God of Love explains that clerics write books about women's purported ills and teach their young pupils to be wary of them. Ovid's *Remedia Amoris* (*Remedies for Love*), a treatise on ways to fall out of love that relies upon unappealing descriptions of women, was often used as a Latin-language textbook.[24] But clerics, Christine's God of Love says, are among the most lascivious of men: they seek only wanton women with interests like their own. They do not know honorable women, so how can they purport to speak about *all* women? Further, old men blame women in order to deflect attention from their own impotence. Even if there are some evil women, as a matter of principle women as a group should not be blamed (vv. 651–58).

One defense advanced by the God of Love reaches back into theological commentary on the Creation story. Clerics conceded certain "privileges" to Eve, and thus to women: for example, women were made of bone, a finer material than the earth from which Adam was formed (vv. 596–601); man was born outside the earthly paradise, whereas Eve was the first to be born inside it (vv. 602–6).[25] Incongruously familiar with the story of Jesus, Cupid further says that the biblical books about Jesus speak only good of women (vv. 558–73), and it was a woman who was worthy of carrying the son of God (v. 578). Truly noble men, such as the knights Othon de Grandson and Hutin de Vermeilles, would not dream of

24. See Elisabeth Pellegrin, "Les 'Remedia amoris' d'Ovide: Texte scolaire médiéval," *Bibliothèque de l'Ecole des Chartes* 115 (1957): 172–79; and James G. Clark, Frank T. Coulson, and Kathryn L. McKinley, eds., *Ovid in the Middle Ages* (Cambridge and New York: Cambridge University Press, 2011).

25. See Blamires, "Eve and the Privileges of Women," in *The Case for Women*, 97–125.

defaming women; they should serve as exemplars (vv. 225–32, 233–39); this "naming of profeminine men," in Blamires's view, "is a new development."[26]

Pushing Back 2: The Debate of the Roman de la Rose: *Voices Carry*

Some two years after composing the *Epistre* Christine's criticism of the *Roman* took a different turn. She entered into an epistolary exchange with the humanists Jean de Montreuil, Provost of Lille (1354–1418), and Gontier Col (ca. 1350–1418), joined by Pierre Col, Gontier's brother and canon of Notre-Dame de Paris, all of whom admired the *Roman*. Jean Gerson (1363–1429), chancellor of the University of Paris, supported Christine's view of the *Roman*, and he wrote against it in his *Traité contre le Roman de la Rose* (*Treatise against the Romance of the Rose*).[27] It is not known what events occurred in the roughly two years between the *Epistre* and the first Debate letter. It appears that in 1399 Jean de Montreuil had not yet read the *Roman*; when he did, he wrote in praise of it, circulating his appreciation in a now-lost treatise. In his letters, he was high-handed with Christine, refusing, as Emma Cayley has underscored, to address her directly, and referring to her through a third party as "she."[28] In a Latin letter of 1402 sent to an unidentified poet—perhaps Eustache Deschamps (ca. 1340–1404/5), or the Benedictine cleric Honorat Bovet (ca. 1340–ca. 1410)—Montreuil compared her to the Greek courtesan Leontium, a pupil of Epicurus who had dared to write against "the great philosopher," Theophrastus.[29] Christine did not flinch in her response to Montreuil's slur: "may it not be attributed to folly, arrogance, or presumption that I, a woman, dare to reprimand and refute so subtle an author [Jean de Meun] and to divest his work of its renown, when he, just one man, dared undertake to defame and

26. Blamires, *The Case for Women*, 45.

27. In addition to the English translation of all the Debate documents in *DR* ed. and trans. Hult, Gerson's treatise against the *Romance* is translated in *Jean Gerson: Early Works*, trans. Brian Patrick McGuire (New York: Paulist Press, 1998), 378–98. For a fuller understanding of Montreuil and the circles in which he moved, see Gilbert Ouy, "Paris, l'un des principaux foyers de l'humanisme en Europe au début du XVe siècle," *Bulletin de la Société de l'Histoire de Paris et de l'Ile de France* 94–95 (1967–68), 71–98; Ezio Ornato, *Jean Muret et ses amis Nicolas de Clamanges et Jean de Montreuil: Contribution à l'étude des rapports entre les humanistes de Paris et ceux d'Avignon (1394–1420)* (Geneva and Paris: Droz, 1969), and André Combes, *Jean de Montreuil et le chancelier Gerson: Contribution à l'histoire des rapports de l'humanisme et de la théologie en France au début du XVe siècle* (Paris: J. Vrin, 1942).

28. Emma Cayley, *Debate and Dialogue: Alain Chartier in His Cultural Context* (Oxford: Clarendon Press; New York: Oxford University Press, 2006), 78.

29. *DR* ed. Hicks, 42–43; *DR* ed. and trans. Hult, 103. After Aristotle fled from Athens, Theophrastus succeeded him at the Lyceum. Leontium's criticisms of the philosopher were called out by Cicero, who attacked the Epicureans for having "emboldened a loose woman like Leontium to write a book refuting Theophrastus." See Cicero, *De natura deorum*, ed. and trans. Harris Rackham (London: William Heinemann, 1933), 1.33.93.

condemn without exception an entire sex."[30] Montreuil was also embarrassed to be writing in the vernacular instead of Latin, the language deemed appropriate to humanist reflection and dialogue;[31] it fell to the Col brothers to respond further in French. Christine herself glossed the Debate as *non haineux* (not vicious), but her adversaries could be both condescending and rude.[32]

Christine would have caused consternation among her opponents when she prepared a dossier of the Debate letters and sent it to Queen Isabeau (ca. 1370–1435), wife of King Charles VI, and to Guillaume de Tignonville (d. 1414), Provost of Paris—especially since the dossier included, along with the dedicatory letter to the queen and one to Tignonville, only her own letters and two by Gontier Col. Of her own letters, the lengthy letter to Montreuil, a rebuttal of his praise of the *Roman*, may have been indebted to the genre of the newly developing vernacular prose treatise, at which Christine was trying her hand.[33] Andrea Valentini has persuasively argued that Christine probably saw her collected letters in the Debate as an integral literary work on their own.[34] (By 1402 she had fully launched her literary career and had every reason to think of herself as an author: in addition to her collected lyric poetry, she had completed three courtly narratives—the *Dit de Poissy*, the *Deux Amans*, and the *Trois Jugemens*—as well as the learned *Epistre Othea*, was working on the nearly 24,000-line universal history, the *Mutacion de Fortune*,[35] and was considering or had already begun the *Chemin de longue étude*, another learned composition.) It is also plausible that her exclusion of Pierre Col's letter of late summer 1402, with its forceful response to her arguments, was deliberate.[36]

Implicit to the Debate is the simulated orality of the *Roman* itself, voice, or voices. Christine regarded the *Roman*'s many contradictory voices as a failure to

30. *DR* ed. Hicks, 22; *DR* ed. and trans. Hult, 63.

31. *DR* ed. Hicks, 30–31; *DR* ed. and trans. Hult, 65. See also Valentini's comments in *Epistres du debat sus le* Rommant de la Rose, 119 and n. 25.

32. Nor was such condescension restricted to the Middle Ages. In 1969, John Fleming called Christine a "minor poet" whose role in the debate was "rather inflated . . . by modern feminists and should probably not be taken too seriously." See *The* Roman de la Rose: *A Study in Allegory and Iconography* (Princeton, NJ: Princeton University Press, 1969), 47. Fleming's comment bears witness to the ground Christine Studies have covered since he wrote.

33. Virginie Greene's suggestion in "Le débat sur le *Roman de la Rose* comme document d'histoire littéraire et morale," *Cahiers de recherches médiévales et humanistes/Journal of Medieval and Humanistic Studies* (*CRMH*) 14 Spécial (2007): 297–311, at 297 (accessible online at <https://journals.openedition.org/crm/2586>). Christine's letter to Montreuil was dated summer 1401 (*DR* ed. Hicks, 11–22; *DR* ed. and trans. Hult, 50–63).

34. Andrea Valentini, ed., *Epistres du debat*, 107.

35. According to Suzanne Solente, Christine began writing this work in 1400. See *Le Livre de la Mutacion de fortune*, ed. Suzanne Solente, 4 vols. (Paris: Picard, 1959–1966), 1:xi.

36. See *DR* ed. Hicks, 89–112; *DR* ed. and trans. Hult, 130–58.

provide the morally uplifting closure that a single narrating voice, with a single, instructive message, could furnish and which would signify the work's *utilitas*.[37] In the *Epistre* Christine sets this right by channeling many voices through the single voice of Cupid, and through the clarity of his point of view. But Cupid's voice is unavoidably thick with the trace of other voices: Meun's voice of Cupid and then Ovid's figure of the god, upon which Meun relied, are funneled through the god of the *Epistre*, to be refuted. One hears the distant buzz of anonymous, clerkly male voices, the fathers of the church, explaining "how women are," and the voices of the deliberate defamers of women, the would-be seducers who take delight in weaving stories of sexual conquest. These voices are made to be heard in the *Epistre* so that all may be identified and condemned by the one voice that articulates the moral standard, that of the God of Love.

Because voice is so crucial to the *Epistre*, some modern readers have lamented that it is Cupid, and not Christine herself, who speaks for the feminine collectivity. Claire Nouvet remarks that in order to give voice to the previously silent "we," the "community of women" who are the poem's plaintiffs, the case against men must be heard through another male voice; as Nouvet puts it, this "feminine plaint, this muted voice, will have to be articulated in the voice that muted it." And because it is Cupid who discloses the damage done to women, he "speaks in women's place the certainty that they cannot speak."[38] Nouvet captures an important difference in expectation as between medieval and modern readers, but Christine's critical technique in both the *Epistre* and the *Dit* depended on rewriting the God of Love as a deliberate and obvious riposte to Meun's god: Christine's god is the exemplar, a male figure whose thoughts and actions are just as Christine would wish, and that is because the God of Love is not speaking *instead of* Christine—rather, he is "being spoken" by Christine. This is a further twist on Christine's talent for "mastering . . . the 'master discourse,' her turning it to speak her own ends," as Maureen Quilligan has observed.[39]

It is in fact voice, material and metaphorical, speaking, reciting, or singing in both the *Epistre* and the *Dit*, that is foregrounded. Emphasized too is the fear that talk could sow chaos, and Christine vehemently condemns it, especially slanderous talk, against which she believed women (and some men) had no recourse. She also made clear in her writing that women had to control what other people

37. On the matter of Christine's approach to responsible writing, see Glenda McLeod, "Poetics and Antimisogynist Polemics in Christine de Pizan's *Le Livre de la Cité des Dames*," in *Reinterpreting Christine de Pizan: Essays in Honor of Charity Cannon Willard*, ed. Earl Jeffrey Richards et al. (Athens, GA: University of Georgia Press, 1992), 37–47.

38. Claire Nouvet, "Writing (in) Fear," in *Gender and Text in the Later Middle Ages*, ed. Jane Chance (Gainesville: University Press of Florida, 1996), 279–305, at 284 and 293.

39. Maureen Quilligan, *The Allegory of Female Authority: Christine de Pizan's* Cité des dames (Ithaca, NY and London: Cornell University Press, 1991), 204.

thought and said about them—that is, women had to "manage" their *fama*.[40] The serious need to do so can be extrapolated from the example of medieval jurisprudence, an indicator of an ethos in the larger society. Without a concept of proof as we know it today, the court testimony of witnesses, called the *fama* of the case, or what people said, "what everyone knew," or common opinion, could serve as proof. Further, an informal but acceptable practice of surveillance by one's neighbors played a regulatory role. In such circumstances, Christine urged women to avoid potentially incriminatory behavior, which could attach especially to them, and she encouraged women to engage instead in conduct that could enhance their good reputations. Both avenues depended on the key factor of self-control, integral to managing one's *fama*. So it was that Christine later wrote the *Trois Vertus* and the cautionary *Duc des vrais amans*,[41] whose married princess, talked about because of her affair with the eponymous duke, pays for her indiscretion with a ruined reputation and an unhappy life. The duke, on the other hand, accused of laziness, restores his good name by going off to fight in foreign wars. In Christine's view, nothing was better evidence of the damage done by talk—or writing—than assertions of women's lasciviousness, greed, dishonesty, and faithlessness, as uttered by characters in the *Roman* such as Old Woman and Jealous Husband.[42] The lack of respect such rumors might engender could effectively erase whatever power and influence women had—running a household, for example, or a kingdom. As Carolyn Collette puts this, a "prudential habit of mind . . . continually assays, weighs, and checks to maintain the strength of the webs of affinity and influence that a woman constructs and which are constructed around her in the social world."[43]

The centrality of language to the project of opposing Jean de Meun is also conveyed in the *Epistre* by the mimicry and displacement that foregrounds certain vocabulary. Old Woman was one of the *Roman* characters Christine found especially offensive, for she is a go-between for clandestine lovers. Further, she counsels young women to profit from their lovers while they can. She observes that young men are seldom reliable, and she advises women not to be so foolish as

40. On *fama*, see Bernard Guenée, *L'Opinion publique à la fin du Moyen Age: d'après la chronique de Charles VI du Religieux de St. Denis* (Paris: Perrin, 2002), and Thelma Fenster and Daniel Lord Smail, eds., *Fama: The Politics of Talk and Reputation in Medieval Europe* (Ithaca, NY: Cornell University Press, 2003).

41. *Le Livre du Duc des vrais amans*, ed. Thelma Fenster (Binghamton, NY: Center for Medieval and Early Renaissance Texts and Studies, 1995); *Le Livre du Duc des vrais amants*, ed. Dominique Demartini and Didier Lechat (Paris: Honoré Champion, 2013); *Le Livre du duc des vrais amans*, in *Œuvres poétiques*, ed. Maurice Roy, 3 vols. (Paris: Firmin Didot, 1886–1896) 3:59–208; *The Book of the Duke of True Lovers*, trans. Thelma Fenster and Nadia Margolis (New York: Persea, 1991).

42. For advice by Old Woman and Jealous Husband, see *RR* ed. Lecoy, vv. 12710–14516, and vv. 8437–9390; *RR* trans. Horgan, 191–224, 130–44.

43. Carolyn P. Collette, *Performing Polity: Women and Agency in the Anglo-French Tradition, 1385–1620* (Turnhout: Brepols, 2006), 37.

to take only one lover; but, she warns, be sure to tell each one that you are faithful to him alone. Old Woman argues that the mistake made by Dido and Medea was to have given all their love in just one place.[44] She puns on the verb *partir*, advising the lady to say to her lover that he alone will have the rose, and "Ja mes autre n'i avra **part**! **Faille** moi Dex se ja la **part**!" (Never will another have a **share** (part)! May God fail me if I **divide** it!").[45] The quite similar pun on *partir* in the *Epistre* is unmissable: the subject (women's alleged promiscuity) is the same, but now its articulation is placed in the mouths of men, the gossiping knights who tease one another about their mistresses' purported sexual adventures:

> Telle t'aimë et tu le jolis fais
> Pour sienne amour, et pluseurs y ont **part**;
> Tu es receu quant un autre **s'en part**!
>
> (Lady so-and-so loves you, and you play the swain / For her love, but many get their part; / You are welcomed as another departs! vv. 128–30)

These echoes of Old Woman's *partir* work intertextually to emphasize that women are seen to act disloyally only in the ribald and self-serving tales told by men.

For Meun's character of Old Woman, a young woman who fails to fleece her lover—that is, *plumer*, or pluck his feathers as if he were a chicken—is a fool.[46] (In Kay's reading, Old Woman says this because men are fickle, and in this way she upends the misogynist discourse of men who so often repeat that women are unfaithful.[47]) The *Epistre* uses the same verb to describe such women as tarts, reprehensible exceptions to the generality of women, but Cupid retorts that he's pleased to have the men who traffic with them dealt with in such a way. As he says: "Si ne remaint en eulz plume a plumer—/ Bien le scevent a leur droit reclamer" (They haven't a feather left to pluck—/ These women know how to claim their due; vv. 513–14).

"Qui sont fames?" *Who Are Women?*

When Christine set out to explain the *nature de femme,* she was working within the long-established formulations of influential Christian male writers, principally Augustine and then the neo-Aristotelian interpretations of Thomas Aquinas.[48]

44. *RR* ed. Lecoy, vv. 13123–42; *RR* trans. Horgan, 203–4.

45. *RR* ed. Lecoy, vv. 13091–92; *RR* trans. Horgan, 202.

46. *RR* ed. Lecoy, vv. 13667–68; *RR* trans. Horgan, 208. Horgan transforms the metaphor of plucking a lover's feathers into plucking love's fruit.

47. Kay, *Romance of the Rose*, 103–4.

48. For a general survey of clerical ideas about women, see Marie-Thérèse d'Alverny, "Comment les théologiens et les philosophes voient la femme," *Cahiers de Civilisation Médiévale: X^{e}–XIIe Siècles*

In discussions of sex and gender, writers seemed to return to a small number of thorny issues, centered in various ways on whether men and women enjoyed complete equality. Souls, which had no sex or gender, were all equals; as incarnate beings, however, women were men's helpers. To answer why woman had been created, Augustine invoked her role in procreation and her divinely ordered place as man's helpmeet.[49] Man's primacy came in part from the order of creation: God created man first, then woman, who was taken from man's side;[50] such arguments from events in the garden were countered by the privileges of women.

A second issue had to do with whether both man and woman were made in the image of God. Saint Paul had declared that only man was the image and glory of God while woman was the glory of man,[51] and for Augustine, woman enjoyed the image of God in her soul alone, which had no gender.[52]

Guilt for the Fall constituted a third topic of importance and was a popular subject for debate. Aquinas argued that since the woman was "more grievously punished than the man, . . . she sinned more grievously than the man." (*ST* II-II.163.4)

Like Augustine, Aquinas believed that women were physically and intellectually weaker than men, but having adopted from Aristotle the more extreme view that woman was a failed man (*mas occasionatus*[53]), he seems to want it both ways. He writes:

> As regards the individual nature, woman is defective and misbegotten, for the active force in the male seed tends to the production of a perfect likeness in the masculine sex; while the production of woman comes from defect in the active force or from some material

---

20 (1977): 105–29. For Christine's ability to read Latin, see Liliane Dulac and Christine Reno, "L'humanisme vers 1400. Essai d'exploration à partir d'un cas marginal: Christine de Pizan, lectrice de Thomas d'Aquin," in *Pratiques de la culture écrite en France au XVe siècle*. Actes du colloque du CNRS (Paris, 16–18 mai 1992), organisé en l'honneur de Gilbert Ouy par l'Unité de recherche 'Culture écrite du Moyen Age tardif,' ed. Monique Ornato and Nicole Pons (Turnhout: Brepols, 1995), 161–78.

49. Augustine, *The Literal Meaning of Genesis*, trans. John Hammond Taylor, 2 vols. (New York and Ramsey, NJ: Newman Press, 1982), 2:72–74. See also Rosemary Radford Ruether, *Women and Redemption: A Theological History*, 2nd ed. (Minneapolis: Fortress Press, 2012), and Kari Elisabeth Børresen, "God's Image, Man's Image? Patristic Interpretation of Gen. 1:27 and I Cor. 11:7" and "God's Image: Is Woman Excluded? Medieval Interpretation of Gen. 1:27 and I Cor. 11:7," in *Image of God and Gender Models in Judaeo-Christian Tradition*, ed. Kari Elisabeth Børresen (Oslo: Solum Vorlag, 1991), 188–207 and 208–27.

50. Augustine, *Literal Meaning*, 1:182–83.

51. 1 Cor. 11:7.

52. Augustine, *Literal Meaning*, 1:98–99.

53. See Joan Cadden, *Meanings of Sex Difference in the Middle Ages: Medicine, Science, and Culture* (Cambridge and New York: Cambridge University Press, 1993), 133.

> indisposition, or even from some external influence. . . . On the other hand, as regards human nature in general, woman is not misbegotten, but is included in nature's intention as directed to the work of generation. Now the general intention of nature depends on God, Who is the universal Author of nature. Therefore, in producing nature, God formed not only the male but also the female. (*ST* I.92.1)

Aquinas was hard-pressed to reconcile that understanding with the church's belief that God could not create a defective being. Blamires observes that not even Aquinas's "best efforts" could "mask" such a "disparity."[54] In the *Cité des dames*, Christine exclaims, "Ha! Dieux, comment peut cecy estre? Car se je ne erre en la foy, je ne doy mie doubter que ton infinie sapience et tres parfaicte bonté ait riens fait qui tout ne soit bon. Ne formas tu toy mesmes tres singulierement femme et dés lors lui donnas toutes teles inclinacions qu'il te plaisoit qu'elle eust? Et comment pourroit ce estre que tu y eusses en rien failli?"[55] (Ah, God! How can this be? For unless I err in my faith, I cannot suspect that your infinite wisdom and very perfect goodness made anything that might not be perfect. Did you not create woman with the greatest care and give her the inclinations you were pleased for her to have? And how could it be that you could have failed in anything?) Viewed in terms of the theological beliefs of her time, Christine's argument is on firm ground.

In the popular sphere, following the appearance of the *Roman* and over the course of the next century, "praise" and "blame" poems about women, in Latin and in the vernacular, came to constitute nearly a literary genre of their own. They stated why women were good or bad, and because they were based on a stock supply of arguments, they could take on the character of literary exercises on a popular subject. More significant for its length and its vitriol was the *Lamentationes Matheoluli* (1290–1291) (*Lamentations of Matheolus*[56]), by the cleric Matthew of Boulogne, a work that rails against women and marriage; it was translated from Latin into French by Jean LeFèvre around 1380, after which LeFèvre wrote a riposte to the *Lamentations* in French, a defense of women called the *Livre de Leesce*

54. Alcuin Blamires, ed., with Karen Pratt and C. W. Marx, *Woman Defamed and Woman Defended: An Anthology of Medieval Texts* (Oxford: Clarendon Press; New York: Oxford University Press, 1992), 89–90.

55. *La Città delle dame*, ed. Earl Jeffrey Richards, trans. [into Italian] Patrizia Caraffi, 2nd ed. (Milan: Luni, 1998), 44.

56. *Les Lamentations de Matheolus et le Livre de Leesce de Jehan Le Fèvre, de Resson: Poèmes français du XIVe siècle*, ed. A. G. van Hamel, 2 vols. (Paris: Emile Bouillon, 1892–1905). A more recent Latin edition with commentary in German is Matheus von Boulogne, *Lamentationes Matheoluli*, ed. Thomas Klein (Stuttgart: Anton Hiersemann, 2014). A summary of the French *Lamentations* is Charles-V. Langlois, "Les Lamentations de Mathieu," in Langlois, *La Vie en France au Moyen Age* (Paris: Hachette, 1925), 2:241–90.

(*Book of Gladness*).[57] Christine disliked the *Lamentations*, as she tells us at the beginning of the *Cité*, where she points out that Matheolus himself confessed to being an old man who blames women for his own impotence, for he is *plain de voulenté, et non puissance* (filled with desire, and not able to act).[58] She does not mention *Leesce*, but the *Epistre* bears a large number of similarities to it.[59] *Leesce* shared arguments with poems that preceded it, and Christine herself was often walking upon well-trodden ground. Her inventiveness in the *Epistre*, however, and the seriousness of her effort, depended not so much on the defense topoi she used, otherwise widespread, but on the larger framework within which she situated them, an illustration of the essential humanity of women and their aptitude for moral virtue.

Brown-Grant has argued that at the heart of Christine's defense of women is a question intended to refute the scurrilous implication of much anti-feminist writing claiming that woman was somehow less than human. In her letter to Pierre Col of October 1402, Christine pointedly asked:

> Qui sont fames? Qui sont elles? Sont ce serpens, loups, lyons, dragons, guievres ou bestes ravissables devourans et ennemies a nature humainne . . . [60]
>
> (Who are women? Who are they? Are they snakes, wolves, lions, dragons, vipers, or rapacious, devouring animals and enemies to human nature?)

Already in the summer of 1401, in her debate letter to Jean de Montreuil, Christine had pinpointed a contradiction in the argument of Meun's character Genius, who advocates sexual relations as often as possible for the continuance of the species, while he elsewhere advises men to flee from the venomous snake: "Fuyez, fuyez,

57. Jehan LeFèvre, *The Book of Gladness / Le livre de Leesce: A 14th Century Defense of Women, in English and French*, trans. Linda Burke (Jefferson, NC, and London: McFarland, 2013) reprints, with minor changes, LeFèvre's French translation from van Hamel's edition.

58. *Cité*, Bk. 1, ch. 8.

59. See Blamires, *The Case for Women*, 5 and 36.

60. Brown-Grant, *Moral Defence of Women*, 14; *DR* ed. Hicks, 139; *DR* ed. and trans. Hult, 181–82. Christine was surely familiar with the tradition of "feminine bestiaries" that linked mostly negative qualities of women with features popularly associated with specific animals. The Anglo-Norman *Blasme des fames* (*The Vices of Women*), for example, compares women with snakes, lions, leopards, foxes, bears, dogs, cats, rats, mice, hedgehogs, falcons, sparrowhawks, titmice, sparrows, blackbirds, bats, and owls; when women are lambs or doves, it is only for superficial attraction. See *Three Medieval Views of Women*: "La Contenance des Fames," "Le Bien des Fames," "Le Blasme des Fames," trans. and ed. Gloria K. Fiero, Wendy Pfeffer, and Mathé Allain (New Haven, CT, and London: Yale University Press, 1989), 120–42.

fuyez le serpent venimeux!"[61] This clearly alludes to the metonymic slide by which Eve and women after her were not merely accused of acting like the serpent, they *became* the serpent.[62] Commenting on Genius's injunction, Brown-Grant observes that it "constitutes a key point of misogynist doctrine which Christine will contest throughout her later writings in defence of women."[63]

The main elements in Christine's argument accentuating women's membership in the human species postdate the *Epistre*, appearing instead in the more accommodating prose of the *Debat* and the *Cité*. In the *Cité*, the character of Rectitude, one of three ladies (with Justice and Reason) who help Christine build the city, says that:

> "Et n'est mie doubte que les femmes sont aussi bien ou nombre du peuple de Dieu et de creature humaine que sont les hommes, et *non mie une autre espece*, ne de dessemblable generacion, par quoy elles doyent estre forcloses des enseignemens moraulx."[64]
>
> (And there is no doubt that women number among God's creatures just as much as men do and are *not another species* or bred in such a dissimilar way that they should be excluded from the teaching of virtue [emphasis added].)

The same reasoning is already present in the *Epistre*. Christine casts the defense in terms associable with natural law theory: *inclinacions*, *meurs*, and their frequent companion word, *condicions*. These three, which Christine brings together for the first time in the *Epistre*, would come to constitute a meaningful semantic field in her writing about women.

"Par droite condicion et inclinacion naturelle" *Through [Their] Rightful Condition and Natural Inclination*

For Aquinas, as D. E. Luscombe puts it, "all beings have within themselves inclinations which direct them to the end that is proper to them."[65] In a passage from the

61. *DR* ed. Hicks, 21; *DR* ed. and trans. Hult, 61.

62. See John A. Phillips, *Eve: The History of an Idea* (San Francisco: Harper and Row, 1984), 38–51.

63. Brown-Grant, *Moral Defence of Women*, 14.

64. *Città*, 376 and 378 (Bk. 2, ch. 54).

65. D. E. Luscombe, "Natural Morality and Natural Law," in *The Cambridge History of Later Medieval Philosophy*, ed. Norman Kretzmann, Anthony Kenny, and Jan Pinborg (Cambridge: Cambridge University Press, 1982), 705–19, at 709. A helpful guide to the *Summa* is Brian Davies and Eleonore Stump, eds., *The Oxford Handbook of Aquinas* (Oxford and New York: Oxford University Press, 2012). See also Stephen L. Brock, "Natural Inclination and the Intelligibility of the Good in Thomistic Natural Law," *Vera Lex*, n.s. 6 (2005): 57–78.

Summa Theologica worth giving in full here, Aquinas explains the inclinations belonging to human beings:

> Wherefore according to the order of natural inclinations, is the order of the precepts of the natural law. Because in man there is first of all an inclination to good in accordance with the nature which he has in common with all substances: inasmuch as every substance seeks the preservation of its own being, according to its nature: and by reason of this inclination, whatever is a means of preserving human life, and of warding off its obstacles, belongs to the natural law. Secondly, there is in man an inclination to things that pertain to him more specially, according to that nature which he has in common with other animals: and in virtue of this inclination, those things are said to belong to the natural law, "which nature has taught to all animals" . . . , such as sexual intercourse, education of offspring and so forth. Thirdly, there is in man an inclination to do good, according to the nature of his reason, which nature is proper to him: thus man has a natural inclination to know the truth about God, and to live in society: and in this respect, whatever pertains to this inclination belongs to the natural law; for instance, to shun ignorance, to avoid offending those among whom one has to live, and other such things regarding the above inclination. (*ST* I-II.94.2)

Inclinations were subject to the action of reason, the higher faculty that separated humans from other animals and gave humans the ability to formulate ethical behaviors. The possibility existed, however, that human beings might not follow the promptings of reason in some instances, and in certain circumstances inclinations could change. Aquinas wrote that "the natural law, in the abstract, can nowise be blotted out from men's hearts. But it is blotted out in the case of a particular action, in so far as reason is hindered from applying the general principle to a particular point of practice, on account of concupiscence or some other passion" (*ST* I-II.94.6). This law of "the natural," it should be noted, appears to be less rigid than the idea of nature in present-day understanding, which tends to posit a rigidly fixed and unchanging drive.[66]

Christine did not directly challenge the gender hierarchy enforced by the church, choosing instead to emphasize the complementarity of gender roles, but she also insisted on fair, equal, and respectful treatment of both men and women. In the *Epistre* (v. 733), she goes even further by stating that men and women are

66. See Diana Fuss, *Essentially Speaking: Feminism, Nature and Difference* (New York and London: Routledge, 1989), 3.

absolute equals, as expressed in the words *per* (equal) and *semblable*, this latter word expressing in Middle French not only similarity, but equality.

It is often noted in modern scholarship that Christine, like others writing in defense of women, often invoked women's role as mothers (as she does in the *Epistre*). As Christine developed her ideas about women's moral virtue, however, she reminded her readers that women also contributed to the well-being of the human group, to the sociability indispensable to its cohesiveness. This was Aquinas's second inclination, "to live in society," and "to avoid offending those among whom one has to live."

Inclinacions

The term *inclinacion*[67] appears only once in the *Epistre*, but its position toward the end of the poem in the God of Love's summation of women's qualities is significant. Further, its pairing with the word *condicions* (discussed at pp. 23–26) is emblematic of Christine's approach. The god says:

> Par ces raisons, conclus et vueil prouver
> Que grandement femmes a approuver
> Font et louer, et leurs **condicïons**
> Recommander, qui **inclinacïons**
> N'ont aux vices, qui humaine nature
> Va dommagant et grevant creature. (vv. 713–18)[68]

67. According to the *Dictionnaire du Moyen Français (1330–1500)* (<http://www.atilf.fr/dmf/>), *inclinacion* is an innate tendency and a spontaneous movement of the soul. Pointing toward astrology, the *DMF* observes that it is particularly what is conferred by the stars at birth, but is susceptible of being modified by free will. Joël Blanchard and Michel Quereuil, *Lexique de Christine de Pizan: Matériaux pour le Dictionnaire du Moyen Français* (Paris: Klincksieck, 1999), 224, gloss it as a general inclination or desire without noting the term's importance to natural law theory or to astrology/astronomy. The *Dictionnaire étymologique de l'ancien français* (*DEAF*), ed. Kurt Baldinger, with Jean-Denis Gendron and Georges Straka (Quebec: Presses de l'Université Laval; Tübingen: Niemeyer; Paris: Klincksieck, 1974–2012), 1: 167, and the *Französisches etymologisches Wörterbuch* (*FEW*), ed. Walther von Wartburg (Bonn: Klopp, 1922–2003, 4: 627b), provide an example taken from the French translation of Aristotle's *On Divination in Sleep* by Nicole Oresme, King Charles V's most forward-looking translator and advisor: s.v. *inclinare*, "Les instruments de Dieu [. . .] qui inclinent les courages de personnes a diverses fortunes" (God's instruments . . . which incline people's hearts toward various fortunes). See Nicole Oresme, *Livre de divinacions*, in G. W. Coopland, *Nicole Oresme and the Astrologers: A Study of His* Livre de divinacions (Cambridge, MA: Harvard University Press, 1952), 50–121, at 66. A definition of *inclinacion* that links it to medieval natural law theory has not yet found its way into glossaries or notes for modern editions of Christine's writings.

68. Earl Jeffrey Richards comments on Christine and natural law in "Justice in the *Summa* of St. Thomas Aquinas, in Late Medieval Marian Devotional Writings and in the Works of Christine de Pizan," in *Christine de Pizan: Une femme de science, une femme de lettres*, ed. Juliette Dor, Marie-Elisabeth

("With this reasoning I conclude and hope to prove / That women do very much to be approved / And praised; and I want to recommend / Their qualities, which show no inclination / Toward the vices that damage / Human nature and harm created beings.")

But *inclinacion(s)* occurs more often in Christine's major defense of women, the *Cité des dames.* Once more, the configuration of *inclinacions/enclin(e)(s)* with *condicion* appears, where *condicion* can be *encline* (inclined). Defending women from the charge that they are gluttonous *par nature*, Christine answers that it is rather *leur condicion, qui n'y est mie encline* (their . . . disposition, which is not so inclined); and even supposing that shame gave them the wherewithal to resist such an *inclinacion naturelle* (natural inclination), that could only be to women's honor.[69]

As human beings wish to know and love God, so does woman:

> Et vrayement je dy et reviens a mon propos que se Nature n'a donné grant force de membres a corps de femme, que elle l'a bien recompensé en ce que **inclinacion** y a mise tres vertueuse, c'est de amer son Dieu et estre cremeteuse de faillir contre ses commandemens, et celles qui sont autres **se desnaturent.**[70]
>
> (I return to my point, telling you truly that if Nature did not give a woman's body great strength, she compensated for that by giving her a very virtuous **inclination**: that is, to love her God and be fearful of violating his commandments. Women who do otherwise act **against their own nature**.)

The term *inclinacion* is in fact a way, for Christine, to make sense of the world. *Inclinacion* explains why some people "naturally" become workers, while others "naturally" become thinkers and still others become civic leaders (or not). In her biography of Charles V, Christine explains the formation of different political and social groups and how labor in them was assigned by princes. She says that some people, *de leur propre inclinacion* (by their own inclination), applied their intelligence to the philosophical arts.[71] And in the *Livre de paix* (*Book of*

Henneau, and Bernard Ribémont (Paris: Honoré Champion, 2008), 95–114. In the *Roman*, Reason claims that both humans and other animals have a *naturiex enclinemenz* (natural inclination) to want to preserve a likeness of self through engendering and nurturing: *RR* ed. Lecoy, vv. 5733–46; *RR* trans. Horgan, 88–89.

69. *Città* 82 (Bk. 1, ch. 10).

70. *Città* 104 (Bk. 1, ch. 14).

71. *Le Livre des Fais et bonnes meurs du sage roy Charles V*, ed. Suzanne Solente, 2 vols. (Paris: Honoré Champion, 1936–40), 1:114. See also 1:17.

Peace), written between 1412 and 1413–1414, she explains why the common people ought not to acquire official positions in the city, because their "general inclination" (*inclinacion generalles* [*sic*]) "is hasty, with little reflection and needing little pretext for action."[72]

Finally, *inclinacion* could be individual. In the *Cité*, in an important autobiographical statement, Christine discusses her personal *inclinacion*. She explains that she took after her father, commenting further that he did not think women worse off for having acquired learning. Her mother was opposed to this, but Christine's *inclinacion naturelle* impelled her to gather *petites goutellettes* (little drops) of knowledge.[73] Again, in the *Mutacion de Fortune*, Christine discusses her upbringing, explaining that her father wished to have a male child, but her "mother" (Nature) prevailed and Christine was the result. Her father had the *tresor*, treasury, of learning, which she too would have liked to have. She adds, however, that in so many ways she is much more like her father than she is her own natural mother, now using *condicions*:

> . . . de toutes choses mon pere
> Bien ressemblay et proprement,
> Fors du sexe tant seulement,
> Mais des façons, de corps, de vis,
> Si bien que il vous fust avis,
> Meismement es **condicions**,
> Que tous semblables les eussions. (vv. 394–400)
>
> (I took after my father well and truly in everything, except for our sex: in our mannerisms, bodies, and faces, even in our **qualities**, so much that you would have thought we possessed all the same ones.)

She compares her longing for learning with the yearning of lovers who can neither see nor hear what they desire:

> Et, combien que femmelle fusse,
> Par quoy l'avoir dessus dit n'eüsse,
> Y avoie **inclinacion**
> De ma droite **condicion**
> Et pour mon pere ressembler. (vv. 447–51)[74]

72. *Livre de Paix*, Bk. 1, ch. 11. See *The Book of Peace by Christine de Pizan*, ed. and trans. Karen Green, Constant J. Mews, Janice Pinder, and Tania van Hemelryck, with the assistance of Alan Crosier (University Park: Pennsylvania State University Press, 2008), 141, 171.

73. *Città* 316 (Bk. 2, ch. 36).

74. *Mutacion*, 1:20–21, 22. An almost complete English translation is Christine de Pizan, *The Book of the Mutability of Fortune*, trans. Geri L. Smith (Toronto: Iter Press; Tempe: Arizona Center for

> (And, although I was a female, according to which I should not have the above-mentioned wealth, I had the **inclination** [to have the treasury of learning] from my own specific **condition**, and to be like my father).[75]

In Psalm 31 of the *Sept Psaumes allegorisés*, a devotional text, Christine's supplicant asks God, "chaces de moy toute *inclinacion* de pechié car, se de toy ne vient, je n'ay force de contrester a ma mauvaise *inclinacion* . . . "[76] (banish from me every *inclination* to sin, for, if I don't receive that from you, I haven't the strength to resist my bad *inclination*).

This same argument about individual inclinations having been divinely bestowed leads Justice, in the *Cité*, to defend both women and men who like finery and pretty little things on the grounds that it would be hard for them to eradicate that taste, which they possess "par droite condicion et inclinacion naturelle" (through their rightful condition and natural inclination).[77] It is worth noting that the argument about personal, natural inclinations brings theological import to what might otherwise be thought a uniquely literary point in the *Debat*. Pierre Col defends characters such as Old Woman and Jealous Husband on the grounds that in what they say they are being true to their natures (inclinations); he says that Jean de Meun "makes each personage speak according to what pertains to him—the Jealous Man like a jealous person, the Old Woman like an old woman, and likewise for the others."[78] Like Boccaccio and Christine, they too behave according to their inclinations.

Condicions

Often paired with *inclinacion* is *condicions*, independently the more frequent of the two, perhaps due to its wide range of meanings, and, as we shall see, to its transregional literary applications.[79] Christine uses it to mean character, attribute,

---

Medieval and Renaissance Studies, 2017).

75. Evidence for this is also found among other late medieval writers. Boccaccio, for instance, invoked his personal, natural inclination: he was prepared by nature ("in his mother's womb") to follow his natural inclinations, that is, to follow poetic meditations. See Filippo Andrei, *Boccaccio the Philosopher: An Epistemology of the Decameron* (Cham, Switzerland: Palgrave Macmillan, 2017), 72.

76. *Les Sept Psaumes allegorisés*, ed. Bernard Ribémont and Christine Reno (Paris: Honoré Champion, 2017), 7.

77. *Città* 408 (Bk. 2, ch. 62).

78. "fait chascun personnage parler selonc qui luy appartient: c'est assavoir le Jaloux comme jaloux, la Vielle comme la Vielle, et pareillement des autres" (*DR* ed. Hicks, 100; *DR* ed. and trans. Hult, 144).

79. In the *DMF*, *condition* has a variety of meanings: something that makes something or someone what they are; a manner of being; a state or situation. For Christine the plural *condicions* can indicate

feature, characteristic, trait, quality, property, and the like—pretty much the range of meanings to be found in Aquinas's writing, where it does not have the systematic valence that *inclinatio* carries for him. English translators of Thomistic natural law theory most often translate *conditio* or its declensions as "conditions": *diversas hominum conditiones*, in English translation, can be "various conditions of men," while *conditiones particulares* may be simply "conditions," and *aliae conditiones* "other conditions."[80]

After qualifying the *nature de femme* in some detail, Christine concludes that:

> Et telles sont par nature sens doubte
> **Condicïons de femme**, somme toute. (vv. 677–78)
>
> (Such are certainly by nature / **Women's qualities**, in sum.)

Should a woman lack these *condicions*, she *se desnature* ("distorts her nature," v. 680), but she nonetheless remains a woman. Such women are not "other"; rather, they are on a scale, *enormales* (v. 656), meaning not "abnormal" but "excessive." The *nature de femme* is found not always, but *selon le commun cours* ("according to what is usual," v. 657), a rendering in French that seems to parallel the Thomistic phrase *ut in pluribus*, "for the most part,"[81] and this leads Christine to emphasize that blaming all women for the defects of a few is wrong. In conclusion, Cupid says:

> . . . moult leur fist le hault Dieu courtoisie
> D'elles fourmer sens les **condicïons**
> Qui gent mettent a griefs perdicïons (vv. 694–96)

characteristic traits or qualities; it can signal the physical or mental state of a person, one's social position and/or rank. In the *Lexique de Christine de Pizan*, condition is glossed as a *façon de se conduire* (comportment) and *nature, façon d'être* (nature, way of being), and it gives the following example from Christine's *Trois Vertus*: " . . . toutes gens ne sont mie d'une **condicion** et qu'il est assez d'ommes et de femmes si pervers que quelque bonne correction et enseignement que on leur donne, si suivront ilz tousjours leur fole ou mauvaise **inclinacion**" (not all people are of one condition and there are enough men and women who are so perverse that whatever good correction or teaching one may give them, they continue to follow their foolish or evil **inclination** (*Lexique de Christine de Pizan*, 84).

80. See Ludwig Schütz, *Thomas-Lexikon*, online at <http://www.corpusthomisticum.org/tl.html>. For the range of possible English translations of Thomas's *conditio*, see Roy J. Deferrari and M. Inviolata Barry, with the technical collaboration of Ignatius McGuiness, *A Lexicon of St. Thomas Aquinas* (Washington, DC: Catholic University of America Press, 1948–49), 199–200.

81. For this observation and for much information on other related points, we are grateful to Fr. Brian Davies, O. P.

> (. . . God on high did women a courtesy / By forming them without the **qualities** / That lead people to grievous perdition.)

The god assures his listeners that women are in fact inclined *not* to do evil, in a formulation which includes *condicions* but also *taches*:

> Et s'on me veult dire que mie **enclines**
> **Condicïons** ne **taches** femenines
> Ne soit a ce, n'a user de batailles,
> N'a gens tuer në a faire fouailles
> Pour bouter feu, në a telz choses faire,
> Pour ce, nul preu, louange, ne salaire
> Ne leur en puet ne doit appartenir
> D'elles souffrir de telz cas, ne tenir,
> Mais sauve soit la grace des diseurs,
> Je consens bien qu'elles n'ont pas les cuers
> **Enclins** a ce, në a cruaulté faire. (vv. 659–69)

> (And if someone wants to say to me / That women's **traits** and **qualities** are not **inclined** / Toward that, or to do battle, / Kill people, or prepare the torches / To start a fire, or to do any such things, / And so no special praise, credit, or reward / Can or should belong to them / For abstaining from things like that, or resisting /—Begging pardon from those who say so—/ I indeed agree that women haven't hearts / So **disposed**, nor toward doing deeds of that sort.)

Christine stands out for her exploration of woman's nature as a group of *condicions*, but she is not alone in applying the term to perceived character traits. In his *Archiloge Sophie*, for example, Christine's contemporary, Jacques Legrand, uses it in a more condemnatory fashion:

> Femme raisonnablement doit avoir deux **condicions**, c'est assavoir honte de mesprendre et paour de desobeÿr a sa partie: car lors femme est perdue et dissolue quant elle n'a en soi honte ne paour. Si est chose moult a reprandre de veoir femmes hardies et dissolues et prestes a faire pluseurs maulx: teles sont celles qui par leurs manieres villes et dissolues, et par leurs regars vains et luxurieux attraient les hommes a mal faire.[82]

82. Jacques Legrand, *Archiloge Sophie. Livre de bonnes meurs*, ed. Evencio Beltran (Geneva: Slatkine; Paris: Honoré Champion, 1986), 371.

> (A woman must reasonably have two **qualities**, that is, shame in wrongdoing and fear of disobeying her spouse: for a woman is lost and dissolute when she has no shame in herself or fear. There is much to blame at the sight of bold and dissolute women ready to commit much evil: such are those who by their vile and dissolute comportment, and by their frivolous and lecherous glances, entice men into evildoing.)

Finally, "conditions" was part of a transcultural French literary vocabulary. In a study of "individuality" in medieval English literature, Blamires notes that for Chaucer *condiciouns* was a preferred word for dealing with "the moral attributes forming part of the rhetorical coding of literary portraiture."[83] Taken as well with the evidence from Boccaccio concerning his own "natural inclination" to pursue poetic meditation (see note 75), Christine was thus applying a late-medieval lexical practice to the portrayal of an entire group.

Meurs

Of the three terms discussed here, *meurs* or *mours*[84] (*mœurs* in modern French) denotes an especially important and subtle piece in the pragmatics of Christine's moral outlook. It is central to her emphasis on women's virtue (*meurs femenins*).

The word *meurs* is derived from the Latin *mores*, the plural form of *mos* (manner, custom, usage, or habit). In modern English, the word "mores," or social norms, does not connote something moral (athough the adjective *moral* does), but in fifteenth-century French and therefore in Christine's usage, *meurs* had a strong moral component. On this, Nicolas Oresme (d. 1382), probably the leading intellectual in Charles V's court, translated Aristotle as follows: "la vertu morale est faite et causee en nous par **meurs**, et pour ce son nom est dirivé de '**meur**' et en differe peu" (moral virtue is made and caused in us by *meurs*, and for this reason its name is derived from *meur* and differs little from it); to this is added Oresme's explanation that in Latin *mos* meant *coustume*,[85] given in Middle French as "manière de faire ou de se comporter, usage, habitude" (a way of doing something or of behaving, a usage, or a habit).[86]

83. Blamires, "Individuality," in the *Oxford Handbook of Medieval Literature in English*, ed. Elaine Treharne and Greg Walker, with the assistance of William Green (Oxford, UK; New York: Oxford University Press, 2010), 478–95, at 490.

84. According to the *DMF*, *meurs* denotes one's conduct or comportment, manner of living (morally), or one's habits and tastes; it may also refer to one's nature.

85. Nicole Oresme, *Le Livre de Ethiques d'Aristote*, ed. Albert D. Menut (New York: Stechert, 1940), 146.

86. *DMF* s.v. *coutume*, A.1.

In five instances in the *Epistre* Cupid refers to *meurs*, translatable variously as manners, ways, practices, comportment, and the like. In three cases, a particular set of habits is said to belong to women: there are *meurs femenins*, v. 200 (women's practices), and as a group, *leurs meurs*, v. 260 (women's conduct, habits). In his *Remedia Amoris*, according to Cupid, Ovid attributes *moult de vilaines mours*, v. 282 (many nasty habits) to women. A comment on Ovid's *Art of Love* shows that *meurs/mours* can be taught: Cupid claims that it "n'enseingne **condicïons** ne **mours** / De bien amer, mais ainçoiz le contraire," vv. 370–71 (doesn't teach the **behaviors** or **ways** / Of loving truly, but rather the opposite). To be underlined here is the verb *enseingne*, teach, which recalls that *mours* can be acquired. This is fundamental to Christine's impulse to compose the *Epistre* and to her advocacy of men's exercise of reason so as to practice virtuous behavior toward women.

At the very beginning of the *Cité*, Christine's narrator refers to the chorus of male voices who have formed the bad *fama* (the common opinion, or what everyone knows) about women. Joining *enclins* with *meurs*, Christine's narrator says:

> . . . generaument auques en tous traictiez, philosophes, pouetes, tous orateurs desquieulx les noms dire seroit longue chose, semble que tous parlent par une mesmes bouche et tous accordent une semblable conclusion, determinant les **meurs femenins enclins** et plains de tous les vices[87]
>
> (. . . generally in nearly all treatises, philosophers, poets, all orators whose names would be tedious to mention, it seems that all speak with the same mouth and all agree upon one conclusion, determining **feminine practices** to be **inclined** toward, and filled with, all vices).

Later in her writing, as Christine moved toward fuller discussion of virtue ethics for women, *meurs* would be central. Once more, a cluster of expressions at the opening of the *Cité* sets the tone of the book as a whole: there are *meurs femenins* (feminine comportment), *meurs comme femme naturelle* (comportment as a natural woman), and *natureulz meurs et condicions femmenines* (natural comportment and conditions of women). She pairs *meurs* with *vertu* or *vertus*, referring to an *edifice de vertu et de meurs*[88] (the realization of virtue and comportment), a formulation she uses again in the *Corps de policie*, telling her readers that she will remind them of the *edifice de bonnes meurs*.[89] Delphine Videt-Reix, examining the *Cité* in particular, observes that with phrases like *perfeccion des*

87. *Città* 42 (Bk. 1, ch. 1).

88. *Città* 42 (Bk. 1, ch. 1).

89. *Le Livre du Corps de policie*, ed. Angus J. Kennedy (Paris: Honoré Champion, 1998), 1.

meurs et des vertus (perfection of comportment and virtue) Christine develops a "nouvelle poétique de la prudence et de la justice à travers l'illustration concrète des vertus" (a new poetics of prudence and justice through the concrete illustration of virtues).[90] Christine offers individual exemplars: Artemisia, a queen and warrior in the *Cité*, possesses *force en vertu et sagece de meurs et prudence en gouvernement*[91] (strength in virtue and wisdom in her comportment and prudence in government). In the *Duc des vrais amans*, the wise Sebile, herself an example of a virtuous older woman, sends a letter to the young princess counseling against her illicit love affair with the eponymous duke. She stresses that the princess must be excellent in *bonté et sagece, meurs, condicions et manieres* (goodness and wisdom, habits, qualities, and comportment) so as to be an example to other women.[92] In addition to the personal harm the princess's adultery causes, it raises the specter of men's misogynous generalizations about women: men's pronouncements on women create a rupture in direct woman-to-woman exemplarity by discouraging women from thinking of themselves as agents capable of virtue.

The Intellectual Life of the Laity and the Place of the Epistre

With some exceptions, attempts to evaluate and place Christine's individual works have left the *Epistre* somewhat at the periphery of her body of writing.[93] Its philosophical statement is more cursory than that offered by the *Cité*, and as a courtly composition it lacks the story element that shapes Christine's love debate poems. But is the atmosphere of the poem, as Eric Hicks maintained, not intellectual or literary? Does the misogyny described in the poem, as Hicks described it, have primarily to do with hypocritical lovers and furtive love affairs, pretended courtliness and amorous conquests, in a game played against other men, rather than

90. See Delphine Videt-Reix, "Christine de Pizan et la poétique de la justice," Diss., Aix-Marseille Université, 2011 (<www.theses.fr/2011AIX10006.pdf>), 117; Earl Jeffrey Richards, Liliane Dulac, and Delphine Reix, "Creating New Political and Allegorical Forms of Discourse and the Meaning of the Word 'Moral' in the Works of Christine de Pizan," in *"Ton nom sera reluisant aprés toy par longue memoire": Etudes sur Christine de Pizan*, ed. Anna Loba (Poznan: Uniwersytet im. Adama Mickiewicza, 2017), 85–103.

91. *Città* 136 (Bk. 1, ch. 21).

92. *Duc des vrais amans*, 172. The translation here is revised as against that in *Duke of True Lovers*, trans. Fenster and Margolis, 112. The letter is repeated in the *Trois Vertus* (Bk. 1, ch. 25).

93. In "*L'Epistre au dieu d'amours* ou 'l'origine du monde' auctorial," Tania van Hemelryck points out that Christine's career as an author begins in the *Epistre*, where she uses the term *ignorant petite femmelette* (v. 548) with the intention of refuting it. See also Nadia Margolis, "Christine de Pizan, mangeuse de savoir," in *L'Offrande du cœur: Medieval and Early Modern Studies in Honour of Glynnis Cropp*, ed. Margaret Burrell and Judith Grant (Christchurch, NZ: Canterbury University Press with Massey University, 2004), 45–60.

with a more learned misogyny?[94] Hicks's comments may have the potential to drive the *Epistre* into the margins of Christine's participation in the Debate and in her writing generally, whereas it in fact marks the opening chapter of her lifelong intellectual and personal preoccupation, persistently argued in the philosophical vocabulary the *Epistre* introduces. The courtly tone and framework of the *Epistre* can indeed lead the reader away from its serious import, and the God of Love's amusing critique of a type of foolishness identified with men certainly captures its readers' interest. But the poem's verve should not be allowed to mislead the reader: it is speaking to both a lay and clerical audience, educating both.[95]

Christine's shaping of her argument in the terms of contemporary theological thinking, and in the vernacular, reflected the educational spirit of the court of Charles V and would have contrasted with the lack of any communal interest in learning under Charles VI. Like French kings before him, but far more extensively, Charles V—known as "Charles the Wise"—had created a library of translations into French of the Latin *auctoritates.*[96] He employed the best translators of the day, those who had spent their lives studying Latin, because he saw that transmitting ancient learning to the aristocracy could be an effective means of articulating his own governing policies. According to Serge Lusignan, Charles was to all intents and purposes the first of his line to consider his library an instrument for ruling; for Lusignan, this was so marked that it constituted a break from previous royal practice and a new direction in the way knowledge was acquired and in who

94. "L'atmosphère de l'épître n'a rien d'intellectuel ni même de 'littéraire,' dans la mesure où la science et la littérature s'écartent de la vie de cour,—dans la mesure, précisément, où la littérature ne serait plus *fête*. [. . .] S'il est exact qu'elle vise une misogynie, c'est une misogynie hypocrite et suave, complice des amours furtives, de galanteries feintes, de conquêtes amoureuses faites plus encore par jeu que par luxure [. . .]; *DR* ed. Hicks, xxx).

95. On Christine's philosophical and theological learning, see Benjamin M. Semple, "The Critique of Knowledge as Power: The Limits of Philosophy and Theology in Christine de Pizan," in *Christine de Pizan and the Categories of Difference*, ed. Marilynn Desmond (Minneapolis: University of Minnesota Press, 1998), 108–27. On February 1, 1402 (n. st. [the dedicatory letter to Guillaume de Tignonville was undated]), Christine submitted the dossier of Debate letters to Queen Isabeau, but in spite of its sandwiching between the putative dinner in January and the poem's recitation a month later, Hicks warns that the *Dit* and the *Epistre*, by their nature as poetic compositions rather than prose commentary, should not be considered part of the *Debat du Roman de la Rose* (*DR* Hicks, xxix–xxx). Here again, however, strict demarcation on formal grounds alone may not be helpful; the *Epistre*, with its open criticism of an iconic (male-authored) work by a woman, would surely have helped to draw attention to Meun's work.

96. Previous royal bibliophiles included Philip IV the Fair (1268–1314), Philip VI the Fortunate (1293–1350), and John II the Good (1319–1364). For a list of manuscripts held in Charles's library, see Léopold Delisle, *Recherches sur la librairie de Charles V, roi de France, 1337–1380* (Paris: Honoré Champion, 1907).

could acquire it.[97] Latin, the hegemonic vehicle for erudition, had been the exclusive property of learned clerics. Translation into the vernacular changed that, and it changed what the laity could know.

Lusignan sees Charles's efforts as the culmination of an important earlier idea, *translatio studii*: the geographic passage of *chevalerie* and *clergie* (chivalry and learning) from Greece and Rome to France, a concept articulated by the twelfth-century poet Chrétien de Troyes in his prologue to *Cligès*.[98] By the end of the thirteenth century French was "firmly established as a language of written culture," Lusignan observes, but not in the case of learned writing.[99] Beginning in the early fourteenth century, however, the French royal court began to see the value of translating learned writing from Latin into French, although it was not until Charles V became king that a concept of ancient learning's capacity to enhance royal power took shape: study and wisdom were linked with political accomplishment.

Charles's translators often commented on the severe challenges presented by translation from Latin into French, given that the French of the time lacked the lexical equivalents to the Latin philosophical vocabulary. They remedied the shortcoming by creating neologisms.[100] Among Charles's translators, Nicole Oresme stands out, as previously noted. Oresme was a perspicacious advisor who saw the political and linguistic ramifications of the translation project. He understood and supported Charles's ambitions, embracing the opportunity to form the French aristocracy to Charles's program of government. This was an effort at the formation of an educated laity, and Oresme was a willing and talented instructor. For his vernacularization of Aristotle's *Ethics*, for example, Oresme created a glossary and commentary explaining the meanings of the new French vocabulary he had forged. That crucial vocabulary, Oresme saw, would furnish French with the competence to express learned ideas,[101] while ancient learning, he astutely realized, could endure only by being translated into the vernacular languages.

97. Serge Lusignan, "La topique de la *translatio studii* et les traductions françaises de textes savants au XIVe siècle," in *Traduction et traducteurs au Moyen Age*, Actes du colloque international du CNRS (Paris, Institut de recherche et d'histoire des textes, 26–28 mai 1986), ed. Geneviève Contamine (Paris: CNRS, 1989), 303–15, at 310.

98. Chrétien de Troyes, *Cligès*, vv. 30–39.

99. Lusignan, *Translatio studii*, 6–7.

100. Margolis has rightly dubbed this "the golden age of the neologism," due especially to the activity of Charles's translators; see "Les terminaisons dangereuses: Lyrisme, féminisme et humanisme néologiques chez Christine de Pizan," *Le Moyen français* 39–41 (1996–97): 381–404, at 381.

101. Serge Lusignan, "Nicole Oresme, traducteur, et la pensée de la langue française savante," in *Nicolas Oresme: Tradition et innovation chez un intellectuel du XIVe siècle*, ed. Pierre Souffrin and Alain-Philippe Segonds (Paris: Les Belles Lettres, 1988), 93–104.

Joan Cadden has argued that Oresme's French translation of Aristotle's *Livre de divinacions* and the resulting discussions of astrology in Charles's court "suggested the existence of another set of contexts—the intellectual life of the laity, the social dynamics of the court, and the political interests of the monarchy."[102] Cadden's observation broadens our understanding of the rationale for the translations in that it looks at the place of education for the laity as a way of making Charles's vision work. To take Cadden's point is to recognize that there were not two mutually exclusive spheres, courtly or learned, and that Charles V's translation program went a long way toward eradicating that distinction.

Like other evidence that suggests an erosion of boundaries between the learned and the secular—that is, between the university and the court, Latin and the vernacular—so too Jean de Meun's *Roman*, with its encapsulations of major philosophical and theological ideas not in Latin but in French verse. Indeed, the *Roman* stood at a threshold where learned ideas could be discussed in the vernacular. The *Epistre*'s learned language and its courtly context should not be construed as separate, much less opposing, entities.

The Dit de la Rose *and Chivalric Orders*

The staging for the *Dit*, composed for Valentine's Day 1402, is a Parisian residence of the Duke of Orléans, where noble guests enjoy exquisite dishes, witty conversation, and poetic competitions. It presents yet a further retort to the *Roman* by rewriting the symbol of the rose, elevating it from sexual symbol to metaphor for the honor of women.[103] We do not know whether the Order of the Rose, whose founding the *Dit* records, actually existed, but certainly the poem is intended to introduce a new kind of chivalric order: like other orders, it will be dedicated to honoring women, but unlike others, its authority and administration will come not from men, but from women. Lady Loyalty[104] has selected Christine as her

102. Joan Cadden, "Charles V, Nicole Oresme, and Christine de Pizan: Unities and Uses of Knowledge in Fourteenth-Century France," in *Texts and Contexts in Ancient and Medieval Science: Studies on the occasion of John E. Murdoch's Seventieth Birthday*, ed. Edith Sylla and Michael McVaugh (Leiden, New York, and Cologne: Brill, 1997), 208–44, at 209–10. See also Edgar Laird, "Astrology in the Court of Charles V of France, as Reflected in Oxford, St. John's College MS 164," *Manuscripta* 34 (1990): 167–76, and Laird, "Christine de Pizan and the Controversy Concerning Star-Study in the Court of Charles V," *Allegorica* 18 (1997): 21–30.

103. Lori Walters observes that Christine "reappropriates and reworks the major metaphor of Jean's text" by present[ing] her version of what Jean's 'Rose' would have said had the character spoken in her own voice." See "Fathers and Daughters: Christine de Pizan as Reader of the Male Tradition of *Clergie* in the *Dit de la Rose*," in Richards et al., *Reinterpreting Christine*, 63–76, at 63.

104. Christine's Lady Loyalty was perhaps inspired by the debate that unfolded in the late fourteenth century in Jean le Seneschal's *Les Cent Ballades* as to whether Loyalty (Loyauté) or Falseness (Fausseté) brings more joy in love. See Jean le Sénéchal, *Les Cent Ballades: Poème du XIV*e *siècle composé par Jean*

earthly representative, and she has given her a mandate to select other women who in turn will choose candidates for membership in the Order.[105]

The Order of the Rose bears comparison with the Order of the Dame Blanche à l'Ecu Vert (the White Lady on the Green Shield) and the Cour amoureuse dite de Charles VI (Court of love attributed to Charles VI), both created within a few years of the *Dit*'s composition. The Order of the White Lady on the Green Shield, whose members pledged themselves to protecting women, was founded April 11, 1400 and thus followed the *Epistre* by less than a year. The order was an initiative of the famous Jean II le Meingre (1366–1421), known, like his father, as "Boucicaut," a war hero and champion of the late-medieval reprise of chivalric ideals.[106] Christine knew of the Order's founding and celebrated it in her Autre Balade XII (no doubt composed between April 1400 and 1402) while exhorting women to pray for the success of the Order, whose members "l'escu vert aux dames belles / Portent sanz estre deffaillans" (carry the green shield with beautiful ladies without flinching).[107] In the ballade, she asks that good may be said of them and that they be remembered always.

Boucicaut's anonymous biographer, in his report of the Order's founding in *Le Livre des fais du bon Messire Jehan le Maingre, dit Bouciquaut* (*Book of the Deeds of the Good Sir Jean Le Meingre, called Boucicaut*), uses terms strikingly like those uttered by the God of Love in his account of the circumstances impelling him to write the letter. Boucicaut's biographer reports that:

> . . . avint que aucunes **complaintes** vindrent devers le roy comment plusieurs **dames et damoiselles, vesves et autres**, estoient oppressees et traveillees d'aucuns poissons hommes qui par leur force et

---

le Seneschal avec la collaboration de Philippe d'Artois, comte d'Eu, de Boucicaut le jeune et de Jean de Crésecque, ed. Gaston Raymond (Paris: Firmin Didot, 1905).

105. Both Loyalty and the motif of the dream vision, perhaps a rewriting of Lover's dream in the *Roman*, are firsts in Christine's *œuvre*. In the *Chemin*, published soon after the *Dit*, the Cumaean Sibyl descends to a sleeping Christine and takes her on a voyage to faraway places, including Jerusalem and up to the heavens.

106. Charity Cannon Willard has suggested that Boucicaut's Order of the White Lady on the Green Shield was the inspiration for Christine's Order of the Rose. See Willard, "Christine de Pizan and the Order of the Rose," in *Ideals for Women in the Works of Christine de Pizan*, ed. Diane Bornstein (Detroit: Michigan Consortium for Medieval and Early Modern Studies, 1981), 51–67, at 58. The fourteenth century had in any case been a time of chivalric revivalism that encouraged the establishment of several knightly orders, the most famous of which is still Edward III's Order of the Garter, founded in 1348 in England. In 1369 in France, Louis of Bourbon founded the order of the *Ecu d'Or* (Golden Shield), welcoming knights who promised they would honor ladies. In 1394 Louis, Duke of Orléans, at the occasion of his son Charles's baptism, created the *Ordre du Porc-Epic* (Order of the Porcupine; also known as the *Ordre du Camail*, Order of the Cameo).

107. *Œuvres poétiques*, 1:220–21.

> puissance les vouloient **desheriter** de leurs terres, de leurs avoirs et de **leurs honneurs**, et avoient les aucunes desheritees de fait.[108]
>
> (. . . it happened that certain complaints came before the king [about] how many ladies and demoiselles, widows and others, were oppressed and made to suffer by certain powerful men who, by their force and might intended to deprive them of their lands, their possessions and their reputations, and had in fact disinherited certain women).

For his part, the God of Love had earlier said that *sont venues complaintes* (complaints have come, v. 9) from *dames et damoiselles* (v. 11) asking for his help, for without it they will be *desheritees / De leur honneur* and *ahontees* ("robbed / Of their honor and shamed," vv. 15–16). Of special interest is the Boucicaut biographer's inclusion of widows. Christine, as a widow, was forced to file lawsuits after her husband's death to hold on to threatened property.[109] Because of the similarities between the biographer's comments and the God of Love's reasons for writing, Christine's failure to mention widows is notable, especially as she would soon make her sympathies known in Autre Balade VI, which begins:

> Ou donc trouveront reconfort
> Pouvres vesves, de leurs biens despoillées,
> Puis qu'en France qui sieult estre le port
> De leur salut, et ou les exillées
> Seulent fouïr et les desconseillées,
>   Mais or n'i ont plus amistié?
> Les nobles gens n'en ont nulle pitié,
> Aussi n'ont clers li greigneur ne li mendre,
> Ne les princes ne les daignent entendre.[110]
>
> (Where shall they find comfort / Poor widows, robbed of what they had, / Since in France, which used to be the harbor / Of their safety, and where the banished / And disconsolate are used to going, / But

108. *Le Livre des Fais du bon Messire Jehan le Maingre, dit Bouciquaut, Mareschal de France et gouverneur de Jennes*, ed. Denis Lalande (Geneva: Droz, 1985), 160–61. For purposes of this introduction, translated excerpts from Boucicaut are ours. A translation appears in *The Chivalric Biography of Boucicaut, Jean II Le Meingre*, trans. Craig Taylor and Jane H. M. Taylor (Woodbridge: Boydell and Brewer, 2016).

109. Charity Cannon Willard, *Christine de Pizan: Her Life and Works* (New York: Persea, 1984), 39. See also Maureen C. Curnow, "'La Pioche d'Inquisicion': Legal-Judicial Content and Style in Christine de Pizan's *Livre de la Cité des* Dames," in Richards et al., *Reinterpreting Christine*, 158–60.

110. *Autres Balades*, in *Œuvres poétiques*, 1:213. This poem is repeated in the *Advision*, where Christine describes her trials as a widow (*Advision*, Bk. 3, ch. 6).

> where they no longer find friendship? / Nobles no longer pity them / Nor clerics, great or small, / And princes don't deign to hear them.)

Boucicaut surely knew Christine, and may have had her in mind. In a passage remarkably like the sentiments of Autre Balade VI, the biographer says that Boucicaut felt great pity for women, and reflects that:

> . . . moult grant honte estoit a si **noble royaume comme cellui de France**, ou est la **fleur de la chevalerie et noblece du monde**, souffrir que dame ne damoiselle ne femme d'onneur quelconques eust cause de soy plaindre que on lui [eust] tort fait ne grief, et que elles n'eussent, entre tant de chevaliers et escuyers, nulz champions et deffendeurs de leurs querelles, par quoy les mauvais et villains de courage estoient plus hardis a leur courir sus par mains oultrages leur faire, pour ce que femmes sont foibles, et elles n'avoient qui les deffendist.[111]
>
> (. . . what a great shame it was that **such a noble realm as France**, where the **flower of chivalry and worldly nobility exist**, should tolerate that a lady, demoiselle, or honorable woman might have cause for complaint and not have, from among so many knights and squires, champions or defenders of their cases, because of which evil men and those of base intention grew bolder at pursuing them by committing many an outrage, because women are weak and have no means of defending themselves).

A second important and much larger society founded almost a year later, ostensibly for the protection of women, was the Cour amoureuse dite de Charles VI (Court of love attributed to Charles VI), created in 1401 by Philip the Bold of Burgundy (1342–1404) and Louis II, Duke of Bourbon (1337–1410). The Cour brought together a group of nine hundred fifty nobles, clergy, merchants, and humanists, pledged to promote the "*tres loees vertus, c'est assavoir humilité et leauté, à l'onneur, loenge et recommandacion et service de toutes dames et damoiselles*"[112] (the very estimable virtues of humility and loyalty, to the honor, praise and esteem and service of all women). The membership included most of the highest-ranking nobles of France: Charles VI, Louis of Bourbon, and Philip of Burgundy, followed by the king's younger brother, Louis I, Duke of Orléans (1372–1407); John, Duke of Berry (1340–1416), the king's uncle; John of Burgundy (Jean sans Peur, John the Fearless), son of Philip (1371–1419), and Philip's other son, Anthony of

111. *Livre des Fais*, ed. Lalande, 161–62.

112. Carla Bozzolo and Hélène Loyau, *La Cour amoureuse, dite de Charles VI.* 3 vols. (Paris: Le Léopard d'Or, 1982–92), 1:41.

Brabant (1384–1415); and Louis VII, Duke of Bavaria (ca. 1368–1447), brother of the queen. Guillaume de Tignonville, Pierre and Gontier Col, Jean de Montreuil, and Christine's son Jean de Castel (ca. 1384–ca. 1425) also held important positions in the Cour. Other members included the poet Eustache Deschamps; the writer Antoine de la Sale (ca. 1386–ca. 1462), author of *Le petit Jehan de Saintré*; the poet and diplomat Alain Chartier (ca. 1385/90–ca. 1430); and Waléran III of Luxembourg (ca. 1355–1415), appointed Constable of France in 1411.[113]

The first meeting of the Cour amoureuse took place in the Paris residence of the Duke of Burgundy on Valentine's Day, 1401, a day when male lovers were to choose a sweetheart to serve in the coming year (as Christine says in the *Dit*, vv. 639–42). Members were forbidden to write anything, whether in rhyme or in prose, that might dishonor, reproach, belittle, or blame women, and no one could be a member who said or caused another to say *vilaines ne vituperables paroles* (ugly or shameful words) about any woman, for whatever reason, in any place whatsoever.[114]

It is perhaps the very efflorescence of other chivalric orders dedicated to the defense of women around the time the *Tale of the Rose* was composed that contributes to explaining why Christine wished to create the Order of the Rose. Certainly she would have viewed the founding of an order in which women, not men, elected the Order's members as an appropriate remedial measure. Who better than a woman could judge a man's service to women? As in the case of the *Epistre*, a defense of women written by a woman, an order that espoused giving women some control over their own fortunes was another way for a woman to write the book.

To the extent that the chivalric orders as a whole recalled earlier popular literary narratives, especially Arthurian-inspired tales such as those by Chrétien de Troyes and others, the Order of the Rose retroactively edits the ethos they advance, which called upon champions, if willing, to defend ladies' honor. In that sense, the late medieval orders revived and formalized a literary ideal, and they also institutionalized the obligation to act on behalf of complainants. In literature, women were not always sure of finding a champion and thus were at men's mercy. Christine's Order of the Rose therefore brought women the agency required to choose a champion already sworn to act.[115] Given the name of the Order and the

113. Christine honored various members of the Cour by mentioning them in her poetry. She addressed her *Trois Jugemens* to Jean III de Werchin (1374–1415), the seneschal of Hainaut (*Love Debate Poems*, 155); Jean de Chateaumorand (d. 1429) and Guillaume de Montrevel, "l'Hermite de la Faye" (d. 1413), are named in the *Deux amans, Love Debate Poems*, vv. 1627, 1641–42); Chateaumorand is also in the *Chemin* (vv. 4519–20; 4544); and Jean de Torsay (d. after 1428) is celebrated in Autre Balade XII (*Autres Balades,* in *Œuvres poétiques*, 1:220–21).

114. Bozzolo and Loyau, 43.

115. Douglas Kelly, reading the *Epistre*, has suggested that at this point in her career Christine still believed in the value of the courtly paradigm and of love for a woman as a knight's inspiration to

title of its founding poem, this new order must also be considered a further challenge to Jean de Meun's *Roman.*

The issuing of the poem itself is the second of two events. The first would have been the dinner party at which the Order of the Rose was created, which Christine tells us occurred in mid-January 1402. The second involved the composition or presentation of the poem about the dinner party, possibly at a second dinner party dated Valentine's Day, 1402 (the feast day of Valentina Visconti, wife of Louis of Orléans). Thus the gathering at which the Order was founded would have taken place well before and completely outside the reading of the poem, as Eric Hicks stresses. Hicks goes on to surmise that the ballades inserted into the poem, brought by Lady Loyalty[116] and integral to aspirants' induction into the Order, must have been composed by Christine before the rest of the poem was written so as to be of use at the January dinner. Hicks's assumption that the founding dinner was not a fiction is plausible. It would otherwise be difficult to explain Christine's careful dating of the event a month before the poem appeared; were it a fiction, the founding of the Order and the feast could simply have been placed, not inappropriately, at Valentine's Day, along with the *Dit.* Regrettably, in spite of Hicks's meticulous reconstruction of both the event and its commemoration, we have no independent information that the duke's dinner party in fact occurred, or that the Order of the Rose really existed. But even if the Order was nothing more than a fiction, the point—that women could, and should, make decisions about matters affecting their own lives—had been made.

Manuscripts

These editions of the *Epistre au dieu d'Amours* and the *Dit de la Rose* are based on the four extant manuscripts supervised by Christine de Pizan that contain these texts; all of these manuscripts are large volumes of her collected works. Three of

---

chivalric deeds; she would change her opinion later, in such works as the *Duc des vrais amans.* See *Christine de Pizan's Changing Opinion: A Quest for Certainty in the Midst of Chaos* (Cambridge: D. S. Brewer, 2007), 108–12.

116. For Tracy Adams, the *Dit* is marked by an "absent and impotent God of Love" because Loyalty, not Cupid, comes to Christine in her sleep—a hint at the dysfunction of Charles VI's court. See "The Political Significance of Christine de Pizan's Love Poetry," *Cahiers de recherche médiévales et humanistes/Journal of Medieval and Humanistic Studies (CRMH)* 17 (2009): 353–71, at 366 (accessible online at <https://journals.openedition.org/crm/11539>). But by making Loyalty the God of Love's messenger, Christine signals that loyalty in love is a principal ethical point of the *Dit.* As noted earlier, she appears to accept and even promote the foundational principles of humility and loyalty specified in the statutes of the Cour amoureuse, that is, "comme dit est que nostre amoureuse Court et seignourie est principanment [*sic*] fondee sur les deux vertus d'umilité et leauté" (as it is said that our loving Court and seigneury is founded principally on the two virtues of humility and loyalty). See Bozzolo and Loyau, 41.

the four (L_1, L_2, and *R*) are believed to have been copied by the author.[117] There are but two copies of the *Dit*: Chantilly, Bibliothèque du Château 492 (L_1), and Paris, BnF, fr. 12779 (L_2). All four volumes contain the *Epistre*: the aforementioned two plus Paris, BnF, fr. 835 (*D*), and London, BL, Harley MS 4431 (*R*). We use the sigla coined by James Laidlaw and widely adopted since: *L* for *Livre* (Book), *D* for Duke's manuscript, and *R* for Reine (Queen).[118]

As indicated earlier, we have opted for a genetic presentation, choosing the earliest manuscript as our base and showing in the variants the changes the author made from one copy to the next. This approach allows us to trace the evolution of the texts under the author's direction and to focus on the specific changes she introduced from version to version.

In the case of the *Dit* Christine made very few changes in her second edition, L_2, which was executed soon, if not immediately, after L_1. There are changes nonetheless. For example, for v. 534, she corrected the verb form *veulz* to *veult*, and in v. 33, she opted for a slight textual modification, substituting the conjunction *et* and noun *assemblee* for the verbal phrase *ot assemblé*. Not all changes were deliberate: the recopying of v. 22 led to the omission of the word *eulx* and a resulting hypometric line.

The evolution of the *Epistre* unfolds over a longer period of time—some dozen years—and is consequently more complex. The larger number of changes for the *Epistre* made between L_1 and L_2 indicate that Christine worked on this text more than she did the *Dit*. She introduced a variety of changes in L_2, including correction of the number of syllables in v. 74; substitution of the non-ambiguous pronoun *elz* for *ilz* in v. 683; and new wording in vv. 129 (*mais* for *et*), 388 (*long* for *loinz*), and 421 (*desprisant* in place of *mesdisant*). All of these changes were maintained in *D* and *R*. Christine did not keep some of the L_2 modifications in preparing later copies, where she reverted to the text of L_1 (see vv. 244 and 258). More often, however, she continued working on the *Epistre*, introducing new modifications in *D*, most of which were kept in *R*. These involved such corrections as syllable count in verses left uncorrected in L_2 (vv. 165, 201, 436); the introduction of an improved rhyme (v. 600: *omme/somme* instead of *omme/fourme*); numerous lexical changes (vv. 83, 101, 164, 171, 185, 212, 213, 345, 350, etc.); the reworking of an entire verse (v. 599); changes of word order (vv. 84, 114, 504, 546, 96, 705, 778); and the addition of new verses (vv. 250 a, b), the repositioning of others (810 a, b), and the elimination of still others (vv. 487–88, 561–62). The Queen's manuscript (*R*) shows that Christine continued working on the *Epistre*, introducing still further variations in word order (v. 57); improving a verse stylistically (v. 397); making lexical changes to some already made in *D* (v. 525); and introducing modifications that intensify the criticism of men (vv. 338, 361). In

117. Ouy et al., *Album*, 194, 222, 325, 340.

118. Laidlaw, "A Publisher's Progress."

sum, we may imagine Christine—the author, editor, and publisher of her own writings—working continuously on them, taking time to bring to them metrical, lexical, and stylistic refinements, and sharpening their ideological focus.

Our edition lists at the end, for comparison's sake, the variants of the *Epistre* contained in a manuscript anthology of poetry dating ca. 1430–1440, Westminster Abbey 21 (*W*), which also includes a copy of Christine's *Dit de la pastoure* (but not the *Dit de la Rose*). As the reader will see, this copy contains a considerable number of errors when compared with those produced under the author's supervision, and it well illustrates the defects that could creep into a text once it had left the author's oversight.

We do not include variants from three other manuscripts that are imperfect copies of the two *L* manuscripts: Paris, BnF, fr. 604, a mid-fifteenth-century paper copy of Chantilly 492 and its companion Chantilly 493, and two eighteenth-century paper copies of BnF, fr. 12779, made for the celebrated medieval scholar and collector Jean-Baptiste de La Curne de Sainte-Palaye (1697–1781): Paris, BnF, Moreau 1686, and Paris, Arsenal 3295. The latter is the more faithful of the two, containing the same lacunae as the original and even an identical cross-out. Moreau 1686 lacks three of the works contained in L_2: the *Oroison Nostre Dame*, the *Quinze Joyes Nostre Dame rimees* and the *Dit de la pastoure*, and changes the ordering of two works, putting the *Enseignemens moraulx* before the *Epistres sur le Roman de la rose.*

L_1 Chantilly, Bibliothèque du Château, 492

This manuscript is the first of two volumes numbered 492 and 493 in the Bibliothèque du Château in Chantilly that together form the first copy of Christine's collected works owned by the French queen, Isabeau of Bavaria. The volumes were compiled over the course of some six years, between 1399 and 1405, and probably presented in installments. The table of contents written on fol. 1v of Chantilly 492 lists twenty-one works and states that the volume was begun in 1399 and "completed and written" in 1402 on the eve of the birth of Saint John the Baptist; that is, June 23.[119] The twenty-one works listed, beginning with the *Cent Balades* (*One Hundred Ballades*) and ending with the *Quinze joyes Nostre Dame rimees* (*Fifteen Joys of Our Lady in Rhyme*), do not account for the entire contents of the current two volumes, nor even for those of the first.[120] The author increased

119. "Cy commencent les rebriches de la table de ce present volume fait et compilé par Cristine de Pizan demoiselle; commencié l'an de grace mil. ccc. iiij^{xx}.xix eschevé et escript en l'an mil quatre cens et deux la veille de la nativité saint Jehan Baptiste" (Here begin the rubrics for the table [of contents] of the present volume, [which was] written and compiled by Demoiselle Christine de Pizan; begun in the year of grace 1399, completed in the year 1402, the eve of the birth of Saint John the Baptist).

120. A scratched-out passage on fol. 163v at the end of the *Quinze Joyes* in all likelihood corresponds to an original *Explicit*; see *DR* ed. Hicks, lix.

the initial twenty-one works by five: the *Oroison Nostre Seigneur* and the *Pastoure* were added to current ms. 492 in fols. 164–182, plus the *Chemin*, *Mutacion*, and *Epistre a la reine* that comprise the current second volume, Chantilly 493, probably completed shortly after the date of the last work (Oct. 5, 1405). The *Epistre* is found on fols. 67c–73d of Chantilly 492; the *Dit* follows immediately on fols. 74a–79a. They are the fourteenth and fifteenth items, respectively.

The two volumes were early on bound into a single volume.[121] Separated into two before its acquisition by Henri of Orléans, Duke of Aumale (1822–1897), in November 1887 from the bookseller Damascène Morgand,[122] the volumes were bequeathed to the Institut de France upon the duke's death a decade later. Nothing has been discovered about its travels during the nearly five hundred intervening years.

Written on parchment, Chantilly 492 measures 291 x 240 mm (justification 205 x 184 mm), and contains 182 written folios preceded and followed by four parchment leaves. The text is presented in two columns of 32 lines (35 for the *Pastoure*). Almost all texts are copied in dark brown ink, with the ink of the *Pastoure* and the table of contents in a lighter brown, indicating their separate execution. Rubrics are a bright red throughout, except for the rubric accompanying the table of contents, which is orange-red. There remains a faint trace of a signature on fol. 2r. Catchwords are generally written in the bottom space between the two columns; the last two, accompanying the two added works (*Oroison Nostre Seigneur* and *Pastoure*), are written more rapidly and aligned with the end of the second column.[123] Fourteen miniatures illustrate various texts, of which six accompany the *Epistre Othea*; neither the *Dit* nor the *Epistre* is illustrated. The artist for the first thirteen miniatures has been named by Inès Villela-Petit the Pastoure Master ("Maître de la Pastoure") for his creation of the charming scene of the *Pastoure* in BnF, fr. 12779, that features shepherdesses, a shepherd, and their flock; this artist works with light colored washes over ink drawings set off against a background of orange, dark pink, or blue wash decorated with scrollwork.[124] The fourteenth miniature in the volume was executed by the artist Villela-Petit

121. Tania van Hemelryck and Christine Reno, "Dans l'atelier de Christine de Pizan. Le manuscrit Harley 4431," in *Du scriptorium à l'atelier: Copistes et enlumineurs dans la conception du livre manuscrit au Moyen Age*, *Pecia* 13 (2010): 267–86, at 271; Gilbert Ouy et al., *Album*, 199–200; Olivier Delsaux, Gilbert Ouy, Christine Reno, and Inès Villela-Petit, "Le premier recueil de la reine," *Médiévales* 53 (2012): 46–55.

122. See *Chantilly. Le Cabinet des livres. Manuscrits*, 3 vols. (Paris: Plon-Nourrit, 1900), 2:84–86. On fol. 2r is inscribed the shelf number 1667 that the manuscript was assigned in the Duke of Aumale's collection.

123. They were probably written before the rubrics, as the catchword on fol. 73v corresponds to the first words of the text on fol. 74r rather than with the rubric that opens that folio.

124. Ouy et al., *Album*, 110–17. An image of the miniature can be viewed at the Gallica website: https://gallica.bnf.fr/ark:/12148/btv1b60001038/f317.image.r=manuscrit%20francais%2012779 (fol. 157r).

has called the Chantilly Blue-yellow-pink Master ("Maître bleu-jaune-rose de Chantilly") because of his work with those three colors both in this painting and in those of the second volume, Chantilly 493.

The *Dit* opens with a six-line blue and gold filigreed letter with a dark blue interior dotted with red, one of fifteen in the volume. The letter is extended in the margin by a nine-line blue and gold festoon composed of half fleurs-de-lys. The *Epistre* begins with a much simpler two-line red ink letter against a dark blue filigreed background. Red and blue paragraph marks are used throughout both texts, and indeed throughout the volume; of the two colors, blue is predominant.[125]

The volume features a luxuriously tooled, late nineteenth-century red morocco binding made by the Parisian company Belz-Niedree.[126] The inside of the binding is lined with blue leather decorated with gold, and the first and last flyleaves are doubled with blue taffeta.

Bibliography

Bulletin mensuel de la librairie Damascène Morgand, vol. 4, no. 23 (November 1888), n° 15958; • *Chantilly. Le Cabinet des Livres. Manuscrits*, 2:84–86; • Delsaux et al., "Le premier recueil de la reine"; • *Epistre Othea*, ed. Gabriella Parussa (Geneva: Droz, 1999), 94–95, 106–7; • Laidlaw, "A Publisher's Progress," 35–52, 68–69; • Gianni Mombello, *La Tradizione manoscritta dell' "Epistre Othea" di Christine de Pizan: Prolegomeni all'edizione del testo* (Turin: Academia delle Scienze, 1967), 106–16; • *Œuvres poétiques*, 1:xix–xx; • Ouy et al., *Album*, 186–200; • Gilbert Ouy and Christine Reno, "Les hésitations de Christine: Etude des variantes de graphies dans trois manuscrits autographes de Christine de Pizan," *Revue des Langues Romanes* 92 (1988): 265–86; • *Répertoire général et méthodique de la librairie Morgand et Fatout* (Paris: Damascène Morgand and Charles Fatout, 1882), n° 1482; Van Hemelryck and Reno, "Dans l'atelier de Christine de Pizan," 271–72; • Frédéric Vergne, *La Bibliothèque du Prince. Château de Chantilly. Les Manuscrits* (Paris: Editerra, 1995), 222.

L_2 **Paris, BnF, fr. 12779**

Written on parchment, this one-volume manuscript lost several folios through the theft of miniatures.[127] It initially contained the same works as Chantilly

125. There are minor discrepancies in the placement of the paragraph marks between this manuscript and the following, BnF, fr. 12779, which are close to identical in layout.

126. Ouy et al., *Album*, 199.

127. Five miniatures have disappeared: three from the *Epistre Othea* between fols. 106–107 and 108–109, one at the beginning of the *Debat de deux amans* (fol. 49 is missing), and one from the *Oroison Nostre Seigneur* (the entire poem has been removed between fols. 156 and 157). The folios were numbered after the theft(s). Folios 35 and 36 are also missing: they contained most of the *Lay leonime*, of which only the last eighteen lines appear on fol. 37r; however, this poem is not illustrated in any other manuscript.

492, arranged in exactly the same order. In fact, the layout of most folios in the two manuscripts is identical; in the case of the *Epistre*, the layout is congruent throughout, while for the *Dit* it is identical until the final two columns, where a discrepancy of one line is introduced. The manuscript can be confidently dated to 1402 for most of the works copied therein,[128] with the *Pastoure*, dated May 1403, added to the corpus, as it was in Chantilly 492. A couple of corrections and improvements made over against the Chantilly manuscript indicate that fr. 12779 is the latter of the two.[129]

The volume consists of 172 folios measuring 326 x 251 mm (justification 215 x 184 mm), preceded and followed by three paper flyleaves; the text is in two columns of 32 lines. The bulk of the folios (between 26r–156v) have text written in dark brown ink, whereas the ink of the folios before and after is medium brown in color. Existing rubrics are a bright red; however, the majority of rubrics have not been executed. Nine miniatures remain, the product of the Pastoure Master; the assistance of the Master of Jeanne Ravenelle has been identified in three that accompany the *Epistre Othea*.[130] As in Chantilly 492, neither the *Epistre* nor the *Dit* is illustrated. Both of these texts begin with large blue and gold letters against a background of dark blue and red filigree; that of the *Epistre* is four spaces high, that of the *Dit* is six. Red and blue paragraph marks punctuate the text, with the colors alternating regularly. There are traces of three different series of signatures; catchwords begin toward the end of the second column and often continue into the margin.

A fifteenth-century sanguine-colored signature [?] ("Hagar") fills the column that was left blank on fol. 77b at the end of the *Dit*; it is accompanied by a motto ("Y doth myn"[?]) The volume belonged to the great medievalist and collector La Curne de Sainte-Palaye and subsequently to the Cabinet des Chartes, perhaps the marquis de Paulmy, and to Georges-Jean Mouchet (1737–1807), Sainte-Palaye's collaborator on the *Glossaire de l'ancien langage françois* (shelfmark "Mouchet n° 6" on fol. 1r). Another old shelfmark is S-F 6259 (Supplément français of the Bibliothèque nationale de France).

Bibliography

BnF Gallica, <https://gallica.bnf.fr/ark:/12148/btv1b60001038> (digitized version of the entire manuscript); *DR* ed. Hicks, lxxi–lxxii; • James Douglas Farquhar and Eric C. Hicks, "Christine de Pizan's *Dit de la Pastoure:* Membra

128. The *Rose* debate letters lack Christine's letter to Pierre Col dated Oct. 2, 1402. As with Chantilly 492, the *Autres Balades* do not include poems written after 1402: for example, n° 38 dated 1403, and n° 42, which is a lamentation on the death of Philip the Bold, Duke of Burgundy (April 27, 1404).

129. For example, vv. 129, 230, 388 and 421 of the *Epistre* and vv. 33, 216, 352 and 534 of the *Dit*. See also Ouy et al., *Album*, 218n25.

130. Ouy et al., *Album*, 224–25; identification by Inès Villela-Petit.

disjecta," *Scriptorium* 30 (1976): 196, 198; Laidlaw, "A Publisher's Progress," 42–52; • Mombello, *Tradizione*, 63–70; • *Œuvres poétiques*, 1:xviii–xix, xx n. 1; • Ouy and Reno, "Les hésitations"; • Ouy et al., *Album*, 214-26; • Lucie Schaefer, "Die Illustrationen zu den Handschriften der Christine de Pizan," *Marburger Jahrbuch für Kunstwissenschaft* 10 (1937): 181–83 and fig. 113; • Inès Villela-Petit, *Le Gothique international: L'art en France au temps de Charles VI* (Paris: Hazan / Musée du Louvre, 2004), 108; • Charity Cannon Willard, "Christine de Pizan's Clock of Temperance," *L'Esprit créateur* 2 (1962): 149–54.

_D_ Paris, BnF, fr. 835

This manuscript constitutes the first component of a very large volume that by 1510 had been divided, and consists today of five manuscripts in the *fonds français* of the BnF: fr. 835, 606, 836, 605 and 607.[131] The ensemble includes a number of works composed after the enlarged *Livre* of 1405.[132]

The original volume was intended for Louis I, Duke of Orléans, but acquired by his uncle, John, Duke of Berry, in 1408, following Louis's assassination in November 1407. It evidences some reordering of the early elements of the collection,[133] plus some last-minute modifications that reflect the change of patrons. These involve large alterations, such as the removal of the *Dit* (given its association with the Duke, including its setting in one of his Paris residences), and the transformation of another work dedicated to Louis, the *Livre de la Prodommie de l'omme* (*Book of Man's Integrity*), into the *Livre de Prudence* (*Book of Prudence*), by means of deft changes made to the already-copied text.[134]

The initial plan of the collection called for changing the placement of the *Epistre* and the *Dit*, which for the first time would not have followed each other directly. The *Epistre* is numbered "viij" in the collection, and immediately follows the *Autres Balades*, which are titled here *Pluseurs balades de divers propos* (*Several Ballades on Different Topics*). The *Epistre* occupies fols. 45a–50a. Had the *Dit* not been removed, it would have come in eleventh place, after the *Debat de deux amans*, the final column of which (64a) has been recopied in lighter ink, and the *Trois Jugemens*, begun on fol. 64b in the same light ink.[135]

Fr. 835 consists of 103 parchment folios, preceded by three flyleaves (two paper, one parchment) and followed by one parchment and one paper flyleaf.

131. Laidlaw, "A Publisher's Progress," 52–59.

132. The *Duc des vrais amans*, the *Epistre a Eustace Morel*, the *Proverbes moraulx*, and the *Cité*.

133. See Ouy et al., *Album*, 178–79.

134. Ouy et al., *Album*, 177–80; Liliane Dulac and Christine Reno, "Rhétorique, critique et politique dans le *Livre de Prudence* de Christine de Pizan: quelques aperçus." In *La Vertu de prudence entre Moyen Âge et l'âge classique*, ed. Evelyne Berriot-Salvadore, Catherine Pascal, François Roudaut and Trung Tran (Paris: Classiques Garnier, 2012), 193–222, at 199–203.

135. Ouy et al., *Album*, 231n19.

Folios measure 348 x 260 mm (justification 233 x 180 mm). The text is copied in dark brown ink up to fol. 63v, and in lighter brown ink from thereon to the end. Rubrics are in bright red, and there are also running titles bearing the title of each work and its place in the volume in Roman numerals from I to XIV; these are in reddish orange.

The volume is embellished by six miniatures. The first five are the work of the Epistre of Othea Master, and the last, accompanying the *Dit de Poissy*, by the Egerton Master. The *Epistre au dieu d'Amours* is among the works illustrated, on fol. 45a. In the Epistre of Othea Master's composition, the God of Love sits on a grassy seat against a backdrop of a trellis covered with pink roses; three birds fly overhead. He wears a long, pink houppelande (over-garment) fringed in white, his large blue wings with golden feather outlines spread behind him. He holds two long arrows in his left arm, and with his right hand holds out a folded letter to the young noble kneeling on one knee at his side. The young man wears a short orange houppelande, the right sleeve of which is decorated with clovers, and particolored orange and white hose.[136]

In keeping with the high quality of the illustrations, the volume has fairly elaborate ancillary decorations, including a luxurious border on fol. 1r, executed by one of the most celebrated artisans of the day, Pierre Gilbert.[137] Six works begin with large illuminated letters, including a four-line pink C on gold leaf, filled with a double-curved vine. Two-line champ initials (that is, gold on a blue and red background) and champ paragraph signs complete the decoration.

After the Duke of Berry acquired this edition of Christine's collected works, the volume passed to his daughter Marie, Duchess of Bourbon (a Bourbon signature appears at the bottom of fol. 28r). The collection became part of the library of Francis I (1494–1547) in 1523 when he seized the goods of the Bourbons. There are three seventeenth-century shelfmarks from the former Royal Library (now the Bibliothèque nationale de France): *cinq cents nonante trois* (Rigault), 466 (Dupuy), and 7217 (Regius).[138] BnF, fr. 835 is bound in late eighteenth-century red morocco decorated with a triple thin gold line around the edges.

Bibliography

Laidlaw, "A Publisher's Progress," 52–59, 70–72; • Millard Meiss, *French Painting in the Time of Jean de Berry: The Late Fourteenth Century and the Patronage of the Duke*, 2 vols. (London and New York: Phaidon, 1967), 1:242, 300, 398n77, 416; • Millard Meiss, with Sharon Off Dunlap Smith and Elizabeth Home

136. The image, on fol. 45r, can be seen at <https://gallica.bnf.fr/ark:/12148/btv1b8449047c/f97.image.r=manuscrit%20francais%20835>.

137. Ouy et al., *Album*, 72–75, 235; identification by Inès Villela-Petit.

138. These three different shelfmarks were assigned by royal librarians in 1622, 1645, and 1682, respectively.

Beatson, *French Painting in the Time of Jean de Berry: The Limbourgs and their Contemporaries*, 2 vols. (New York: Pierpont Morgan Library / George Braziller, 1974), 1:37–38, 292–93, 440n150; 2: figs. 139, 145; • *Œuvres poétiques*, 1:v-xii; • Gilbert Ouy, "Une énigme codicologique: Les signatures des cahiers dans les manuscrits autographes de Christine de Pizan," in *Calames et Cahiers: Mélanges de codicologie et de paléographie offerts à Léon Gilissen*, ed. Jacques Lemaire and Emile van Balberghe (Brussels: Centre d'Etude des Manuscrits, 1985), 119–31; Ouy et al., *Album*, 59–67, 72–74, 131–42, 178–80, 228–38; • *Paris 1400: Les arts sous Charles VI*, ed. Elisabeth Taburet-Delahaye, François Avril et al. (Paris: Arthème Fayard / Réunion des musées nationaux, 2004), n° 62A and 135; Paris, BnF, Moreau 1655, fols. 204r–205v, n° 577.

_R_ London, BL, Harley MS 4431

This final collection of Christine's works, presented to Queen Isabeau of Bavaria in 1414, is the largest and the most luxurious.[139] Three works have been added to those contained in the Duke's manuscript: the *Complainte amoureuse*,[140] *Encore autres balades*, and the *Cent balades d'amant et de dame*. The *Epistre a la reine* (*Letter to the Queen*), dated October 5, 1405, was initially included but later erased (fol. 255a–c). There is no sign that the *Dit* was ever meant to be included in the collection. The *Epistre*, found on fols. 51b–56c, is here numbered xij and is preceded and followed by *Encore autres balades* and the *Complainte amoureuse*, respectively.

Initially a very large single volume of 398 parchment folios, the codex was divided into two at the time of its rebinding in 1962, at which time paper leaves were inserted to protect the paintings.[141] The first volume contains 179 folios measuring 366 x 280 mm,[142] preceded by five flyleaves (three paper and two parchment) and followed by a single paper flyleaf; the second contains 223 folios measuring 366 x 279 mm, preceded by four and followed by three paper flyleaves. Justification varies.[143]

The volume contains 132 miniatures in all, the vast majority attributed by Inès Villela-Petit to the Cité des Dames Master and his workshop, and five to the

139. Digital images of the Queen's manuscript can be seen online at <www.pizan.lib.ed.ac.uk/gallery/index.html>. For the dating of the manuscript, see James Laidlaw, "The Date of the Queen's MS" (2005), 2, also accessible online at <www.pizan.lib.ed.ac.uk/harley4431date.pdf>.

140. This same title was used by a different poem in the Duke's manuscript; it is here renamed *Autre complainte amoureuse*.

141. The binding is the house binding of the British Museum, green leather with gold tooling.

142. The volume contains two folios whose numbers 51 and 52 have been crossed out and do not figure in the numbering, which stops in this volume at 177.

143. See Ouy et al., *Album*, 322, 338–39.

Bedford Master.[144] The *Epistre* is illustrated on fol. 51b by an image similar to that in the Duke's manuscript. Here, the crowned god is seated on a grassy throne against a background of green and blue trees and four large birds. His wings are a brilliant yellow rimmed with orange; he wears a dark red houppelande decorated with golden wing motifs and carries both a slim bow and two arrows in his left hand. With his right, he hands a letter to the young noble dressed in blue and white with a red scarf kneeling on one knee before him.

Several works in the two volumes begin with large decorated letters. The *Epistre* begins with one of 21 large initials found in the collection: a five-line blue C on a gold leaf background, prolonged in the middle column by black pen vines with gold leaves. Several of the works have small decorated initials and champ paragraph marks, but the *Epistre* does not.

The Harley volume was brought to England in the 1420s by John of Lancaster, first Duke of Bedford (1389–1435), and given to his second wife, Jacquetta of Luxembourg (1415/16–1472); her signature is on fols. 1r, 51v, 52v; her motto, *sur tous autres* (above all others), appears on fols. 1r and 387r, and her name is scratched into the miniature on fol. 115r. The volume passed to her son Anthony Woodville (1442–1483) by her second marriage to Richard Woodville, first Earl Rivers (1405–1469); Anthony's motto *nulle la vault* (she has no equal) and signature are on fol. 1r as well.[145] (The volume also contains the signature of the Flemish courtier and nobleman Louis de Gruuthuse [ca. 1427–1492] on fol. 1r, but there is no corroborating evidence that he actually owned it.) By 1676 the volume belonged to Henry Cavendish, second Duke of Newcastle (1630–1691), whose ex-libris appears on fol. 1r. After his death it passed to his granddaughter Dame Henrietta Cavendish Holles, who married the bibliophile and arts patron Edward Harley, second Earl of Oxford (1689–1741), in 1713. Their manuscripts were sold to the British nation in 1753.

Bibliography

Marilynn Desmond and Pamela Sheingorn, *Myth, Montage, and Visuality in Late Medieval Manuscript Culture: Christine de Pizan's Epistre Othea* (Ann Arbor: University of Michigan Press, 2003); • *Epistre Othea*, ed. Parussa, 103–4; • Mary Weitzel Gibbons [Landor], "The Bath of the Muses and Visual Allegory in the *Chemin de long estude*," in *Christine de Pizan and the Categories of Difference*, ed. Marilynn Desmond (Minneapolis: University of Minnesota Press, 1998), 128–45; • Ilona Hans-Collas and Pascal Schandel, with Hanno Wisjman, *Manuscrits enluminés des anciens Pays-Bas méridionaux*, vol. 1: *Manuscrits de Louis de Bruges* (Paris: BnF, 2009), 15; • Christian Heck, "De la mystique à la raison: La spéculation

144. Ouy et al., *Album*, 327, 343.

145. See note 151 below.

et le chemin du ciel dans le *Livre du chemin de long estude*," in *Au champ des escriptures*, ed. Eric Hicks, with Diego Gonzalez and Philippe Simon, Actes du IIIe colloque international sur Christine de Pizan (Lausanne, 18–22 juillet 1998) (Paris: Honoré Champion, 2000), 709–22; • Sandra Hindman, "The Composition of the Manuscript of Christine de Pizan's Collected Works in the British Library: A Reassessment," *British Library Journal* 9 (1983): 93–123; • Sandra Hindman, "With Ink and Mortar: Christine de Pizan's 'Cité des Dames,'" *Feminist Studies* 10 (1984): 457–83; Sandra Hindman and Stephen Perkinson, "Insurgent Voices: Illustrated Versions of Christine de Pizan's *Le Livre du duc des vrais amans*," in *The City of Scholars: New Approaches to Christine de Pizan*, ed. Margarete Zimmerman and Dina De Rentiis (Berlin and New York: Walter De Gruyter, 1994), 221–23; • Noriko Kobayashi, "La dernière étape de l'enluminure des oeuvres de Christine de Pizan," *Art de l'enluminure* 18 (Sept.–Nov. 2006): 2–65; • Laidlaw, "A Publisher's Progress"; • Laidlaw, "Christine and the Manuscript Tradition," in *Christine de Pizan: A Casebook*, ed. Barbara K. Altmann and Deborah L. McGrady (New York and London: Routledge, 2003), 231–49; • Laidlaw, "Christine's Lays: Does Practice Make Perfect?," in *Contexts and Continuities*: Proceedings of the IVth International Colloquium on Christine de Pizan (Glasgow, July 21–27, 2000), published in honour of Liliane Dulac, ed. Angus J. Kennedy et al. (Glasgow: University of Glasgow Press, 2002), 2:467–81; • Laidlaw, "The Date of the Queen's MS"; • Laidlaw, "Christine de Pizan: The Making of the Queen's Manuscript (London, British Library, Harley 4431)," in *Patrons, Authors and Workshops: Books and Book Production in Paris around 1400*, ed. Godfried Croenen and Peter Ainsworth (Louvain, Paris, and Dudley, MA: Peeters, 2006), 297–310; • "*Livre de la Cité des dames*: Kritische Text-edition auf Grund der sieben überlieferten 'manuscrits originaux' des Textes," ed. Monika Lange, Diss., University of Hamburg, 1974, xli–xlviii, lxv; • "The *Livre de la Cité des dames of Christine de Pisan: A Critical Edition*," ed. Maureen Cheney Curnow, PhD diss.,Vanderbilt University, 1975, 372–78; • *Le Livre du Duc des vrais amans*, ed. Thelma Fenster (Binghamton, NY: Center for Medieval and Early Renaissance Texts and Studies, 1995), 38–43; • Deborah McGrady, "What is a Patron? Benefactors and Authorship in Harley 4431, Christine de Pizan's Collected Works," in Desmond, *Categories of Difference*, 195–214; • Meiss et al., *The Limbourgs and their Contemporaries*, 1:24, 39–40, 290, 292–96, 379, 436n51, 437n73, 440n156, 163, 165; 2: figs. 38, 42, 45, 114, 136–137, 142, 148, 151, and 154–55; • Meiss, *Late Fourteenth Century*, 1:89, 356; • Ouy et al., *Album*, 180–84, 317–47; • *Paris 1400*, n° 55; • Gabriella Parussa, "Veoir, oïr, entendre: *L'Epistre Othea* et le cycle iconographique de deux manuscrits," in *Favola, mito ed altri saggi di letteratura e filologia in onore di Gianni Mombello*, ed. Antonella Amatuzzi and Paola Cifarelli (Alessandria: Edizioni dell'Orso, 2004), 335–57; • Schaefer, "Die Illustrationen," 119–208 and figs 1–40; • Charles Sterling, *La peinture médiévale à Paris 1300–1500*, 2 vols. (Paris: Bibliothèque des

Arts / Fondation Wildenstein, 1987–90, 1:287, 292, and fig. 196; Van Hemelryck and Reno, "Dans l'atelier de Christine de Pizan"; Inès Villela-Petit, "La France et le gothique international (1360–1430)," in *L'Art du Moyen Age en France*, ed. Philippe Plagnieux (Paris: Citadelles et Mazenod, 2010), 382–441, at p. 389; Willard, "Christine de Pizan's Clock of Temperance."

W London, Westminster Abbey MS 21

Measuring 281 x 204 mm, the manuscript consists of 80 folios of paper, bound at the end with two treatises on parchment of Charles the Bold, Duke of Burgundy, that apparently served as wrappers.[146] Several folios were severely damaged, but were skillfully restored.[147] Only two watermarks are found throughout: the first, a flower, and the second, a *P* ending in a trilobe and topped with a cross.[148] The disposition of watermarks points to the organic quality of the volume, which was not assembled from disparate pieces but rather compiled intentionally. Another feature pointing to the volume's organicity is the use of dry point ruling throughout, despite different patterns of ruling that are adapted to the different types of poems contained therein.[149] The copying was done by multiple hands using uniform dark ink.

The volume contains some sixty-eight distinct works, none of whose authors is identified. Most of them are poems, especially ballades that occupy one side of a folio or a column. The longest are Christine de Pizan's *Epistre au dieu d'Amours* (fols. 52r–64v) and her *Dit de la pastoure* (fols. 65r–75v).

146. We have been unable to verify the collation of Robinson and James, perhaps done when the manuscript was being rebound. See J. Armitage Robinson and M. R. James, *The Manuscripts of Westminster Abbey* (Cambridge: Cambridge University Press, 1909). 77.

147. The first folio is a mere tongue of paper 120 x 15 mm mounted on a whole new leaf; fols. 2–4 are jagged remnants on which the writing has partially disappeared; almost all the remaining folios have received minor repair, particularly in the bottom corner. There is at least one folio missing between fols. 45 and 46. In addition, the writing on fols. 6v and 7v is partially obscured by stains that occur elsewhere but do not affect legibility.

148. The flower is located on folios 10, 11, 12, 14, 71, and 78–80; the *P* on fols. 16, 18–20, 23, 28, 30, 32, 33, 36, 38, 40, 41, 43, 45, 46, 48, 50, 52, 55, 57, 59–62, and 69. The P is closest to Briquet 8485, dating from the 1430s in the area of Rouen. The flower does not resemble any attested in the standard watermark references for the period (*The New Briquet, Jubilee Edition. A Facsimile of the 1907 edition with supplementary material contributed by a number of scholars*. Edited by Allan Stevenson. 4 vols. Amsterdam: The Paper Publications Society, 1968; Gerhard Piccard, *Wasserzeichen: Blatt, Blume, Baum*. Stuttgart, W. Kohlhammer, 1982).

149. One finds, for example, a single vertical line that sets the left margin, which is the case for the *Epistre*, or a double vertical that creates the space for initial capitals, or, in the case of folios with two columns of writing, a double vertical at left for the first column and a single vertical that situates the second column.

The volume lacks signatures and catchwords, and is tightly bound in half-morocco, which makes it difficult to distinguish quire structure. What is clear is that the *Epistre*, beginning on fol. 52r, was apparently not copied immediately after the works that precede, as fol. 51v was left blank, and was filled later with drafts of two letters, two versions of the first in Latin and one version of the second, in English, the latter beginning "Trysty and welbelovyd Master Gyles. . . . "[150] In fols. 1–51r, initial capitals are all uniformly highlighted with a stroke of ochre, another feature indicating a hiatus, however brief, between the copying of the *Epistre* (and following works) and those that precede. These strokes have faded over time.

The *Epistre* bears, at the end (fol. 64v), the signature "Scales," embellished with elaborate cadels. It is not clear whether the signature belongs to a scribe or an owner.[151] The version of the *Epistre* found in the Westminster manuscript is very close to that contained in manuscript *R*, indicating that it might have been copied from it or from a manuscript close to it. Frequent tiny marginal marks throughout correspond for the most part to paragraph marks in the Harley manuscript. *W* contains a relatively large number of errors, however, evident in the list of variants. The French used throughout the manuscript bears no trace of Anglo-Norman.

Bibliography

Paul Meyer, "Notice d'un recueil manuscrit de poésies françaises du XIIIe au XVe siècle, appartenant à Westminster Abbey," *Bulletin de la Société des Anciens Textes Français* 1 (1875): 25–36; • Robinson and James, *The Manuscripts of Westminster Abbey*, 77.

Versification

Reading Christine's Poetry

Christine's skill as a poet is apparent in her handling of meter and rhyme as well as in her lively treatment of other poetic ornaments. She liked to try her hand at different types of narrative poems, composing ten-, eight-, and seven-syllable narrative verses. Her lyric poetry included ballades, rondeaus, virelais, and other short, sometimes challenging, types of short poems, particularly lais. She liked to mix verse and prose (as in the *Epistre Othea*, a book of moral instruction), or lyric and narrative verse (as in the *Duc des vrais amans*).

150. We are grateful to Christine Reynolds, Assistant Keeper of the Muniments at Westminster Abbey, for the information that the formula "Trysty and welbelovd" was a common opening in letters of the Tudor period.

151. We have not been able to find any trace of scribes bearing that name. Scales was a barony from the thirteenth through the fifteenth century; its last official lord was Anthony Woodville, second Earl Rivers, who inherited the Harley manuscript from his mother. Born in 1442, he was executed in 1483 at the behest of the future Richard III.

Where today we expect prose, the most frequent organizing principle of French narrative was poetry, especially the rhyming couplet. The octosyllabic couplet, in particular, was used for many types of medieval poetry, as in the *Dit*. In contrast, the *Epistre* is written in decasyllables, a meter that better suits its declamatory register: compare the *Epistre*'s stasis with the gaiety and movement of the *Dit*.[152] The *Dit*'s inserted ballades and rondeau, a first example of Christine's mixing of narrative and lyric,[153] introduce variety and heighten the effect of the fixed-form poems. Varying line length sets off the closing sections of the *Epistre*: verses 797–800 are probably to be read as two couplets of heptasyllabic lines; the octosyllabic couplets of vv. 801–20 name the gods and goddesses; finally, the last two lines of the poem, vv. 821–22, the god's signature lines, are once again heptasyllabic.

Given the nature of the French language itself, in which stress predictably falls on the final syllable of a word or group of words, the counting of syllables rather than the stressed foot is fundamental to French verse. (Because English has relatively unpredictable word stress, English verse depends upon varying word stress and thus allows for rhythmic patterns such as iambs, trochees, dactyls, anapests, and the like.) Rhyme affects syllable count, and line-final rhymes are "feminine" or "masculine": if rhyme words end in *–e* or *–es*, as on nouns, verbs, or adjectives, or on the sixth person *–ent* verbal ending, they are deemed feminine, and their final syllable will not be counted; otherwise, they are deemed masculine, and their final syllable does count.

For example, verses of the *Epistre* may be scanned as in the following couplet:

Et / Jehan / de / Meun / ou / *Ro* / *mmant* / *de* / *la* / *Rose*:
1 2 3 4 5 6 7 8 9 10

Quel / loinz / pro / cez! / Quel / di / ffi / ci / le / chose! (*Epistre* vv. 387–88)
1 2 3 4 5 6 7 8 9 10

The final *e* at the rhyme in *Rose* and *chose* does not figure in the syllable count; the *–se* is pronounced not as a full syllable but as a short off-glide. Where a final *–e* appears within a line before a word beginning with a consonant, it does count; thus the final *–e* of *difficile* was pronounced (as it still is in modern French poetry, if not in modern spoken French). Hence *difficile*, which is three syllables in current spoken French, counts as four syllables in the second line above. In position

152. See Daniel Poirion, *Le Poète et le prince: l'évolution du lyrisme courtois de Guillaume de Machaut à Charles d'Orléans* (Grenoble: Allier, 1965; rpt. Geneva: Slatkine, 1978), 449.

153. See the comments of Maureen Barry McCann Boulton, *The Song in the Story: Lyric Insertions in French Narrative Fiction, 1200–1400* (Philadelphia: University of Pennsylvania Press, 1993), 117–18.

before another vowel line internally, –*e* was elided in principle, as *peine a* (*pei-na*) and *quelque acointance* (*quel-qacointance*) in these lines:

> Au / tres / me / ttent / grant / pei / n*e* a / pro / cu / rer
> 1 2 3 4 5 6 7 8 9 10
> Par / me / ssa / ge / sou / par / quel / qu*e* a / coin / tance (*Epistre*, vv. 60–61)
> 1 2 3 4 5 6 7 8 9 10

On the other hand, the instability of –*e* [ə] in Old and Middle French offered poets metrical flexibility, sometimes allowing for their full pronunciation, as in *cë* of this verse:

> Je / leur / re / spons / que / ceulz / qui / cë / es / crirent
> 1 2 3 4 5 6 7 8 9 10 (*Epistre*, v. 311)

The –*e* of *cë*, which precedes another vowel, would normally elide, but that would make the line hypometric. The modern editor has suggested how this verse should scan by adding the diaresis over the –*e* to indicate that it should be fully pronounced. (The third person plural –*ent* verb ending follows the rule for final –*e* at the rhyme, as noted above.)

A masculine rhyme is produced when both rhyme words end in a consonant or a vowel other than an unstressed –*e*, as in these verses:

> S'en / tre / di / ent: / "Je / sçay / bien / de / tes / **fais**:
> 1 2 3 4 5 6 7 8 9 10
>
> Te / lle / t'ai / më / et / tu / le / jo / lis / **fais** (*Epistre*, vv. 127–28)
> 1 2 3 4 5 6 7 8 9 10

(In the first line above, *fais* is a noun meaning "deeds." In the second, *fais* is the second person singular of the verb *faire*, "to do, to make.")

> Sa / be / lle / suer / de / cuer / es / **lit**,
> 1 2 3 4 5 6 7 8
>
> M'ot / a / ppres / té / un / trop / beau / **lit**: (*Dit*, vv. 273–74)
> 1 2 3 4 5 6 7 8

The Ballades and Rondeau

Each of the three ballades in the *Dit de la Rose* is composed of three *huitains* (stanzas of eight lines, which are here decasyllabic), the form Christine used most often.[154] All three rhyme in *ababbcbc*. Each eighth line of a *huitain* is a refrain: in the first (vv. 129–52), Loyalty explains that she has come with important news; in the second (vv. 153–76), she announces the conditions for accepting the roses, and, in the refrain, each recipient is enjoined to uphold the honor of ladies. In the third (vv. 197–224), participants take the Order. This final ballade is unique among the three in containing an envoi (an added stanza of four lines, making the poem four lines longer than the other two). The envoi was a novelty at the time, and may have been added to emphasize the performative significance of this third ballade. As a group, then, the refrains coalesce around three key points: Loyalty's bringing of the news; the requirement for accepting the symbolic rose; and the taking of the oath.

The rondeau follows a conventional format: each of its first two stanzas is of two lines; the refrain of the second stanza consists of the first line of the first stanza. In the last stanza the refrain consists of both lines of the first stanza.

Rhyme

Both Daniel Poirion and John Fox have observed that Christine's rhymes are in general more careful and more sophisticated than those of many of her contemporaries.[155] Christine often strove for rich rhyme, which required the identical pronunciation of the consonant preceding the stressed vowel, as in ***nouvel: revel*** (*Dit*, vv. 19–20). This differs from simple rhyme, which calls for the identity of the final stressed vowel and all following sounds but not the consonant preceding the final stressed vowel: *d'avan**ture***: *l'en**dure*** (*Epistre*, vv. 87–88) or *ch**ose***: *cl**ose*** (*Dit*, vv. 31–32).

So-called "grammatical rhymes" are paired words having a shared etymology but different prefixes or no prefix at all, as *jure*: *parjure* (*Dit*, vv. 629–30), *commise*: *remise* (*Dit*, vv. 599–600), *apportees*: *portees* (*Dit*, vv. 529–30), *honnourees*: *deshonnourees* (*Epistre*, vv. 29–30), and *couvrir*: *descouvrir* (*Epistre* vv. 139–40). But Christine occasionally exploits a like technique to highlight antonyms which have no etymological connection, some of which serve to emphasize the themes of the poem:

> Et qui dire ne les veult mie **appertes**
> Les monstre au doy par parolles **couvertes**. (*Epistre*, vv. 157–58)
> or
> Adont fut la sale **estourmie**,
> Il n'y ot personne **endormie**, (*Dit*, vv. 113–14)

154. See Poirion, *Le Poète et le prince*, 374.

155. Poirion, *Le Poète et le prince*, 434; John Fox, *The Lyric Poetry of Charles d'Orléans* (Oxford: Clarendon Press, 1969), 133–34. See also the comments of Peter V. Davies in "La rime chez Christine de Pizan: Quelques cas particuliers," in *Au champ des escriptures*, ed. Hicks et al., 819–32.

Homonyms, words that have the same spelling but mean different things, supplied another poetic ornament. Some are usual in poetry of the time, as the following pair:

> Partis s'en sont, congié ont **pris**, (took, from *prendre*)
> Emportant la rose de **pris** (value) (*Dit*, vv. 263–64)

Other examples include:

> Si comme pour faire en **present** (gift)
> A celle gent nouvel **present**. (in attendance) (*Dit*, vv. 111–12)
>
> Noble paÿs ou gentillesse **regne**. (reigns, third pers. pres. of *regner*, to rule)
> Mais a present elles sont en ce **regne**, (kingdom) (*Epistre*, vv. 27–28)
>
> Et aucuns sont qui jadis en mes **laz** (snares, lit. nets)
> Furent tenus, mais ilz sont d'amer **laz** (weary) (*Epistre*, vv. 493–94)
>
> L'amour d'elles qui leur cuer tient en **serre** (grip)
> Dont l'un se plaint, a l'autre le cuer **serre** (tightens) (*Epistre*, vv. 39–40)

Sometimes, however, homonyms at the rhyme do not rise to such cleverness; some, in fact, are not completely successful: **sont / sont** (*Epistre*, vv. 207–8), which both mean "are," and **non / non** (*Dit*, vv. 617–18), which both mean "no."[156]

Another category of admired rhyme, called the *rime équivoque* or *équivoquée*, is a punning rhyme in which one word of two or more syllables rhymes with two or three words in the next verse. Sometimes this could be the other way around, as in:

> Vers la sienne: de corps, **de vis**
> Et de beau maintien, a **devis** (*Dit*, vv. 95–96)
>
> Qui autelle comme celle **fourme a**;
> Car oncques Dieu nulle riens ne **fourma** (*Epistre*, vv. 583–84)
>
> Le mal laissent. Les bonnes vueillent **en ce**
> Prendre vouloir d'avoir **perseverence**, (*Epistre*, vv. 769–70)

There are times, however, when something less than a full rhyme occurs. That is, a rhyming pair may differ in one or more phonemes even though the orthography suggests sameness. Consider the following pair:

156. Cited in Davies, "La rime chez Christine de Pizan," 824.

Si sont de son hostel tous **ceulx**,
Et n'y avoit pas un tout **seulz** (*Dit*, vv. 43–44)

The *l* in *seulz* would have been pronounced, whereas that in *ceulx* would have had to be silent. This would also have led to different pronunciation values as between *–eu* in *ceulx* and *–eu* in *seulz*, so that the vowels would not have rhymed either. The result is called an "eye-rhyme," in this case twice, as there is a mismatch for both the *–l* and the *–eu*.

The following rhymes could be called "approximate":

Or ay conclus en tous cas mes **raisons**
Bien et a droit; n'en desplaise a nulz **homs** (*Epistre*, vv. 747–48)

The form *homs* is an alternative way of spelling *homme* and would be pronounced [ɔm], whereas *raison* would have had a close (nasalized) [õn], with final *n* conceivably still lightly pronounced. The final –s would not have been pronounced, but it is worth noting that the *–s* of *raisons* marks the plural, while the *–s* of *homs* is a case marker that reaches back to an earlier period of French. Thus, in the Middle French period, much was available to poets wanting to adjust the toilette of their poetry.

Enjambment

Enjambment, often useful to vary the rhythm of a couplet or group of couplets, occurs when a phrase is continued beyond the rhyme into the next verse; the continued phrase is a *rejet*.[157] Combined with homonymic rhyme, enjambment nicely sets the stage in the *Dit* for Lady Loyalty to visit Christine at night. In the following verses, the phrases *Et m'endormy*, *Si m'apparu*, *Clere et luisant*, and *Me merveillay* are skillful *rejets*, and internal rhyme—*nue* with *m'apparu*, and *luisant* with both *dormant* and *formant*—add to the euphony of the passage:

La me couchay seulette et *nue*
Et m'endormy. Lors une *nue*
Si m'appar*u* en mon dorm*ant*,
Clere et luis*ant*; de ce form*ant*
Me merveillay que pouait estre. (*Dit*, vv. 283–87)

157. On Christine's enjambment, see Peter Davies, "'Si bas suis qu'a peine / Releveray': Christine de Pizan's Use of Enjambement," in John Campbell and Nadia Margolis, eds., *Christine de Pizan 2000: Studies on Christine de Pizan in Honour of Angus J. Kennedy* (Amsterdam and Atlanta, GA: Rodopi, 2000), 77–90.

Sometimes, however, Christine's enjambments can seem particularly bold, even jarring, as, for instance, where the name Hutin de Vermeilles is divided over two lines and is interrupted by the word *exemple*, needed for the rhyme with *emple*:

> Ne prennent pas au bon Hutin exemple
> De Vermeilles, ou bonté ot si emple (*Epistre*, vv. 225–26).

A similar enjambment occurs in the *Deux amans*, in the case of l'Ermite de la Faye.[158]

Vocabulary

Christine's acquaintance with the chancellery left its stamp on her style. The *style clergial* or *curial*, developed in Latin by clerks of the Roman curia but imitated in the vernacular languages, is apparent in her use of terms like *dessus dictes*, "above-mentioned" (*Epistre*, v. 17), *combien que*, "notwithstanding," "although," and by her use of legal vocabulary more or less in its technical sense, as in *complaintes*, "complaints" (*Epistre*, v. 9), *a la relacïon*, "on the testimony" (*Epistre*, v. 800). Use of ecclesiastical terms such as *excommunier*, excommunicate (*excommenye*, *Epistre*, v. 781) was widespread. Maureen Curnow has observed that this legal register is "a clear touchstone of erudition, further proof of the affinity of women for learning."[159] This is of course especially appropriate in the God of Love's official act.

Pairs of synonyms or near-synonyms suggest curial style, and were also routinely employed by the king's translators, who feared that readers might not understand words translated from Latin. In the *Dit*, Loyalty reports that Cupid both "commands" and "mandates" (*commande* and *mande*, vv. 525–26) that the Order of the Rose be placed in good hands; at the end of the same poem, Christine herself both "gives" and "relinquishes" (*donne* and *habandonne*, vv. 623–24) the power to bestow the Order.

The varying forms of *onc*, *oncque(s)*, donc, *doncque(s)*, and *com*, *comme*, are part of a stock of sanctioned practices available to poets to adjust syllable count: *onc*, *donc*, and *com* are one syllable each, whereas *oncque(s)*, *doncque(s)*, and *comme* count as two syllables.

Presentation of French Texts

In conformity with modern editorial practices, we have distinguished between the letters *i* and *j*, and *u* and *v*. We have employed modern punctuation for capitalization and used the apostrophe after the article. The adverb *presque* is written

158. *Love Debate Poems*, 125.

159. Maureen C. Curnow, "'La Pioche d'Inquisicion,'" in Richards et al., *Reinterpreting Christine*, 157–72, at 157.

in two words (*pres que*), as in the base manuscript. The varying presentation of the adverb *tres*, written in the manuscripts with either final or intermediate *s* and correspondingly separated from or attached to its related adjective, is followed in our transcription.

In accordance with the guidelines established by Mario Roques regarding accents, we add the acute accent only on tonic *e*, whether occurring alone or followed by *s*; it is not used when tonic *e* is followed by another *e* denoting a feminine form.[160] Where two contiguous vowels that could be diphthongized or reduced to one sound by elision threaten proper syllable count, we add the dieresis on one of the vowels to signal that both must be pronounced.

Textual variants are listed in two groups, the first comprised of rejected readings from our base manuscript L_1, and the second of variants from the other author-supervised manuscripts (L_2, *D* and *R*). As stated earlier, variants from *W* are listed separately at the end of the *Epistre* variants. We have exercised due caution in rejecting readings in the base manuscript, doing so only when obviously faulty readings risked impeding comprehension of the text. Variants do not include spelling differences such as *age/aige* and *ue/eu* that were common at the time. Orthographic changes that serve the purpose of making an eye-rhyme or introducing textual ambiguity (as in v. 67) are not recorded in the variants, but are pointed out in the notes. No diacritical marks are used on variants.

Interlinear additions in the manuscript are inscribed in slashes (\ /), both in the text and in the variants.

Note on the Translations

By offering editions with facing-page translations, we invite readers not thoroughly conversant with Christine de Pizan's Middle French to read in dual fashion, attending to both the French poem and its English rendering. We strove to capture Christine's liveliness and to make the English as contemporary to modern readers as the French would have been to Christine's medieval readers. As in any translation of this kind, we endeavored to stay as close as possible to the French wording, although the occasional lack of a strict French-English equivalency required interpretation to avoid a potentially baffling word-for-word translation. Similarly, the syntax of octosyllabic or decasyllabic verse, with its ellipses and clauses reordered to suit syllable count and rhyme, requires a habit in reading that is unfamiliar to today's readers; this called for clarification, with the result that English lines may not always appear directly opposite their French verse. Punctuation as between the French and English texts sometimes varies.

160. Mario Roques, "Établissement de règles pratiques pour l'édition des textes français et provençaux." *Bibliothèque de l'École des Chartes* 87 (1926): 453–59, and *Romania* 52 (1926): 243–49.

Our need to focus on the precise English meanings of certain words key to Christine's thought has prompted us to provide our own English translations of selected illustrative phrases from texts by Christine de Pizan other than the *Epistre* and the *Dit*.

L'EPISTRE AU DIEU D'AMOURS

THE GOD OF LOVE'S LETTER

L'Epistre au dieu d'Amours

[fol. 67c] *Ci commence l'epiltre au dieu d'amours*

Cupido, par la grace de luï
Dieu des amans, sens aide de nullui
Regnant en l'air du ciel tresreluisant,
Filz de Venus, la deesse puissant,
Sire d'amours et de tous les obgiez,
A tous noz vrays loyaulx servans subgiez:
Salut, amour, familiarité.
Savoir faisons en generalité
Qu'a nostre court sont venues complaintes
Par devant nous, et moult piteuses plaintes
De par toutes dames et damoiselles,
Gentilz femmes, bourgoises, et pucelles,
Et de toutes femmes generaulment,
Nostre secours requerant humblement;
Ou se ce non, du tout desheritees
De leur honneur seront, et ahontees.
Si se plaignent les dessus dictes dames
Des grans estors, des blasmes, des diffames,
Des trahisons, des oultrages tresgriefs,
Des faulsetez et de mains autres griefs
Que chascun jour des desloyaulx reçoivent,
Qui les blasment, diffament et deçoivent.
Sur tous paÿs se complaingnent de France,
Qui jadis fu leur escu et defense,
Qui contre tous de tort les defendoit,
Comme il est droit, et si com faire doit
Noble paÿs ou gentillesse regne.
Mais a present elles sont en ce regne,
Ou jadis tant estoient honnourees
Plus qu'autre part, des faulz deshonnourees,
Et meismement—dont plus griefment se dueillent—
[fol. 67d] Des nobles gens qui plus garder les seuillent.
Car a present sont plusieurs chevaliers
Et escuiers mains duis et coustumiers
D'elles trahir par beaulz blandissemens
Et se faingnent estre loyaulx amans

The God of Love's Letter

The God of Love's Letter begins here

Cupid, by virtue of his grace
The god of lovers, who reigns alone
In the space of luminous skies;
Son of Venus, the powerful goddess,
Lord of love and of all he commands,
To all our true and loyal servitors:
Greetings, love, and friendship.
We make it publicly known
That complaints have been brought to our court
Before us, and most pitiful plaints
From married and unmarried ladies,
Noblewomen, townswomen, and maidens,
From all women in general,
Humbly begging our help;
Failing which they'll be robbed
Of their honor and shamed.
The above-mentioned ladies complain
Of the great damage, the blame, the defamation;
Of the betrayals and the deeply painful wrongs;
Of the falsehoods and many other grievances
Heard every day from disloyal men,
Who accuse, defame, and deceive them.
Above all countries they complain of France,
Once their shield and defense
Protecting them against wrong by all others,
As is right and should be done
By a noble land where noble conduct rules.
But now in this kingdom,
Where once they were honored more than anywhere else,
They're dishonored by untrue men,
And even (this pains them all the more)
By noblemen accustomed to protecting them.
For at present there exist many knights
And less skilled squires used to
Betraying them with fulsome flattery,
And pretending they're loyal lovers

Et se cueuvrent de diverse faintise;
Si vont disant que griefment les atise
L'amour d'elles qui leur cuer tient en serre,
Dont l'un se plaint, a l'autre le cuer serre,
L'autre pleure par semblant et souspire,
Et l'autre faint que trop griefment empire:
Par trop amer tout soit descoulouré
Et pres que mort et tout alangouré.
Et jurent fort et promettent et mentent
Estre loyaulx, secrez, et puis s'en vantent.
D'aller souvent et de venir se painent,
Par ces moustiers ça et la se pourmainent
En regardant, s'appuyent sur autieulx
Par faulz semblant; moult en y a de tieulx.
Et par rues leur chevaulx esperonnent,
Gays et mignoz, a cliquetes qui sonnent.
Moult font semblant d'en estre embesongniez—
Mules, chevaulx ne sont pas espargniez;
Diligens sont de baillier leurs requestes,
Moult enquierent ou sont nopces et festes,
La vont plusieurs joliz mignoz et cointes.
Si font semblant de sentir de noz pointes
Si qu'a peine les peuent endurer!
Autres mettent grant peine a procurer
Par messages ou par quelque acointance
A mettre a fin ce que leur faulz cuer pense.
Par telz maintiens en plus de miles guises
[fol. 68a] Les faulz amans se cueuvrent de faintises:
C'est assavoir les desloyaulx qui heent
Foy, loyauté et a decevoir beent.
Car les loyaulx ne sont pas en ce compte;
Et ceulx doit on amer et tenir compte,
Car decevoir en nul cas ne vouldroient;
Je leur deffens. Pour ce consens qu'ilz aient
De noz doulz biens savoureux bonne part,
Car a mes gens largement en depart,
Et ceulz tiennent mes vrais commandemens,
Justes et loyaulx et bons enseingnemens.
Si leur defens villenie et meffait,
Et leur command poursuivre honneur de fait,
Estre loyaulx, secrez et voir disans,

And hide behind diverse deceits;
They say they're painfully aflame
With love, which holds their hearts in its grip,
For which this one laments, the other's heart tightens,
The next one pretends to weep and sigh,
While another feigns being woefully worse:
From too much loving he's gone all pale
And nearly dead and languishing.
They swear like mad and promise and lie
They'll be loyal and discreet—and then they boast!
They work at going out and about often,
In those churches here and there
Peering around, and kneeling at the altar
In pretense; so many of them are like that.
They spur their horses through the streets,
Jaunty and handsome, with clacking sounds.
They feign exertion—
Mules and horses aren't spared.
They make their requests diligently,
Asking where the weddings and feasts are—
There many handsome, dapper dandies go.
They pretend to feel our arrows so much
That they can barely endure them!
Others toil at obtaining
By messengers, or through an acquaintance,
The goal their lying hearts intend.
By such behaviors in more than a thousand guises,
False lovers cover themselves in feints:
That is, the disloyal men who hate
Faith and loyalty and aim to deceive.
For the loyal are not among that number,
And those must one love and esteem,
For in no case would they wish to deceive;
I forbid them. Therefore I grant to them
A good portion of our sweet and delectable store,
For I share that generously with my followers
And they keep my true commandments,
My just, sincere, and rightful teachings.
I forbid them any base act or misdeed
And command them to pursue honor in their deeds,
To be faithful, discreet, and truthful,

Larges, courtois et fuïr mesdisans,
Humbles et doulz, jolis et acesmez,
Fermes et frans, poursuivre a estre amez,
Armes suir a ceulz qu'il appartient
Loz acquerir. Et qui ainsi se tient,
Savoir de vray puet que ne fauldray mie
A lui donner belle dame et amie;
Car quant ainsi je suis d'aucun servi,
Guerredon lui rens comme il a desservi.
Mais se bien vient a ces faulz d'avanture,
N'est pas droit bien, combien que je l'endure,
Car en tous cas le bien est moult petit
Quant il est pris senz desir n'appetit.
    ¶Et que vauldroit a homs descouragié
Grans viandes, ypocras ou saugié,
Puis que saveur nulle ou pou y auroit?
Mais a cellui qui desirant seroit,
De pain faitis ou d'une miche blanche
[fol. 68b] S'attaindre y puet, Dieu scet comme il la trenche
Joyeusement et de grant cuer s'en paist:
Ainsi de toute riens desiree est.
    ¶Ainsi se trop ne sont apparceües,
Sont maintes fois les dames deceües
Car simples sont, ne veulent se bien non,
Dont il avient souvent, vueillent ou non,
Qu'amer leur fault ceulx qui si les deçoivent;
Trahies sont ains qu'elles l'apparçoivent!
Mais quant ainsi sont fort enveloppees,
Les desloyaulx qui les ont attrappees—
Or escoutez comment ilz s'en chevissent:
Ne leur souffist dont ainsi les traïssent,
Ains ont compains de leur male alïance;
Si n'y remaint ne fait ne convenance
Qui ne soit dit l'un a l'autre; et trop plus
Qu'ilz n'ont de bien, se vantent que reclus
Sont devenus en la chambre leurs dames
Dont amez sont; puis jurent corps et ames
Comment du fait il leur est avenu,
Et que couchié braz a braz y ont nu.
Les compaignons ce dient es tavernes,
Et les nobles font leurs pers et leurs sernes

Generous and courtly, and to flee slanderers,
To be humble and kind, loving and refined,
Firm and noble, to strive to be loved,
And to pursue arms, if they would seek
To earn praise. He who holds to that purpose
May be sure I won't fail
To give him a lovely lady and sweetheart,
For when I'm served in such wise by someone,
I grant him the reward he's deserved.
But if by chance good comes to false lovers,
It's not truly just, though I put up with it,
For in any case the pleasure is very small
When it is received without desire or appetite.
    And to a man lacking appetite, what would
Exquisite fare, herbed wine or spiced, be worth
Since they would have little taste or none?
But a man who would covet
Some simple bread or a loaf of white
If he can get it, God only knows how joyfully
He carves into it and feasts with all his heart.
And thus it is desired above all else.
    So if ladies aren't alert,
Time and again they're deceived.
For they're simple, wanting nothing but good,
Because of which it often happens, whether they wish it or not,
They're compelled to love their deceivers;
Betrayed before they see it coming!
But once those disloyal men have caught them
And have them completely enthralled,
Listen to how they finish the job:
It's not enough to betray them thus,
Rather they have partners in their criminal pact.
There remains no act or promise
That isn't told from one to the next; and the more
They've failed, the more they boast of being secluded
In the chambers of their ladies
By whom they're loved. Then they swear on body and soul
How things unfolded for them,
And how they lay naked, arms entwined.
Their pals tell it in taverns,
And nobles share the news and form their circles

En ces grans cours de nos seigneurs les ducs,
Ou chiez le roy, ou ailleurs espandus.
Et la tiennent de telz plais leurs escoles.
Plusieurs y a qui deussent leurs parolles
En bons comptes drecier sens bourderie
A raconter pris de chevalerie.
¶Mais aux grans feux a ces soirs ou sur couches,
La rigolent l'un l'autre, et par reprouches
S'entredient: «Je sçay bien de tes fais:
[fol. 68c] Telle t'aimë et tu le jolis fais
Pour sienne amour, et pluseurs y ont part;
Tu es receu quant un autre s'en part!»
La diffament les envïeux la belle
Senz achoison, ne nul mal savoir d'elle.
Et lors cellui qui en est rigoulé
Monstre semblant qu'il en soit adoulé;
Mais moult lui plaist de ce qu'on l'en rigole,
Et de son bec mainte parolle vole
Qui blasme vault, combien qu'il s'en excuse;
En excusant celle nomme et accuse,
Et fait semblant de celer et couvrir
Ce que lui plaist a dire et descouvrir.
¶D'autres y a qui le rigol commencent
A celle fin que les autres s'avancent
D'eulz rigoler et d'eulz ramentevoir
Ce qu'ilz veulent a tous faire assavoir;
Si s'en rient, et tout en accusant
Se vont du fait laschement excusant.
¶Sy en y a qui se sont mis en peine
Qu'on les amast, mais perdu ont leur peine;
Si sont honteux dont ilz sont refusé,
Ne veulent pas qu'on croye que musé
Aient en vain. Pour ce de ce se vantent
Qu'onques n'avint; et se en ce lieu hantent
Par aucun cas ou pour quelque acointance,
De tout l'ostel conteront l'ordonnance
Pour enseingnes de confermer leurs bourdes.
La sont dictes maintes parolles lourdes,
Et qui dire ne les veult mie appertes
Les monstre au doy par parolles couvertes.
La sont femmes moult laidement nommees

In those great courts of our lords, the dukes,
Or at the king's residence, or elsewhere bandied about.
And there, with words like these, they teach their lessons.
Many there should turn their talk
To telling good stories without lies,
Recounting the worth of chivalry.
But before great fires on those evenings, or lolling on couches,
They rib one another, reproachfully
Saying: "I know what you're up to:
Lady so-and-so loves you, and you play the swain
For her love, but many get their part;
You are welcomed as another departs!"
There the envious defame the lovely lady
Without cause, knowing no ill of her.
And then he who's being ribbed
Makes believe he's ever so sad;
But he's deeply pleased to be so teased
And from his beak flies many a word
Worth blame, however much he excuses what he's done.
In making excuse, he names the lady and accuses her
And affects to hide and conceal
The very thing he's pleased to reveal.
There are others who begin the teasing
To the end that the rest will step up
To make fun of them and remind them
Of what they want made known to all;
They laugh about it, and while accusing themselves,
Those cowards make excuses for the deed.
Still others have worked hard
To be loved, but they've wasted their effort;
So they're ashamed of being refused
And don't want others to think they tried
In vain. That's why they boast
It never happened; and if they frequent her place
By chance or through an acquaintance,
They'll relate how the rooms are placed
As the proof that confirms their lies.
Many boorish words are uttered there,
And whoever doesn't want to speak them openly
Points to them through innuendo.
There, in the most shameful terms, women are named

[fol. 68d] Souventesfoiz, et sens cause blasmees,
Et meismement d'aucunes grans maistresses,
Tant ayent ilz blondes ou brunes tresses.
Dieux, quelz parleurs! Dieux, quelles assemblees
Ou les honneurs des dames sont blasmees!
Et quel prouffit vient d'ainsi les diffamer
A ceulz meismes qui se deussent armer
Pour les garder et leur honneur defendre?
Car tout homme doit avoir le cuer tendre
Envers femme, qui a tout homme est mere
Qui ne lui est ne diverse n'amere,
Ainçoys lui est souevë et amiable,
A ses besoings piteuse et secourable,
Qui tant lui a fait et fait de services
Et de qui tant les euvres sont propices
A corps d'omme souëfvement nourrir.
A son naistrë, au vivre, et au mourir
Lui sont femmes aidans et secourables
Et piteuses, douces, et serviables;
Si est cellui non congnoissant et rude
Qui en mesdit, et plain d'ingratitude.
¶Encor dis je que trop se desnature
Homme qui dit diffame, ne laidure,
Ne reprouche de femme en la blasmant,
Ne une ne deux ne tout generaulment.
Et supposé qu'on en trouvast de nices
Ou raemplies de plusieurs divers vices,
Senz foy n'amour ne nulle loyauté,
Fieres, males, plaines de cruauté,
Ou pou constans, legieres, variables,
Cauteleuses, faulses et decevables:
Doit on pour tant toutes mettre en fremaille
[fol. 69a] Et tesmoingnier qu'il n'est nulle qui vaille?
¶Quant le hault Dieu fist et fourma les angels,
Les cherubins, seraphins, et archangels,
N'en y ot il de mauvais en leurs fais?
Doit on pour tant angels nommer mauvais?
Mais qui male femme scet, si s'en gart
Senz diffamer ne le tiers ne le quart,
Ne trestoutes en general blasmer,
Et tous leur meurs femenins diffamer.
Car moult en fu, et sera de telles

Time and again, and blamed without cause,
And especially certain great ladies,
Whether they're blonde or brunette.
Lord, how they blather! Lord! what assemblies
Where the honor of ladies is brought low!
And what profit does slander offer
To the very men who should take up arms
To protect women and defend their honor?
For every man should have a tender heart
Toward woman, who is his own mother
And is never hostile or cruel toward him.
Rather, she is pleasant, gentle, sweet,
Merciful and helpful when he's in need,
And has done and still does so many services for him,
And whose good works favor
The gentle nourishing of the body of man.
At his birth, during his life, and at his death
Women come to his aid and help him,
Compassionate, kind, and obliging.
And thus that man is an ignorant boor
Who slanders them, and is filled with thanklessness.

Furthermore, I say that a man is greatly at odds with his nature
Who utters slander or ugly slurs
Or reproach of woman, blaming her,
Be it one woman or two, or all of them.
And supposing there are foolish women
Or ones filled with many different vices,
Without faithfulness, love, or loyalty,
Puffed-up, evil, and filled with cruelty,
Or faithless, fickle, and capricious,
Scheming, false, and deceitful:
Must we therefore lock all of them up
And claim there's not a worthy one to be found?

When sovereign God made the angels,
Cherubim, seraphim, and archangels,
Did not some of them go wrong?
Must one therefore say that angels are bad?
But whoever knows an evil woman, let him avoid her
Without defaming even a third or a quarter
Or blaming all in general,
And decrying what women do.
For there have been and will be many

Qui a louer font com bonnes et belles,
Et ou vertus et graces sont trouvees,
Sens et valour en bonté esprouvees.
¶Et de blasmer celles qui le mains valent,
Ceulx qui ce font, encor dis je qu'ils faillent
Si les nomment, disant qui elles sont,
Ou demeurent, quoy ne quelz leurs faix sont,
Car le pecheur on ne doit diffamer,
Ce nous dist Dieux, n'en publique blasmer.
Les vices bien peut on et les pechiez
Forment blasmer, sens ceulz qui entechiez
En sont nommer, ne encuser nullui;
Ce tesmoingne l'escript ou je le lui.
¶De telz parleurs en y a a grans sommes,
Dont grant honte est tel vice en gentilz hommes.
Je dy a ceulz qui en sont entechié,
Non mie a ceulz qui n'y ont nul pechié,
Car maint y a de nobles si vaillans
Que mieulx perdre vouldroient leurs vaillans
Que de telz faiz restez ne reprouvez
Feussent pour riens, n'en telz cas pris prouvez.
Mais les mauvaiz dont je fais mencion,
[fol. 69b] Qui n'ont bon fait ne bonne entencion,
Ne prennent pas au bon Hutin exemple
De Vermeilles, ou bonté ot si emple,
Qu'onques nulz homs n'y sçot que reproucher,
Ne nul mesdit en diffamant n'ot cher.
Souverainement porta honneur aux fammes,
D'elles ne pot avoir ne blasme ne diffames;
Chevalier fu preux, saige et bien amé,
Pour ce fu il et sera renommé.
¶Le bon Othe de Grançon le vaillant,
Qui pour armes tant s'ala travaillant,
Courtois, gentil, preux, bel et gracïeux
Fu en son temps; Dieux en ait l'ame es cieux!
Car chevalier fu moult bien entechié;
Qui mal lui fist, je tiens qu'il fist pechié,
Non obstant ce que lui nuysi Fortune.
Mais de grever aux bons elle est commune,
Car en tous cas je tiens qu'il fu loyaulx,
D'armes plus preux que Thalamon Ayaulx;
Onc ne lui plot personne diffamer,

Who should be praised as good and fine
And in whom virtue and grace are found,
Wisdom and worthiness proven by their goodness.
As for blaming those of lesser worth,
Those who do that, I say again that they err
If they name them, saying who they are,
Where they live, or what they've done,
For one must not defame the sinner,
—God tells us that—or blame him in public.
One may indeed condemn vices and sins
Most vigorously, without naming those
Tarnished by them, or slandering anyone.
The text I've read attests to that.
Gossipers like that come in droves;
In noblemen such a vice is a great shame.
I'm speaking to those who have that vice,
Not to those who haven't sinned,
For there are many nobles who are so worthy
They'd rather lose everything they own
Than be accused of or reproved for such acts
For any reason, or be caught at them.
But the wicked men I mention here,
Who've done nothing good and intend no good,
Don't follow the example of worthy Hutin
De Vermeilles, whose goodness was so great
That no man could find anything to reproach,
Nor was he fond of scandalmongering.
He honored women above all
And could not have them blamed or defamed.
He was a noble, wise, and beloved knight;
For that reason he was and will be renowned.
Good Othon de Grandson, a valiant man
Who labored so at arms,
And was courtly, noble, fine, and gracious
In his time; may God receive his soul in heaven!
He was deeply imbued with knightly qualities.
Whoever did him wrong did sin, I hold,
And though Fortune brought him harm,
She often harms those who are good,
For I maintain that he was loyal in everything,
And braver at arms than Ajax, son of Telamon.
He was never pleased to slander anyone,

Les dames volt servir, prisier, amer.
D'autres plusieurs furent bons et vaillans;
Estre doivent exemple aux defaillans.
Encor en est maint (il est bien mestiers)
Qui des vaillans suivent les bons sentiers.
Honneur suivent, vaillance les y maine,
A acquerir pris et loz mettent peine
En ce royaume, ailleurs et oultre mer.
Mais je me tays de cy leurs noms nommer
Qu'on ne deïst que ce feust flaterie,
Ou qu'il peut tourner a vanterie.
Et telz doivent gentilz hommes a droit
[fol. 69c] Estre, autrement gentilesce y fauldroit.
    ¶Si se plaingnent les dessus dittes dames
De plusieurs clers qui leur seurmettent blasmes:
Dictiez en font, rimes, proses et vers,
En diffamant leurs meurs par moz divers;
Si les baillent en matiere aux premiers,
A leurs nouveaulx et jeunes escolliers,
En maniere d'exemple et de doctrine
Pour retenir en aage tel doctrine.
    ¶En vers dient: Adam, David, Sanson,
Et Salmon, et autres a foison
Furent deceuz par femme main et tart;
Et qui sera dont li homs qui s'en gart?
    ¶Li autres dit que moult sont decevables,
Cauteleuses, faulses et pou valables;
Autres dient que trop sont mençongieres,
Variables, inconstans et legieres.
D'autres plusieurs grans vices les accusent
Et blasment moult, sens que riens les excusent.
Et ainsi font clers et soir et matin,
Puis en françoiz leurs vers, puiz en latin,
Et se fondent dessus ne sçay quelz livres,
Qui plus dient de mençonges q'uns yvres.
Ovide en dit, en un livre qu'il fist,
Assez de maulx (dont je tiens qu'il meffist)
Qu'il appella *Le Remede d'Amours*,
Ou leur met sus moult de vilaines mours:
Ordes, laides, plaines de villenie.
Que telz vices aient, je le lui nye;
Au deffendre par bataille je gaige

And he wished to serve, treasure, and love ladies.
Many other men were good and valiant,
And they should be examples to the faltering.
There still are many (and they're much needed)
Who follow the good paths of the worthy;
Honor guides them, valor leads them there,
They strive to acquire esteem and praise
In this kingdom, elsewhere, and overseas.
But I won't mention their names or who they are
Lest people say it's only flattery
Or lest it give grounds for boasting.
Now *they* are rightly called noble men,
If not, nobility would be lacking.

The above-mentioned ladies also complain
About many learned men who heap blame on them,
Who compose tales in rhyme, in prose, and in verse,
In which they slander women's conduct with cruel words.
They give this matter to their beginners,
To schoolboys who are young and new in class,
By way of example and doctrine,
So they'll keep this teaching when grown.

In verse they say: Adam, David, Samson,
And Solomon, and myriad others,
Were deceived by women both early and late;
What man will protect himself from them?

The next writer says they're treacherous,
And cunning, false, and worthless.
Another one says they're dreadful liars,
Fickle, inconstant, and trifling.
Still others accuse them of many dreadful vices,
And blame them, excusing them in nothing.
That's what clerks do morning and night,
With verses now in French, now in Latin,
Drawing their words from I don't know what books,
Which tell more lies than a drunkard does.
Ovid says of women, in a book he wrote,
Many evil things (for which I say he did wrong)
And named it *The Remedy for Love*,
In which he pins on women many nasty habits,
Repulsive, sordid, and thoroughly wicked.
I say to him that women have no such vices
And I pledge to defend them in battle

S'il est aucun qui contregette gaige;
Voire, j'entens les femmes honnorables,
[fol. 69d] En mes comptes ne mes les non valables.
Si ont les clers aprins tres leur enfance
Cellui livret ou premiere scïence
De gramairë, et a autres l'apprennent
A celle fin que femmes amer n'emprennent.
    ¶Mais de ce sont folz et perdent leur peine,
Ne l'empeschier si n'est fors chose vaine,
Car entre moy et ma dame Nature
Ne souffrerons, tant com le monde dure,
Que cheries et amees ne soyent,
Maulgré tous ceulx qui blasmer les vouldroient,
Et qu'a plusieurs mesmes qui plus les blasment
N'ostent les cuers et ravissent et emblent.
Senz nul frauder ne faire extorcion,
Mais tout par nous et nostre impression,
Ja ne seront hommes si acointiez
Par soutilz clers ne par tous leur dittiez,
Non obstant ce que mains livres en parlent
Et les blasment, qui assez pou y valent.
    ¶Et s'aucun dit c'on doit les livres croire
Qui furent fais d'ommes de grant memoire
Et de grant sens, qui mentir ne daingnerent,
Qui des femmes les malices prouverent,
Je leur respons que ceulz qui cë escrirent
En leurs livres, je treuve qu'ilz ne quirent
En leurs vies fors femmes decevoir.
N'en pouoyent iceulz assez avoir,
Et tous les jours vouloient des nouvelles,
Senz loyauté tenir, ne aux plus belles.
    ¶Qu'en ot David et Salemon le roy?
Dieu s'en courrouça et pugny leur desroy.
D'autres pluseurs, et meismement Ovide,
[fol. 70a] Qui tant en volt, puis diffamer les cuide,
Et tous les clers, qui tant en ont parlé,
Plus qu'autre gent en furent affolé,
Non pas d'une seule, mais d'un millier.
Et se tel gent orent dame ou moullier
Qui ne feïst du tout a leur vouloir,
Et qui meïst peine a les decevoir,
Quel merveille! Car il n'est nulle doubte

If someone throws the gauntlet down.
Indeed, I mean honorable women:
I take no account of unworthy ones.
Thus from childhood clerks have learned
This little book on grammar, the subject one learns first,
And they teach it to others
So they won't fall in love with women.

But they're foolish and waste their time,
And their attempts at dissuasion are vain,
For between my Lady Nature and myself,
We will not tolerate, for as long as the world lasts,
That women not be cherished and loved,
In spite of all who would like to blame them,
Or in the case of men who blame them most
Will we stop women from ravishing and stealing their hearts.
Without cheating or extorting anyone
But entirely through our stamp
Men will no longer be taught as they have been
By subtle clerks or all their poetry,
In spite of the many books that speak of women
And blame them, which are worth very little.

And if anyone says we must believe the books
Which were written by men of great renown
And great wisdom, who never stooped to lying,
Who proved the malice that women do,
I answer that the men who wrote that
In their books, I find they sought
Nothing while they lived but to deceive women.
They couldn't get enough of them
And wanted fresh ones every day,
Without maintaining loyalty, not even to the loveliest.

What did David get, and King Solomon?
God became angry and punished their sin.
And numerous others, especially Ovid,
Who wanted so many, then thought he could slander them;
And all the clerks, who talked of them so much,
Were smitten more than other men,
Not with just one but with a thousand.
If such men had a lady or a woman
Who might not have done all they wished
Or who might have tried to deceive them,
No wonder there! For there's no doubt

Que quant uns homs en tel vilté se boute,
Il ne va pas querant les vaillans dames,
Ne les bonnes, prisees, preudes fammes.
Ne les congnoist ne il n'en a que faire,
Fors ceulz ne veult qui sont de son affaire;
De fillettes se pare et de pietaille.
Est il digne d'avoir chose qui vaille,
Un villotier qui toutes met en compte
Et puis cuide trop bien couvrir sa honte
Quant plus n'en puet et qu'il est ja vieilz homs,
D'elles blasmer par ses soutilz raisons?
¶Mais qui blasmast seulement les donnees
Aux grans vices et les habandonnees,
Et conseillast a celles non suivir
Comme ilz ont fait, bien s'en pourroit suivir,
Et ce seroit chose moult raisonnable,
Enseignement loyal, juste et louable
Senz diffamer toutes communement!
¶Et a parler quant au decevement,
Je ne sçay pas penser ne concevoir
Comment femme puist homme decevoir:
Ne le va pas prier ne requerir,
Ne sur son lieu n'en son hostel querir,
Ne pense a lui, ne ne lui en souvient
[fol. 70b] Quant decevoir l'omme et tempter la vient.
Tempter comment? Voire, par tel maniere
Qu'il n'est peine qui ne lui soit legiere
A endurer ne faissel a porter.
A autre riens ne se veult deporter
Fors a pener a elles decevoir,
Pour y mettre cuer et corps et avoir.
Et par long temps dure la triolaine,
Souventesfois avient, et celle peine,
Non obstant ce que moult souvent y faillent
A leurs esmes, ja soit ce qu'ilz travaillent.
¶Et de ceulx parle Ovide en son traittié
De l'*Art d'Amours*, car par la grant pitié
Qu'il ot de ceulz, compila il un livre
Ou leur escript et enseingne a delivre
Comment pourront les femmes decevoir
Par faintises et leur amour avoir.
Si l'appella *Livre de l'art d'Amours*,

That when a man plunges into such vileness,
He doesn't go looking for worthy ladies,
Or the good, well regarded, honorable women.
He doesn't know them or have to do with them,
He wants only those who play his game,
And adorns himself with whores and tarts.
Does he deserve anything of value,
A rake who lumps them all together,
And then thinks he can hide his shame very well
When, now, an old man, he can't perform,
By blaming women through devious argument?

But should someone blame only those women
Given to great vices and who abandon themselves to men,
And were he to counsel men not to pursue them
As they have done, good might come of it,
And that would be very reasonable,
An appropriate teaching, fair and commendable,
Without defaming all women in general!

And on the subject of deceptiveness,
I cannot imagine or think
How a woman might deceive a man:
She doesn't pursue him or ask where he is,
Nor does she seek out his dwelling.
She doesn't think about him or remember him
When he comes to tempt and deceive her.
And how does he tempt her? Indeed, in such a way
That every exertion strikes him as easy
To bear, every burden easy to lift.
He wants to play at nothing else
But trying hard to deceive women,
Exhausting body, heart, and wealth.
And the torment and toil last a long time,
Returning again and again,
Even though they frequently fail
At their goal, however much they strive.

Ovid talks about such men in his treatise
On the *Art of Love*, for given the great pity
He felt for them, he compiled a book
In which he records and freely teaches
How men can trick women
By subterfuge and get their love.
He called it the *Book of the Art of Love*,

Mais n'enseingne condicïons ne mours
De bien amer, mais ainçoiz le contraire;
Car homs qui veult selon ce livre faire
N'amera ja, combien qu'il soit amez.
Et pour cë est le livre mal nommez,
Car c'est *Livre d'art de grant decevance*—
Tel nom lui don—*et de faulse apparance*!
¶Et comment don\t/ quant fraisles et legieres
Et tournables, nices et pou entieres
Sont les femmes, si com aucuns clers dient,
Quel besoing dont est il a ceulx qui prient
De tant pour ce pourchacier de cautelles?
Et pour quoy tost ne s'i accordent elles
Senz qu'il faille art n'engin a elles prendre?
[fol. 70c] Car pour chastel pris ne fault guerre emprendre,
Et meismement poëte si subtil
Comme Ovide, qui puis fu en exil.
¶Et Jehan de Meun ou *Rommant de la Rose*:
Quel loinz procez! Quel difficile chose!
Et scïences et cleres et obscures
Y met il la, et de grans aventures!
Et que de gent supployez et rovez,
Et de paines et de baraz trouvez
Pour decevoir senz plus une pucelle—
S'en est la fin—par fraude et par cautelle!
A feible lieu faut il dont grant assault?
Comment puet on de pres faire grant sault?
Je ne sçay pas ce vëoir ne comprendre
Que grant peine faille a feible lieu prendre,
Në art, n'engin, ne grant soutiveté
Dont couvient il tout de neccessité,
Puis qu'art couvient, grant engin et grant peine
A decevoir femme noble ou villaine,
Qu'ilz ne soient mie si variables,
Comme aucuns dient, n'en leurs faiz si muables.
¶Et s'on me dist li livre en sont tout plain
—C'est respons a maint dont je me plain—
Je leur respons que les livres ne firent
Pas les femmes, ne les choses n'y mirent
Que l'en y list contre elles et leurs meurs.
Si devisent a l'aise de leurs cuers
Ceulz qui plaident leur cause senz partie;

But he doesn't teach the behaviors or ways
Of loving truly, but rather the opposite;
For a man who agrees to act by that book
Will never love, however much he is loved.
That's why the book is wrongly named,
For it's the *Book of the Art of Great Deception*
And of False Appearances—that's the title I give it!

And how is it that if women are
So frail and fickle and changeable,
Silly and faithless, as some clerks say,
Why is there need for those who woo them
To pursue them with so much trickery?
Why don't women yield right away,
Without cleverness or guile needed to trap them?
A captured castle needs no war,
Especially not for a poet as artful
As Ovid, who was later exiled.

And Jean de Meun in the *Romance of the Rose*:
What a long business! What a difficult thing!
The knowledge both clear and murky
That he puts in it, and the great escapades!
So many people called upon, implored,
So many efforts and ruses found
To trick a maiden, nothing more—
That's his aim—through fraud and scheming!
Why so great an assault against so feeble a place?
How can one leap so far so near the mark?
I can't see or understand why
Great force is needed against so frail a place,
Nor artfulness, ingenuity, or subtlety.
It must necessarily be the case,
Since design, great cunning, and effort are needed
To gull a noblewoman or a peasant,
That they aren't at all as fickle
As some say, nor so changeable in their ways.

And if I'm told that books are filled with such women
—That's the response from many that I'm complaining about—
I answer that books were not written
By women, nor did they put in them
What we read against women and their habits.
So men write on to their heart's content
Pleading their case without opposition;

Senz rabatre comptent, et grant partie
Prennent pour eulx, car de legier offendent
Les batailleurs ceulz qui ne se defendent.
Mais se les femmes eussent les livres fait,
[fol. 70d] Je sçay de vray qu'autrement feust du fait,
Car bien scevent qu'a tort sont encoulpees.
Si ne sont pas les pars a droit coupees,
Car les plus fors prennent la plus grant part,
Et le meilleur pour soy qui pieces part.
¶Encor dient li felon mesdisant
Qui les femmes vont ainsi despisant,
Que toutes sont faulses, seront et furent,
N'oncques encor nulle loyauté n'urent;
Les amoureux, telles, qui qu'elles soyent,
Les treuvent, tous, quant les femmes essaient;
A toutes fins leur est le tort donné,
Qui qu'ait meffait, sur elles est tourné.
¶Mais c'est mauldit, car on voit le rebours,
Car quant a ce qui affiert a amours,
Trop de femmes y ont esté loyales,
Sont et seront, non obstant intervales
Ou faussetez, baraz ou tricheries
Qu'on leur ait fait, et maintes menteries.
¶Que fu jadis Medee au faulz Jason?
Tresloyal! Et lui fist la toison
D'or conquerir par son engin subtil,
Dont il acquist loz plus que autre cent mil;
Par elle fu renommé dessus tous.
Si lui promist que loyal amy doulz
Seroit tout sien; mais sa foy lui menti
Et la laissa pour autre et s'en party.
¶Que fu Dydo, roÿne de Cartage?
De grant amour et de loyal courage
Vers Eneas, qui, exillié de Troye
Aloit par mer, laz, despris et sens joye—
Pres que pery, lui et ses chevaliers.
[fol. 71a] Requeilli fu—dont lui estoit mestiers—
De la belle, qu'il faulsement deçut.
Car a tresgrant honneur elle reçut
Lui et ses gens, et trop de biens lui fist;
Mais puis aprés vers elle tant meffist,
Non obstant ce qu'il lui eust foy promise

They give no quarter, and take the winner's share
For themselves, for readily
Do soldiers attack those who mount no defense.
But if women had written those books,
I know they would read differently,
For women know they're wrongly blamed.
The portions are not divided equally
Because the strongest take the largest cut,
And he who cuts the pieces takes the best.
The nasty scandalmongers further say,
Who go on disdaining women in this way,
That all are false, will be and were,
And not a one has had any loyalty;
And lovers all find them such, whoever they are,
When they put them to the test;
For everything, the fault is women's;
Never mind who did wrong, it's turned against them.
That's detestable, for we see the opposite,
Because when it comes to love,
Many women have been loyal:
They are and they will be, despite the times
When deceptions, ruses, and treachery
Were practiced on them, and many a lie.
In times past how was Medea toward inconstant Jason?
Very loyal! It was through her clever craft
That he won the golden fleece,
From which his fame surpassed a hundred thousand others.
Through her he was renowned above all others.
He promised he'd be a loyal, gentle friend,
Completely hers; but he broke his pledge
And abandoned her for someone else; he left and went away.
And what about Dido, queen of Carthage?
With great love and loyalty
Toward Aeneas; exiled from Troy,
He took to the sea, worn out, bereft, joyless,
He and his knights nearly perishing.
He was rescued—and he needed it—
By this beautiful woman, whom he falsely deceived.
For with very great honor she received
Him and his men, and treated them very well;
But then later he did her great wrong,
Even though he'd pledged his faith to her

Et donnee s'amour, voire en faintise!
Si s'en parti ne puis ne retourna
Et autre part la sienne amour tourna,
Dont en la fin celle, pour s'amittié,
Mouru de dueil, dont ce fu grant pitié.
¶Peneloppe, la femmë Ulixés,
Qui raconter vouldroit tout le procés
De la dame, trop trouveroit a dire
De sa bonté, ou il n'ot que redire;
Tresbelle fu, requise et bien amee,
Noble, saige, vaillant et renommee.
D'autres pluseurs—et tant que c'est senz nombre—
Furent et sont et seront en ce nombre.
Mais je m'en taiz adez d'en plus compter,
Car long procez seroit a raconter.
Si ne sont pas femmes si desloyales
Comme aucun dist, mais sont pluseurs loyales.
Mais il avient, et c'est de commun cours,
Qu'on les deçoit et trahit en amours.
Et quant ainsi se treuvent deceües,
Les aucunes des plus apparceües
S'en retrayent; de ce font grant savoir.
Doivent elles doncques ce blasme avoir?
Est ce doncques, se Dieux vous doint santé,
Mal ne folour, barat ne fausseté?
Nennil certes! Ains est grant sens ainçois!
[fol. 71b] Mais je congnois de vray et apparçois
Que se amans tenissent verité,
Foy, loyauté senz contrarïeté,
Vers leurs dames feïssent leur devoir,
Comme amans doivent faire par droit devoir,
Je croy que peu ou nulle fausseroit,
Et que toute femme loyal seroit.
(Au mains, le plus riglé n'est qui ne faille,
De toute riens n'est pas tout bien senz faille.)
Mais pour ce que pluseurs faulsent et mentent,
Et en maint lieux par desloyauté hantent,
Leur faulse l'en, et c'est tout par leur coupe
Que l'en leur fait de tout autel pain soupe!
¶Et aucuns sont qui jadis en mes laz
Furent tenus, mais ilz sont d'amer laz,
Par vïeillesse ou defaulte de cuer.

And given his love, deceitfully indeed!
He left and never returned
And bestowed his love elsewhere;
Because of which, in the end, for love of him, Dido
Died of grief, which was a great pity.

Penelope, Ulysses' wife:

Whoever might recount everything this lady
Went through, would find a great deal to say
About her irreproachable goodness;
She was very beautiful, sought after, and loved,
Noble, wise, brave, and renowned.
Many others, so many they're without number,
Were and are and will be in the count.
But from here on I'll say no more,
For the telling would be a long affair.
Thus women aren't so disloyal
As some say; rather, many are loyal.
But it happens, and quite commonly,
That they are deceived and betrayed in love,
And when they find they've been betrayed,
The most prudent among them
Withdraw; in that they show great wisdom.
Should they be blamed for that?
If God should give you health,
Is it evil or madness, trickery or falseness?
Certainly not! Rather, it is great good sense!
But in truth, I perceive and recognize
That if lovers held to the truth,
Were faithful and loyal without exception,
If they did what they should toward their ladies,
As lovers are responsible for doing,
I believe that few women or none would cheat,
And that every woman would be loyal.
(At least, even he who lives by the rules may slip;
In all things no good can be without a flaw.)
But because many men deceive and lie
And go calling here and there disloyally,
They're tricked in turn, and it's all their fault
If they're served up the same dish!

Now there are some who formerly
Were held in my snares, but they're weary of loving
Because of old age or lack of pluck.

Si ne veulent pas amer a nul fuer;
Et convenant m'ont de tous poins nÿé,
Moy et mon fait guerpy et regnÿé,
Comme mauvais serviteurs et rebelles.
Et telle gent racontent telz nouvelles
Communement, et se plaingnent et blasment
Moy et mon fait et les femmes diffament
Pour ce que plus ne s'en peuent aidier
Ou que leurs cuers de moy veulent vuidier.
Si les cuident faire aux autres desplaire
Par les blasmer, mais ce ne peuent faire.
Si hé tel gent trop plus qu'autre riens, certes,
Et les paye souvent de leurs dessertes,
Car en despit de leurs males parolles,
Eulz assoter d'aucunes femmes folles
De peu d'onneur, males, mal renommees,
[fol. 71c] Je faiz yceulz; de telz gens sont amees.
Si ne remaint en eulz plume a plumer—
Bien le scevent a leur droit reclamer.
La sont seurpris et bien enveloppé
Ceulz qui le mieulx cuident estre eschappé!
Comme il affiert sont tel gent avoyé;
Si leur est bien tel meschief employé.
¶Et encor piz, car ceulz qui plus souvent
Vont les femmes par grant soing decevant,
Et qui le plus se peinent et travaillent,
N'il ne leur chault qu'il leur couste ou qu'ilz baillent,
Ne quel peinë ilz doivent endurer
Pour a grant soing leur vouloir procurer,
Tant qu'ilz tant font par malices trouvees,
Par faulz sermens, par choses controuvees,
Qu'ilz attraient plusieurs a leurs cordelles
Par leur engin et par faulses cautelles,
Et puis aprés s'en moquent et s'en vantent,
Et vont disant que femmes se consentent
Legierement, com legieres et frailles,
Et qu'on ne doit avoir fiance en elles.
C'est maul jugié et trop male sentence
De trestoutes pour tant mettre a la dance.
Mais s'aucunes attraient par tel guise,
Quel merveille! Ne fu pas par faintise,
Par faulz consaulz, par trahison bastie,

They refuse to love again at any price
And have denied a pact with me in every way,
Rejecting and abandoning me and what I do,
Like bad and rebellious servants.
These men repeat such gossip
Publicly, and complain and blame
Me and what I do, and defame women
Because they can no longer perform,
Or because they wish to rid their hearts of me.
They think they'll make women disagreeable to others
By blaming them, but that they cannot do.
I hate such men more than anything else, that's for sure,
And I often pay them their just desserts;
For in spite of their nasty words
I make them fall madly for prostitutes,
Who've little honor, who're sinful and disreputable.
They're loved by men like that,
Who haven't a feather left to pluck—
These women know how to claim their due.
There they're caught and bound,
Those men who most thought they'd escape!
As is fitting, they're led astray;
And such woe on them is well-applied.
    But there's worse, for those who most often
Assiduously deceive women,
Who strain and strive the most,
Without a thought to cost or what they'll give,
Or to what pain they have to endure
To get what they want with great effort;
They do so much by their concocted evil,
By fraudulent oaths, by invented schemes,
That they rope in many women
By their wiliness and chicanery,
And then afterward they laugh and boast
And go around saying that women
Give themselves readily, like weak and easy targets,
And that no faith should be placed in them.
It is badly judged and badly decided
To paint all women with the same brush!
But if men entice some women in that way,
What a wonder! Was it not by dissembling,
False counsel, well-crafted treason,

Par parlemens, engins et foy mentie
La grant cité de Troye jadis prise,
Qui tant fut fort et toute en feu esprise?
Et tous les jours par engins et desroys
Ne trahist on et royaumes et roys?
Trop deçoivent les beaux blandissemens;
[fol. 71d] Tous en sont plains, et livres et rommans.
Si n'est pas chose dont a trop merveillier
Quant pour pener, mentir et travaillier,
On peut vaincrë une chose simplete,
Une ignorant petite femmelette!
Et fëust ou malicïeuse et saige,
Si n'est ce pas en grant vassellage
A homme aigu, de grant malice plain,
Qui peine y met comme il en est tout plain?
Et ainsi sont les femmes diffamees
De pluseurs gens, et a grant tort blasmees
Et de bouchë et en plusieurs escrips;
Ou qu'il soit voir ou non, tel est li cris.
Mais qui qu'en ait mesdit ou mal escript,
Je ne truis pas en livre n'en escript
Qui de Jhesus parle ne de sa vie,
Ne de sa mort pourchacee d'envie
—Et meismement des apoltres les fais
Qui pour la foy porterent maint dur fais—
N'Euvangille, qui nul mal en tesmoingne
Mais maint grant bien, mainte haulte besoingne,
Grant prudence, grant sens et grant constance,
Parfaite amour, en foy grant arrestance,
Grant charité, fervente voulenté,
Ferme et entier couraige entalenté
Le Dieu servir, et grant semblant en firent,
Car mort ne vif, oncques ne le guerpirent.
Fors des femmes fut de tous delaissié
Le doulz Jhesus, navré, mort et blecié.
Toute la foy remaint en une femme:
Si est trop folz qui d'elles dist diffame,
Ne feust ores que pour la reverence
[fol. 72a] De la haulte Roÿne, en remembrance
De sa bonté, qui tant fu noble et digne
Que du filz Dieu porter elle fut digne.
Grant honneur fist a femme Dieu le pere,

Persuasive talk, tricks, and perjured faith
That Troy, the great city, was taken,
And, strong though it was, put to the torch?
And every day, through craft and treachery,
Aren't kings and kingdoms betrayed?
Fine flattery deceives very well;
Books and romances are filled with it.
So hardly is there cause for wonder
When by struggling, lying, and toiling
One may defeat a simple little thing,
A simple little woman!
And should she be malign and sly,
Isn't it when she's in complete vassalage
To some cunning man, full of trickery,
Whose efforts are as great as his subterfuge?
And thus are women defamed
By many people, and wrongly blamed
In both talk and many books:
Whether true or not, that's the word.
But however many have slandered them or written ill,
I do not find in books or in writings
That speak of Jesus or about his life,
Or his death pursued in envy,
—And even in the deeds of the Apostles
Who carried many a hard burden for the faith—
Or in the Gospel, which speaks no ill of them
But many a good thing, many a noble deed,
Great prudence, great wisdom, great constancy,
Perfect love and great attachment to the faith,
Great charity, fervent will,
Firm and steadfast intention desirous of
Serving God, which they showed plainly,
For they never abandoned him in life or in death.
Except for women, sweet Jesus was by all
Abandoned, wounded, stricken, dead.
All faith resided in one woman.
Thus whoever slanders women is foolish,
If only for the reverence
Owed to the exalted Queen, in remembrance
Of her goodness, she who was so noble and dignified
As to be worthy of bearing the Son of God.
God the Father greatly honored womankind,

Qui faire en volt son espouse et sa mere:
Temple de Dieu a la Trinité jointe.
Bien estre doit femme joyeuse et cointe,
Qui autelle comme celle fourme a;
Car oncques Dieu nulle riens ne fourma
De dignité semblable n'aussi bonne,
Fors seulement de Jhesus la personne.
Si est top folz qui de riens les ramposne
Quant femmë est assise en si hault trosne
Coste son filz, a la dextre du Pere:
C'est grant honneur a femenine mere.
        ¶Si ne trouvons qu'oncques les desprisast
Le bon Jhesus, mais amast et prisast.
        ¶Dieu la fourma a sa digne semblance,
Et lui donna savoir et congnoissance
Pour soy sauver, et don d'entendement.
Si lui donna fourme moult noblement:
Et fut faite de moult noble matiere,
Car ne fu pas du lymon de la terre,
Ains fu faite de la coste de l'omme,
Le quel corps ja estoit en toute fourme,
Le plus noble des choses terrïennes.
Et les vrayes histoires anciennes
De la Bible—qui ne puet mençonge estre—
Nous racontent qu'en paradis terrestre
Fut formee femme premierement,
Non pas l'omme. Mais du decevement
Dont on blasme dame Eve nostre mere,
[fol. 72b] Dont s'ensuivi de Dieu sentence amere,
Je dy pour vray qu'onc Adam ne deçut,
Et simplement de l'ennemy conçut
La parolle qui lui donna a croire;
Si la cuida estre loyale et voire.
En celle foy de lui dire s'avance,
Si ne fut donc fraude ne decevance,
Car simplece, senz malice celee,
Ne doit estre decevance appellee.
Nulz ne deçoit sens cuidier decevoir,
Autrement n'est ce decevance voir.
Quelz grans maulz dont en ce peuent estre diz?
Par desservir n'ont elles paradis?
De quelz crimes les puet on accuser?

Who made woman both his spouse and his mother:
God's Temple joined to the Trinity.
Women should be joyful and glad
To have the same form as hers,
For God never formed another being
Of similar dignity or equal goodness,
Except for the person of Jesus.
Anyone who derides them on any score is quite mad
Since woman is seated on such a high throne,
Next to her Son, to the Father's right—
That's a great honor for a woman and a mother.
We do not find that women were ever disdained
By good Jesus, but rather loved and prized.
God created her in his own worthy image,
And gave her the knowledge and intelligence
To save her soul, and the gift of understanding.
He formed her most nobly
And made her from the noblest matter,
For not from the mud of earth did she come,
But from the rib of man,
Whose body was already formed,
The noblest of earthly things.
And the true and ancient stories
Of the Bible—which cannot be lies—
Tell us that in the earthly paradise
Woman was the first to be formed,
Not man. And as for the deception
For which Lady Eve, our mother, is blamed,
Upon which followed God's harsh punishment,
I say in truth that she never deceived Adam,
But in simplicity absorbed the enemy's
Word, which he gave her to believe.
She thought it was true and loyal,
And in that spirit she approached Adam.
It was never fraudulence or deception,
Because simplicity, which has no hidden malice,
Should not be called deceit.
No one deceives without intending to,
Otherwise it's not really deceit.
What great evils can thus be said of women?
Isn't paradise their reward?
Of what crimes can they be accused?

Et s'aucuns folz a leur amour muser
Vuellent, par quoy a eulx mal en couviengne,
N'en peuent mais; qui est saige s'en tiengne:
Qui est deceu et cuidoit decevoir
Nulz fors lui seul n'en doit le blasme avoir.
¶Et se sur ce je vouloye tout dire,
Doubte auroye d'encourir d'aucuns l'ire,
Car moult souvent, par dire verité
Mautalent vient et contrarieté.
Pour ce ne vueil faire comparaisons,
Hayneuses sont a la foiz telz raisons.
Si me souffist de louer sens blasmer,
Car on peut bien quelque riens bon clamer
Senz autre riens nommer mauvaiz ou pire;
Car son bon droit aucunes foiz empire
Cil qui blasmë autrui pour s'aloser;
Si se vault mieulx du dire reposer—
Pour ce, m'en tais. Si en soit chascun juge
[fol. 72c] Et justement selon verité juge;
Si trouvera, s'il vient a droit jugier,
Que le plus grant mal puet pou dommagier.
¶N'occient gent, ne blecent ne mehaignent,
Ne trahison ne pourchacent ne preingnent,
Feu ne boutent, ne desheritent gent,
N'empoisonnent, n'emblent or në argent,
Ne deçoivent d'avoir ne d'eritage
N'en faulz contracts, ne ne portent dommage
Aux royaumes, aux duchiez n'aux empires;
Mal ne s'ensuit gueres, meismes des pires.
Communement une ne fait pas rigle;
Et qui vouldra par histoire ou par Bible
Moy ramposner par moy donner exemple
D'une ou de deux ou de pluseurs ensemble
Qui ont esté reprouvees et males,
Encore en soit celles met enormales,
Car je parle selon le commun cours,
Et moult peu sont qui usent de telz tours.
Et s'on me veult dire que mie enclines
Condicïons ne taches femenines
Ne soit a ce, n'a user de batailles
N'a gens tuer në a faire fouailles
Pour bouter feu, ne a telz choses faire,

And if some madmen want to play at love,
For whom ill treatment would be fitting,
They can't do otherwise; let the wise man abstain:
He who planned to deceive but is himself deceived
Has only himself to blame.
And if I wanted to say everything on this subject,
I'd fear incurring the wrath of certain people,
For very often from speaking the truth
Ill feeling arises, and hostility.
That's why I won't make comparisons,
For such language can at times be hateful.
Let me be content to praise, not blame,
For one may well call some people good
Without also saying who is bad or worse.
For he who blames another just to praise himself
Sometimes casts doubt on his own truthfulness.
It's far better to refrain from talking,
And so I'll hold my tongue. Let each person judge:
If he adjudicates the case truthfully
He will find, if he judges honestly,
That a woman's greatest fault does but little harm.
Women don't kill or wound or mutilate people,
Or chase opportunities for treason.
They don't start fires, disinherit people
Or poison them, or steal gold or silver.
They don't cheat people of their goods or inheritance
With false contracts, and they don't bring loss
To kingdoms, duchies, or empires.
Scarcely is there any harm, even from the worst.
One woman doesn't prove the rule.
Whoever would rebuke me, giving me
Examples from history or the Bible
Of one or two, or many together
Who've been reprobate and corrupt,
Once more, these are only the ones who go too far.
I'm speaking according to what is usual,
For very few exist who practice such tricks.
And if someone wants to say to me
That women's traits and qualities are not inclined
Toward that, or to do battle,
Kill people, or prepare the torches
To start a fire, or to do any such things,

Pour ce, nul preu, louange, ne salaire
Ne leur en puet ne doit appartenir
D'elles souffrir de telz cas, ne tenir.
Mais sauve soit la grace des diseurs,
Je consens bien qu'elles n'ont pas les cuers
Enclins a ce, në a cruaulté faire.
Car nature de femme est debonnaire,
Piteuse, moult paoureuse et doubtable,
[fol. 72d] Humble, doulce, coye et moult charitable,
Amiable, devote, en paix honteuse,
Et guerre craint, simple et religïeuse,
Et en courroux tost appaise son yre,
Ne puet vëoir cruaulté ne martire.
Et telles sont par nature sens doubte
Condicïons de femmes, somme toute.
Et celle qui ne les a d'avanture
Contre le droit toute se desnature;
Car cruauté fait en femme a reprendre,
Ne l'en n'y doit fors toute doulçour prendre.
¶Et puis qu'ilz n'ont meurs ne condicïons
A faire fais de sang, occisïons
N'a autres grans pechiez lays et horribles
Dont sont elles innocens et paisibles,
Voire des grans et enormes pechiez,
—Car chascun est d'aucun vice entechiez—
Si ne seront doncques pas encoulpees
Des grans meffais ou ne sont attrapees.
Si n'en auront në en peine n'en coulpe
Pugnicïon, puis qu'elles n'y ont coulpe.
¶Dont dire puis—ce n'est pas heresie—
Que moult leur fist le hault Dieu courtoisie
D'elles fourmer sens les condicïons
Qui gent mettent a griefs perdicïons,
Car des desirs s'en ensuivent les fais
Dont maint portent sur leur armes griefs fais.
Si vault trop mieux qu'on n'ait pas le desir
Dont l'acomplir fait souvent mort gesir.
Qui soustenir vouldroit seroit herite
Que qui tempté n'est n'a point de merite
Se non pechïer, de soy abstenir.
[fol. 73a] Telles raisons ne font a soustenir,
Car par les sains nous veons le contraire:

And so no special praise, credit, or reward
Can or should belong to them
For abstaining from things like that, or resisting
(Begging pardon from those who say so)
I agree indeed that women haven't hearts
So disposed, nor toward doing cruel deeds,
For woman's nature is sweet and mild,
Compassionate, fearful, and timorous,
Humble, gentle, reserved, and charitable,
Pleasant, pious, reticent in peacetime,
Fearful of war, artless and devout.
When angered, she quickly calms her ire,
And she can't stand to see brutality or suffering.
Such are certainly by nature
Women's qualities, in sum.
She who happens not to have them
Distorts her nature against what's right,
For cruelty in women is to be reproved,
And gentleness alone accepted.

Now since they haven't the habits or penchant
To perform bloody deeds or killings,
Or other grave, ugly, and horrible sins,
Of which they are innocent and from which exempt,
At least from great and enormous sins
—For each of us is tainted by some vice—
So women won't be made culpable
For great misdeeds in which they're not involved,
Nor will they have, through penalty or blame,
Any punishment, since theirs is not the fault.

Thus I may say (and this is not heresy)
That God on high did women a courtesy
By forming them without the qualities
That lead people to grievous perdition,
For from desires come the deeds
From which many bear marks on their souls.
It's far better not to have the desire
Whose satisfying often brings death.
Only a heretic would take the view
That one not tempted shows no merit
By abstaining and not sinning.
Such arguments can't be sustained,
For we see the opposite in the saints.

Saint Nicolas n'eüst sceu pechié faire,
Onc ne pecha n'oncques ne fu tempté;
N'autres pluseurs n'en orent voulenté
Non de pechier quant est mortellement,
(Pechier porent ilz veniellement)
Si sont tous ceulz appellez prëesluz,
Predestinez et de Dieu eslëuz.
¶Par ces raisons, conclus et vueil prouver
Que grandement femmes a approuver
Font et louer, et leurs condicïons
Recommander, qui inclinacïons
N'ont aux vices, qui humaine nature
Va dommagant et grevant creature.
Par ces raisons justes et veritables,
Je preuve que tous hommes raisonnables
Doivent femmes prisier, cherir, amer,
Et ne doivent avoir cuer de blasmer
Elles de qui tout homme est descendu.
Ne leur soit pas mal pour le bien rendu,
Car c'est la riens ou monde, par droiture,
Que homme aime mieulx et de droite nature.
Si est moult lait et grant honte a blasmer
La riens qui soit que l'en doit plus amer
Et qui plus fait a tout homme de joye:
Homs naturel senz femme ne s'esjoye;
C'est sa mere, c'est sa suer, c'est sa mie,
Et peu avient qu'a homs soit ennemie.
C'est son droit per qui a lui est semblable,
La riens qui plus lui peut estre agreable.
Në on ne puet pris ne loz conquester
[fol. 73b] A les blasmer, mais grant blasme acquester.
Il n'est blasme si lait ne si nuisant
Comme tenus estre pour mesdisant,
Voire, encore plus especialement
De diffamer femmes communement.
C'est un vice diffamable et vilain;
Je le defens a homme quant je l'aim.
Si s'en gart dont trestout noble courage,
Car bien n'en puet venir, mais grant dommage,
Honte, despit et toute villlenie;
Qui tel vice a n'est point de ma maisgnie.
¶Or ay conclus en tous cas mes raisons

Saint Nicholas could not have sinned:
He never sinned, and never was tempted.
Many others never had the desire to sin,
That is, to sin mortally
(They could have sinned venially),
And so all those are called the elect,
Predestined and chosen by God.

With this reasoning I conclude and hope to prove
That women do very much to be approved
And praised; and I want to recommend
Their qualities, which show no inclination
Toward the vices that damage
Human nature and harm created beings.
By these fair and truthful arguments
I conclude that all reasonable men
Must prize, cherish, and love women
And not want to denigrate
Those from whom every man is born.
Let none return them evil for good,
For woman is rightly that being in the world
Whom man loves best and by his true nature.
So it's shabby and scandalous to blame
The being one must love the best
And who brings the greatest gladness to every man.
A natural man without a woman has no joy,
For she's his mother, his sister, his sweetheart;
And it seldom happens that she's man's enemy.
She's his proper equal, perfectly like him,
The being most able to please him.
One cannot gain esteem or praise
By blaming women, only blame for oneself.
There is no blame so ugly or damaging
As being thought a slanderer,
And more especially, indeed,
In defaming all of womankind.
That's a shameful, base vice;
I forbid it to a man when I love him.
Let every noble heart avoid it,
For no good can ensue, only great harm,
Humiliation, scorn, and disgrace.
Whoever has such a vice is not of my domain.

Now I've concluded my arguments on each point

Bien et a droit; n'en desplaise a nulz homs,
Car se bonté et valeur a en famme,
Honte n'est pas a homme ne diffame,
Car il est né et fait d'autel merrien.
Se mauvaise est, il ne peut valoir rien;
Car nul bon fruit de mal arbre ne vient,
Telle qu'elle est, ressembler lui couvient;
Et se bonne est, il en doit valoir mieulx,
Car aux meres bien ressemblent les fieulx.
¶Et se j'ay dit d'elles bien et louange,
Comme il est vray, ne l'ay fait par losange
N'a celle fin que plus orgueil en aient,
Mais tout afin que toudiz elles soyent
Curïeuses de mieulx en mieulx valoir,
Senz les vices que l'en ne doit avoir.
Car qui plus a grant vertu et bonté
En doit estre moins d'orgueil seurmonté;
Car les vertus si enchacent les vices.
Et s'aucunes des femmes est de nices,
Ceste epiltre leur puist estre doctrine;
[fol. 73c] Le bien preingnent pour loyale doctrine,
Le mal laissent. Les bonnes vueillent en ce
Prendre vouloir d'avoir perseverence,
Si auront preu, grant honneur, joye et loz,
Et paradis en la fin, dire l'oz.
¶Pour ce, conclus en diffinicïon
Ou des mauvais soit fait pugnicïon:
Qui les blasment, diffament et accusent
Et qui de faulx desloyaulx semblans usent
Pour decevoir elles, si soient tuit
De nostre court banny, chacié, destruit
Et entredis et excommenié
Et tous noz biens si leur soient nÿé;
C'est bien raison qu'on les excommenye.
Et commandons de fait a no mesgnye
Generaulment, a tous noz officiers,
A noz sergens et a tous noz maciers,
A noz prevosts et maires et baillifs
Et vicaires, que tous ceulz malbaillifs
Et villenez soient, treslaidement
Injuriez, pugnis honteusement,
Pris et liez, et justice en soit faite,

Well and rightly. Let no man be displeased,
For if there is goodness and worth in a woman,
That's no shame or disgrace for a man,
For he is born and formed of the same matter.
If she is bad, he can have no worth,
For no good fruit comes from a bad tree.
He must resemble her as she is,
And if she's good, he is the worthier,
For sons resemble their mothers.
If I've uttered good and praise of her,
As it is the truth, I haven't done it to flatter
Or so that women may be more arrogant,
But entirely so they may always try to be
Desirous of being worth more and more,
Without the vices which one ought not to have.
For the more a person has great virtue and goodness,
The less should that person be consumed by arrogance,
For the virtues drive out the vices.
And if there are among women some foolish ones,
May this epistle be their teaching.
May they take the good for loyal doctrine
And abandon evil. May good women
Acquire from this the will to persevere
And they'll have merit, joy, honor, and praise,
And paradise in the end, I dare say.
With that, I conclude:
Let punishment be dealt to evil men
Who blame, defame, and accuse women,
And who use false and disloyal subterfuges
To trick them. And thus let all
Be chased from our court, banished and disgraced,
Banned from all rites and excommunicated,
And let all our favors be denied to them;
We're indeed justified in excommunicating them.
And we emphatically command our household
Generally, as well as our officers,
Our bailiffs and all our sheriffs,
Our provosts, mayors, judges,
And deputies, that all such men be shamed
And treated with contempt,
Discredited, punished in disgrace,
Seized and bound, and let justice be done

Senz plus souffir nulle injure si faite,
Ne plus ne soit souffert telle laidure.
Nous le voulons ainsi, et c'est droiture;
Acompli soit senz faire aucuns delays.
Donné en l'air en nostre grant palays,
Le jour de may, la solennelle feste
Ou les amans nous font mainte requeste,
L'an de grace mil trois cens quatre vins
Et dix neuf, presens dïeux et divins.
[fol. 73d] Par le dieu d'Amours puissant
A la relacïon de cent
Dieux et plus de grant pouoir
Confermans nostre vouloir.
Jupiter, Apollo et Mars,
Vulcans par qui Pheton fu ars,
Mercurïus, dieu de langaige,
Eolus, qui vent tient en cage,
Neptunus, le dieu de la mer,
Glaucus, qui mer fait escumer,
Les dieux des vaulx et des montaingnes,
Des grans forests et des champaignes,
Le dieu des pastours Pan, Saturnus,
Nostre mere la grant Venus,
Pallas, Juno et Lathona,
Cerés, Vesta, Antigona,
Aurora, Thetis, Arequsa,
(Qui le dieu Pluto encusa),
Minerve la bataillerresse
Et Dÿane la chacerresse
Et les dieux qui par nuit obscure
S'en vont pour querir avanture,
Et d'autres dieux no conseillier
Et deesses plus d'un millier.

Cupido le dieu d'Amours
Cui amans font leurs clamours.

Without our enduring any further such villainy,
And may such outrage be tolerated no more.
We wish it thus, and it is just.
Let it be done without any delay.
Enacted in our great palace in the sky
On the first of May, the solemn festival
When lovers bring us many a request,
The year of grace thirteen hundred
And ninety-nine, the gods and deities witnessing.
From the mighty God of Love
On the testimony of a hundred
Gods and more of great power,
Confirming our will:
Jupiter, Apollo, and Mars,
Vulcan, because of whom Phaethon burned;
Mercury, god of language;
Aeolus, who cages the winds;
Neptune, god of the waters;
Glaucus, who churns the foam of the sea;
The gods of valleys and mountains,
Of great forests and of plains.
Pan, the god of shepherds, and Saturn,
Our mother, great Venus,
Pallas, Juno, and Latona,
Ceres, Vesta, Antigone,
Aurora, Thetis, Arethusa,
(Who accused the god Pluto),
Minerva the woman warrior,
And Diana the huntress;
And the gods who in darkest night
Go out to seek adventure,
And other gods, our counselors,
And more than a thousand goddesses.

Cupid the God of Love,
To whom lovers cry out.

Rejected Readings and Variants to the French Edition of the Epistre au dieu d'Amours

Readings Rejected from *L_1* (Chantilly, Bibliothèque du Château, 492)

271 q. pou s.
307 doit les hommes
415 le livre
547 On ne peut
621 Desquelz
679 celles
706 n'e. senz

Variants from *L_2* (Paris, BnF, fr. 12779), *D* (Paris, BnF, fr. 835), and *R* (London, BL, Harley MS 4431)

Rubrique *om. L_2*; Ci c. *om. D*
1 C. dieu par *DR*
2 Roy d. a. *DR*
5 ses o. *DR*
39 leurs cuers *R*
41 et en s. *R*
44 Ou p. q. m. ou t. a. *D*
45 Si j. *R*
50 semblans *L_2DR*; mains en *DR*
51 Par mi r. *DR*
54 n'y s. *DR*
57 mignos jolis *R*
62 De m. *DR*
65 deshoiaulz *D*
74 *1st* et *om. L_2DR*
81 suivir *R*
82 Et *om. DR*; q. en ce point se t. *DR*
83 Sache pour v. *DR*; ne lui f. *DR*
84 dame belle *DR*
95 m. chaude blanche *R*
101 n'y pensent se *DR*
105 a. le\s/ ont en. *R*
108 s. ce qu'ainsi *DR*
114 sont amez *DR*
128 T. est t'amie *D*

129 seue a. *R*; a. mais L_2*DR*

140 Ce qu'il *DR*

142 Ad *D*

144 savoir *R*

152 s'en L_2*D*; s'en cellui l. *R*

153 Pour a.c. *DR*; par q. *R*

162 Tout a. *DR*; brunes ou blondes *R*

163 q. paroles *R*

164 s. emblees *DR*

165 les *om. DR*

169 qui est sa chiere mere *DR*

170 Et ne l. *DR*

171 A. souefve doulce et *DR*

172 son besoing *DR*

178 et amiables serviables *R*

179 mau congnoissant *DR*

184 .ij. *DR*

185 qu'il y en ait de *DR*

200 Ne t. *DR*

201 fu est et *DR*; celles *DR*

206 se f. *R*

207 S'ilz *DR*

212 Tresfort b. *DR*

213 ne diffamer n. *DR*

214 Le t. *R*

219 des n. *DR*

220 Qui *R*

222 tel c. *R*

230 *2nd* ne *om.* L_2; ne peust/pot ouir d'elles blasme ou d. *DR*

239 nuise *D*

240 est *om. D*

244 prisier servir L_2

249 H. les duit *DR*

250a, b *D and R contain here two more verses, lacking in* L_1 *and* L_2: De nobles meurs bien entechiez se perent / Par leurs beaulz fais leurs vaillances apperent

252 t. d'eulz (*corr. over erasure*) \et/ l. *R*

255 par droit *DR*

258 que sus leur metant L_2

266 Salemon L_2*D*; Salomon *R*

271 q. pou s. L_2

278 menconge *R*

282	de moult *DR*
286	Contre tous ceulz qui giter vouldront gage *DR*
287	des f. *DR*
290	l. en *DR*
291	a *om.* L_2; aux *DR*
296	t. qu'on *D*
303	n'en *DR*
304	ne pour *DR*
307	doit les hommes L_2
309	daignent *D*
316	nez aux *DR*
317	le *om. D*
326	Ou q. *DR*
338	D'elles trayr *R*
341	a elles *DR*
344	digne j. et louable *D*; \juste/ et digne et l. *R*
345	generaument *DR*
349	E. pas ne cherchier ni querir *DR*
350	l. prier ne requerir *DR*
361	s. ilz f. *R*
388	Q. long L_2*DR*
390	Mist il y la *DR*
397	p. ne v. *R*
400	Ou il c. t. *R*
403	Qu'elz *DR*
405	tuit pl. *DR*
406	le r. *DR*
414	batailleux *D*
415	*1st* les *om. DR*; le livre L_2; li livre *R*
418	a droit les pars *D*
421	f. desprisant L_2*DR*
425	Et qu'amoureux *D*; Et que teles amans qui *R*
426	treuve L_2; Toutes treuvent quant *DR*
428	sus *D*
429	et on *DR*
431	est *expunctuated bef.* esté *D*
433	b. et *D*
435	aux *D*
436	Tresloialle *D*; Tres loyale *R*
438	.C. *D*
439	dessur *R*
457	a la f. *DR*

470	d. ains *DR*
476	donc de ce *DR*
480	de voir *DR*
484	amant doit *DR*
487–488	*om. DR*
489	par c. q. *D*
492	Se on *DR*
495	Ou par *DR*
496	v. plus *DR*
497	tout point L_2; f. de touz poins r. *D*
504	c. veulent de moy v. *DR*
507	Je he *R*; \trop/ *R*
512	tel gent *DR*
514	B. les *DR*
518	tout m. *DR*
521	s'en p. *R*
525	m. celees *D*; m. prouvees *R*
526	faulz semblans *DR*
528	engins *DR*
534	en dance *DR*
535	en t. g. *R*
545	pas *om. DR*; dont chose *DR*
546	mentir pener *DR*
547	On ne peut L_2
549	f. ores *DR*
557	ne mal *D*
559	ou de *D*
560	Ou de *DR*
561–562	*om. DR*
569	De D. *DR*
571	de\s/ *D*; du tout d. *DR*
599	Mais seulement de la c. *DR*
600	estoit s'en est la somme *DR*
618	Ou aultrement decepvance n'est voir *DR*
621	Desquelz L_2
623	V. a eulx par quoy *DR*
626	Nulz *om. DR*; lui tout seul *DR*
629	pour d. *DR*
631	n'en *D*
632	maintesfois *D*
637	Cellui *DR*
640	Si justement *R*

641 se v. *DR*

642 Que leurs plus grans maulz peuet (*sic*, n *erased bet.* e *and* t, *space filled w. dash*) pou dommagier *D*; Que leur plus grant maulx peut *R*

644 n'empregnent *DR*

646 n'or *D*

648 et ne *DR*

653 Moy ramp\r/onner pour *D*; Me remprover (remproner?) par *R*

654 .ij. *R*

655 rampronnees *D*; remprouvees *R*

658 Car m. *DR*

661 Ne sont *R*; ad ce *D*

662 fonoilles *D*

664–669 *added in left margin of fol. 55v R*

666 c. n'abstenir *R*

669 ad ce ne a telz choses faire *D*; a ce ne a faiz de tel affaire *R*

671 Moult piteuse p. *DR*

678 femme *DR*

683 elz L_2*DR*

684 n'occisions *DR*

688 techiez L_2*DR*

689 pas doncques *D*

691 n'en p. *R*; ne en c. L_2*DR*

692 que elles *D*; courpe *R*

696 mettent gent *DR*

701 desherite *D*

703 De non *DR*; et de soy *DR*

705 nous veons par les sains *DR*

706 n'e. sen L_2

707 n'en fu *DR*

709 Je di pechier *DR*

710 poirent *D*; pouoient *R*

719 ces preuves *DR*

720 Je conclus *DR*

731 s'amie L_2*DR*

735 n'y p. *DR*

737 N'il *DR*

742 le *om. D*

744 puent *D*

758 louenge *D*

765 en chacent *D*

766 S'il est d. f. aucunes n. *D*; de *om., 2-space dash bef.* nices *R*

767 p. est *D*
771 Si \en/ a. p. joye honneur et loz *R*
772 a la f. *DR*
774 Que d. *DR*
775 acoisent L_2
778 chacie bani d. *DR*
783 G. et a; tous *om. DR*
791 endure tel *R*
795 solempnee *DR*
797 mil iij^{C}.iiij^{xx}. L_2 ; mil CCC.iiij^{xx}. *DR*
798 .xix. *DR*
800 .C. L_2
808 fait mer *D*
810a, b *D and R present here two verses that appear later (819–820) in* L_1 *and* L_2: Et les dieux qui par nuyt obscure / S'en vont pour querir aventure
819–820 *appear after v. 810 DR*
824a Explicit L_2; Explicit l'epistre au dieu d'Amours *R*
824a, b Creintis / Explicit l'epistre au dieu d'Amours *D*

Variants from *W* (London, Westminster Abbey, MS 21)

[Rubric] Cy commence l'epistre au dieu d'amours
1 C. dieu par
5 ses obgiez
19 des o. des griefs
20 *verse om.*
39 leurs cuers
41 et en souppire
45 Si jurent
50 semblans mains
51 Parmy rues; leurs
54 n'y
57 mignoz jolis
62 De mettre
74 *1st* et *om.*
81 suivir
82 Et *om.*; qui en ce point se t.
83 Sache pour v.; que ne lui f. m.
84 dame belle
98 *verse om.*
101 n'y pensent se

105 le sont envelopees

108 souffit ce qu'ainsi

113 leur

114 sont amez

129 seine amour mais

140 Ce qui

144 savoir

152 se cellui lieu

153 Pour aucun cas; par quelque

155 leur

161 a *in* aucunes *lacking (hole in parchment)*

163 quieulx paroles

164 sont emblees

165 les *om.*

169 qui est sa chiere mere

170 Et ne lui

171 Ainçois soueve doulce et

172 son besoing

174 \tant/

178 et amiables serviables

179 mau congnoissant; *unrecognizable word crossed out before* rude

184 .ij.

187 foy n'auront

200 Ne tous

201 fut est et sera de celles

206 se font

207 S'ilz les

209 ~~pes~~ pecheur

212 Tres fort blasmer

213 ne diffamer nullui

214 Le tesmoigne

219 des nobles

220 *verse om.*

222 tel cas; puvez

230 Ne pot ouyr d'elles blasme ou diffames

249 Honneur les duit

250 a, b Des nobles meurs bien entechiez se perent/ Par leurs beaulx fais leurs vaillances apperent

252 je me tais d'eulx et leurs

255 par droit

266 Salomon

282 de moult ~~va~~ villaines

284	~~leur nye~~ lui nye
286	Contre tous ceulx qui getter vouldront gaige
287	des femmes
290	livret en
291	aux autres
303	n'en
304	ne pour
326	Ou qui
328	tel vice
338	D'elle trayr
341	a elles
344	Enseignement a estre digne et louable
345	generaument
349	pas ne cherser ne querir
350	lieu prier ne requerir
361	souvent ilz faillent
370	condicion
374	est il
388	Quel lonc proces
390	Mist il y la
397	pas ne veoir
400	Ou il convient
403	Qu'elz
405–406	*s is crossed out at the end of* plain *in both verses*
406	le respons
409	~~mist~~ list
415	*1st* les *om.*; eussent li livres
422	desprisant
423	ou furent
425	Et que telles amans qui
429	et on
439	desur
449	qui
451	*1st et* doubled; bien
453	ce que
457	a la fin
459	~~uxiles~~ ulixes
470	dit ains
476	dont de ce blasme
480	de voir
484	*verse om.*
487–488	*verses om.*

492	Se on
495	Ou par
496	veulent plus
504	veulent de moy
507	Je he
514	Bien les
518	tout meschef
522	vaillent
525	malices prouvees
526	faulx semblans
528	leurs engins
534	en la dance
535	en tel guise
546	mentir pener
549	feust ores
556	tel est le cas
560	Ou de
561–562	*verses om.*
569	De Dieu
571	du tout
582	joiseuse
599	Mais seulement de la
600	estoit s'en est la somme
607	~~eve~~ dame eve
612	loyale et bonne
618	Ou autrement decevance n'est voir
623	Veulent a eulx par quoy
625	et cuido ce decevoir
626	Nulz *om.*; Fors lui tout seul
628	~~livre~~ l'ire
629	pour dire
634	\bon/
636	*verse om.*
637	Cellui
641	se vient
642	Que leur plus grans maulx peuent pou domagier
644	n'emprennent
648	Ne faulx; et ne
651	~~fait~~ ne fait
653	Me remprover
655	remprouvees
658	Car moult

660 ne *om.*
661 Ne sont
666 cas n'abstenir
669 a ce ne a fais de tel afaire
671 Moult piteuse paouureuse [*sic*]
678 de femme~~nine~~
684 n'occisions
686 \ygnocens/
687 de grans
688 vice tachez
689 pas *om.*
700 souvent fait
705 nous veons par les sains
709 Je dy ~~pes~~ pecher
719 ces premiers justes
720 Je conclus
721 cherir et amer
730 s'esroie
735 n'y peut
746 n'est pas
765 en chassent
766 de *om.*
771 Si en auront preu joie honneur et los
772 a *followed by downstroke* a la fin
774 Que des
778 chacie bani et destruit
783 tous *om.*
791 \ne/ soit endure tel
793 Acomplir
795 solempnee
797 mil $\text{iij}^{\text{C}}\text{iiij}^{\text{xx}}$
798 Et xix; dieux et damez
801 et de plus grant pouoir
809 dieux *om.*
810a, b Et les dieux qui par nuyt ~~os~~ obscure/ S'en vont pour querir aventure
815 Arteusa
Explicit l'epistre au dieu d'Amours/ La non chalant/ Scales

Notes to the Epistre au dieu d'Amours / God of Love's Letter

Incipit, *epiltre*: Alternate spelling for *epistre*.

5 **all he commands** *les obgiez*: Defined in the *DMF* as "everything that is perceptible" ("tout ce qui est perceptible," s.v. *objet*, A.1).

11–13 **From married . . . all women in general** *De par toutes dames . . . toutes femmes generaulment*: A foretaste of Christine's *Livre des Trois Vertus*, a prose conduct book, or "mirror," in which women of all stations are addressed and counseled.

17–32 **complain . . . accustomed to protecting them** *Si se plaignent . . . les seuillent*: On Boucicaut's criticism of France for its failure to protect widows, see pp. 32–33. This cultural criticism is repeated more narrowly in the case of widows in *Autre Balade* VI, a poem that appears again in Christine's *Advision* ("Alas, where shall they find comfort . . . ," Bk. 3, ch. 6).

23–32 **Above all countries . . . protecting them** *Sur tous païs . . . garder les seuillent*: Christine believed that the personal moral conduct of the king and nobles was key to good government. For a brief survey of sources and influences for this view and a discussion of Christine's later development of it, see Barry Collett, "The Three Mirrors of Christine de Pizan," in Green and Mews, *Healing the Body Politic*, 1–18.

31–32 *dueillent, seuillent*: Despite the *-ill* orthography of these rhyme words, which suggests a palatalized *l* and therefore the subjunctive mood, the context here requires the indicative mood. It is likely that there was no call to fully palatalize *-ill* in both rhyme words. See note to vv. 205–6.

35 **fulsome flattery** *beaulz blandissemens*: On the sin of flattery, see "Adulatio," in Carla Casagrande and Silvana Vecchio, *Les Péchés de la langue: Disclipline et éthique de la parole dans la culture médiévale* (Paris: Cerf, 1991), 253–63. This same formulation is repeated at v. 543.

39–40 **in its grip, in thrall** *en serre, serre*: Christine aims here for a *rime équivoque* using a noun, *serre*, and a verb, *serre*, third person singular of *serrer*. A *serre* was also a scythe. See Versification, p. 52.

43 **he's gone all pale** *tout soit descouλouré*: The use of the subjunctive *soit* may bring out the tongue-in-cheek quality of this comment—that is, it shows doubt as to the truth of the claim made by the would-be lover that he is dying of longing. In *Deux amans*, Christine asks where the cemeteries are filled with all those lovers who were dying of love (vv. 987–90).

48 **those churches** *ces moustiers*: Christiane Marchello-Nizia notes a pair of examples of *ces*, "these" or "those," otherwise called a Middle French usage known as "epic" or "emphatic," referring to practices or places that author and readers have in common. See *Histoire de la langue française aux XIVe et XVe siècles* (Paris: Bordas, 1979), 123–24. Robert Martin and Marc Wilmet note the "deictic element inherent in the demonstrative," which can give it an ironic, expressive quality: *Syntaxe du moyen français*, vol. 2 of their *Manuel du français du moyen âge* (Bordeaux: Société bordelaise de diffusion des travaux de lettres et sciences humaines, 1980), 123.

48–56 **In those churches . . . weddings and feasts are** *Par ces moustiers . . . ou sont nopces et festes*: Such advice about where to find women is an echo of Jean de Meun's character Old Woman in the *Roman de la Rose* (*RR* ed. Lecoy vv. 13492–95), which in turn recalls Ovid's counsel in his *Ars amatoria* about finding and seducing women: Ovid, *The Art of Love and Other Poems*, trans. J. H. Mozley, rev. G. P. Goold, Bk. 1, ll. 1–176 (Cambridge, MA: Harvard University Press; London: William Heinemann, 1979). Christine's criticism here turns on its head Matheolus's claims that women cannot be restrained from going out and about and wishing to be seen (*Lamentations*, ed. van Hamel, vv. 942–48), and that, dressed to the nines, they seek out churches, in pursuit of priests and clerics (vv. 963–71).

50 **In pretense** *Par faulz semblant*: The French evokes the character of Faulx Semblant (False Seeming) in the *Romance of the Rose.*

52 **clacking sounds** *cliquetes qui sonnent*: Possibly made by (decorative?) attachments to the horses' harnesses.

58–59 **They pretend . . . endure them** *Si font semblant . . . les peuent endurer*: This mockery of false lovers who exaggerate their lovesickness to entrap young women is also featured in ballade 53 of the *Cent Balades* (*Œuvres poétiques*, 1:54–55).

64 **False lovers** *faulz amans*: A common accusatory formulation in the rhetoric of courtly love.

67–68 *en ce compte, tenir compte*: This is a pun at the rhyme on the word *compte*. *R* uses the spelling *conte* at v. 67, which introduces a double meaning, "count" and "tale."

74 *Justes et loyaulx et bon enseingnemens:* This line is one syllable too long in L_1 but is corrected in L_2, *D*, and *R* by eliminating the first *et*.

76–80 **to pursue honor . . . to be loved** *poursuivre honneur . . . a estre amez*: These brief recommendations recall the much lengthier Commandments of Love that

Cupid gives to the lover in Guillaume de Lorris's portion of the *Roman de la Rose* (*RR* ed. Lecoy vv. 2075–566; *RR* ed. Horgan, 32–39).

92 **herbed wine** *saugié*: A wine infused with sage.

95 **simple bread** *pain faitis*: the reference here is most likely to coarse bread. (But for the view that *pain faitis* was only slightly less fine than white bread, see Félix Lecoy, "Pain bourgeois. Pain faitiz. Pain de retrait," in *Mélanges de philologie offerts à Alf Lombard* [Lund: C. W. K. Gleerup, 1969], 101–7, at 106). Charles, Duke of Orléans (1394–1465), in his rondeau 174, contrasts *pain faitis* with white bread in a similar metaphor of love realized as the consuming of bread. See *Poésies*, ed. Pierre Champion, 2 vols. (Paris: Honoré Champion, 1966–71), 2:389–90. For a discussion of food as an indicator of economic class, see Alice Planche, "La Table comme signe de la classe: le témoignage du *Roman du comte d'Anjou* (1316)," in *Manger et boire au Moyen Age: Actes du colloque de Nice*, Publications de la Faculté des Lettres et Sciences Humaines de Nice, 27–28, ed. Denis Menjot, 2 vols. (Paris: Belles Lettres, 1984), 1:239–60.

96–97 **God only knows . . . all his heart** *Dieu scet . . . desiree est*: This expression of joy in feasting on bread also evokes what Ann W. Astell calls the "eucharistic beauty that is both seen . . . and eaten." See *Eating Beauty: The Eucharist and the Spiritual Arts of the Middle Ages* (Ithaca, NY, and London: Cornell University Press, 2006), 6.

101 **simple** *simples*: The quality of *simplece*, or lack of duplicity, is key to Christine's defense of women. See notes to vv. 547–48, 606–18, and the Introduction, pp. 8–9.

109 **criminal pact** *male aliance*: The French may capture a play on the word *male*, which can mean both "male" and "evil."

119 *ces grans cours*: Marchello-Nizia notes the use of the demonstrative adjective in Middle French to refer to the immediately preceding context: *La Langue française aux XIV*[e] *et XV*[e] *siècles*, 2nd ed. (Paris: Armand Colin, 2005), 154. For the use of "epic" or "emphatic" *ces*, see v. 48 and note.

121 **teach their lessons** *tiennent de telz plais leurs escoles:* A possible allusion to the less-skilled squires of v. 34.

128–62 **Lady so-and-so . . . blonde or brunette** *Telle t'aimë . . . blondes ou brunes tresses*: On this scene, see the Introduction, p. 8.

129–30 **part; . . . departs** *part; . . . part:* These verses, based on an equivocal rhyme, seem to mimic and at the same time alter the similar verses uttered by Old Woman in the *Roman*. See the Introduction, p. 14.

138 **In making excuse, he names the lady and accuses her** *En excusant celle nomme et accuse*: This plays on a proverb, "Qui s'excuse, s'accuse"—"He who makes excuse for himself accuses himself." See James Woodrow Hassell, Jr., *Middle French Proverbs, Sentences, and Proverbial Phrases* (Toronto: Pontifical Institute of Medieval Studies, 1982), 106.

162 *ilz*: The use of a masculine form as an alternative for the feminine plural *elles* here and at v. 403 is not uncommon in Middle French; the substitution very rarely appears in the singular, according to Marchello-Nizia (*Histoire de la langue française*, 175).

165 *Et quel prouffit vient d'ainsi les diffamer*: Eleven syllables in L_1 and L_2; in *D* and *R*, *les* is omitted.

168–80 **For every man . . . thanklessness** *tout homme . . . ingratitude*: The argument that mothers are owed respect was widespread.

193–200 **When sovereign God . . . what women do** *Quant le hault Dieu . . . leur meurs femenins diffamer:* Christine shares this point with LeFèvre (*Leesce*, vv. 1119–29).

201 *Car moult en fu, et sera de telles*: One syllable short in L_1 and L_2, but corrected in *D* and *R* by adding *est* after *fu*; translated, the verse would then read: "For there have been, there are, and there will be."

205–6 *valent, faillent*: in *D* and *R*, *faillent* is emended to *falent*; the correction assures the rhyme with *valent*. See also note to vv. 31–32. Rhymes between *l* and *ill* are frequent in the Middle French period, according to Marchello-Nizia, who interprets this to mean that the palatalized *l* was not very clearly palatalized ("n'était pas très nettement mouillé"; *Histoire de la langue française*, 90–91).

225–26 **Hutin / De Vermeilles . . .** *Hutin / De Vermeilles*: Knight and chamberlain to King Charles V, Hutin de Vermeilles (d. 1390) was married to Marguerite de Bourbon, daughter of Louis I of Bourbon. He appears in Jean le Sénéchal's *Cent Ballades* (One Hundred Ballades, 1389), a love debate, as an older knight who represents fourteenth-century chivalric values not unlike those upon which Boucicaut's Order of the White Lady on the Green Shield and the Cour amoureuse depended (see the Introduction, p. 32). It is worth noting that this category, men who made the defense of women part of their chivalric duty, had crystallized before Christine took up her pen. On the enjambment of Hutin . . . De Vermeilles, see Versification, p. 54.

233 **Othon de Grandson** *Othe de Grançon*: Grandson (1340/1350–August 7, 1397), poet and knight, and the descendant of an important Swiss family. With

others, he was accused of poisoning Count Amédée of Savoy in 1391, although the cause of the count's death was probably tetanus, the result of a wound received in a hunting accident. King Charles VI proclaimed Grandson innocent in 1395, but when the poet sought to recover properties confiscated in 1393, Gérard d'Estavayer, a considerably younger man, challenged him to a duel in which the poet was killed. See Daniel Chaubet, "Le duel Othon de Grandson - Gérard d'Estavayer du 7 août 1397: Une conséquence des événements qui agitèrent la Savoie dans les dernières années du XIVe siècle," in *Othon de Grandson: Chevalier et poète*, ed. Jean-François Kosta-Théfaine (Orleans: Paradigme, 2007), 11–42. See also Arthur Piaget, *Oton de Grandson: sa vie et ses poésies* [Lausanne: Payot, 1941], 11–104). Claude Berguerand suggests that Grandson was among the initiators of the St. Valentine's Day theme of service to ladies: *Le duel d'Othon de Grandson (1397): Mort d'un chevalier vaudois à la fin du Moyen Age* (Lausanne: Université de Lausanne, 2008), 15. In the *Debat de deux amans*, Christine again mentions both Grandson and Vermeilles (*Love Debate Poems*, 124). Grandson's *Complainte de saint Valentin* and *Complainte de l'an nouvel* are known to have influenced Geoffrey Chaucer's *Book of the Duchess*. See Heather Arden, "Othon de Grandson and Christine de Pizan: Love's Martyrs," in *Othon de Grandson: Chevalier et poète*, 103–21, at 117.

242 **Ajax, son of Telamon** *Thalamon Ayaulx*: Telamonius Ajax was a Greek hero of the Trojan War whom Christine also mentions in the *Epistre Othea*: see Gabriella Parussa's edition (Geneva: Droz, 1999), 292.13; 312.14; 332.5; 333.7. Ajax is also mentioned in numerous places in the *Mutacion*. See the Table des Noms Propres in Suzanne Solente's edition (Paris: Picard, 1959–66), 4:105. In the *Debat de deux amans*, Christine claims, erroneously, that he killed Paris in battle (*Love Debate Poems*, 100, and note to v. 651ff.). Another Ajax, also a hero of the Trojan War, was known as Ajax the Lesser.

247–54 **There still are many . . . boasting** *Encor en est maint . . . vanterie*: Christine may be thinking here of Jean II le Meingre (Boucicaut) and his establishment of the Order of the White Lady on a Green Shield. See the Introduction, p. 32. By comparison, Hutin de Vermeilles and Othon de Grandson (see notes to vv. 225–26 and 233) were dead by 1399, so there could be no question of flattery. In her biography of Charles V (Bk. 2, ch. 18) Christine again defends herself against potential charges of being a flatterer, distinguishing between justified and false praise (*Fais et bonnes meurs*, 1:180–84).

251 **overseas** *oultre mer*: While literally meaning "beyond the sea," this expression was understood to refer to Jerusalem and the crusading regions.

253 **flattery** *flaterie*: See note to v. 35.

261 **matter** *matiere*: The *materia* of a work, a term used in literary compositions and law texts, could refer both to subject matter and to "the materials from which it had been composed." See Alastair J. Minnis, *Medieval Theory of Authorship: Scholastic Literary Attitudes in the Later Middle Ages*, 2nd ed. (Philadelphia: University of Pennsylvania Press, 1988), 21.

265–68 **In verse . . . from them** *En vers . . . s'en gart:* This question paraphrases a Latin proverb: "Adam, Samsonem, si David, si Salomonem / Femina decepit, quis modo tutus erit?" (Since woman deceived Adam, Samson, David, and Solomon, how will all the rest be [safe from her]?) The four Hebrew figures, men said to have been beguiled by women, form a standard topos in medieval clerical writing and also appear in vernacular literature. See also vv. 319–20 and note.

281 ***The Remedy for Love*** *Le Remede d'Amours*: Ovid wrote his *Remedia Amoris* as a mock recantation of his *Ars Amatoria* (see *The Art of Love and Other Poems*, trans. Mozley, 2, 179–233). The *Remedia* taught men how to fall out of love, whereas the *Ars amatoria* was a guide to seduction. Both works, examples of didactic poetry on frivolous themes that was popular in Ovid's day, were widely read in the Middle Ages. In the *Lai of Guigemar*, the twelfth-century writer Marie de France describes a wall painting in which Venus is shown burning Ovid's book; those who follow Ovid are to be "excommunicated": *Lais de Marie de France*, ed. Karl Warnke, trans. Laurence Harf-Lancner (Paris: Librairie générale française, 1990), vv. 234–44. "Ovid's book" may refer to the *Remedia*, or perhaps, as Ralph J. Hexter has argued, to the *Ars Amatoria* instead. See *Ovid and Medieval Schooling: Studies in Medieval School Commentaries on Ovid's* Ars Amatoria, Epistulæ ex Ponto, *and* Epistulæ Heroidum (Munich: Arbeo Gesellschaft, 1986), 20n20. Christine's God of Love also finds that false lovers should be *excommenié*, excommunicated; see note to v. 779.

281–92 ***The Remedy for Love*** **. . . won't fall in love with women** *Le Remede d'Amours . . . que femmes amer n'emprennent*: The preference accorded in the medieval trivium to Ovid's *Remedia* is shown by Hexter's tabulation of the number of times in his corpus each appears in student manuals: fourteen for the *Remedia* as against four for the *Ars Amatoria* (*Ovid and Medieval Schooling*, 18–19). He adds that as an "antidote to love," the *Remedia* may have "satisfied some medieval schoolmasters" (20).

290–91 **grammar, the subject one learns first** *premiere scïence / De gramairë*: Grammar, rhetoric, and logic composed the trivium, the first group of subjects taught to young male students. The more advanced group of subjects, the quadrivium, was made up of arithmetic, geometry, music, and astronomy. Together the trivium and the quadrivium constituted the medieval program of the seven liberal arts.

295–97 **between my Lady Nature and myself . . . women not be cherished and loved** *entre moy et ma dame Nature . . . cheries et amees ne soyent*: Christine's objections are based in part on her view of what a man's "natural" inclinations are (see vv. 725–30), and she found clerical misogynous teaching "unnatural." Cf. the term *impression*, v. 302 and note, and see note to vv. 281–92 above, and the Introduction, pp. 9, 27, as well as LeFèvre, *Leësce*, vv. 840–43, in which Love and Nature bring a man and woman together to procreate.

302 **our stamp** *nostre impression*: In Thomistic usage, a stamp or impression could signify the imprint of form on formless matter, as well as the action of stamping a character on something. See Roy J. Deferrari, *A Latin-English Dictionary of St. Thomas Aquinas, based on the* Summa Theologica *and Selected Passages of His Other Works* (Boston: St. Paul Editions, 1960).

316 (var.) *nez*: "Not even," a variant spelling for *neïs*.

317 **David . . . and King Solomon** *David et Salemon le roy*: On David's adultery with Bathsheba, see 2 Samuel 11–12; on Solomon's love for foreign women and God's punishment, see 1 Kings 11. See also vv. 265–68 and note.

319–20 **especially Ovid . . . thought he could slander them** *Ovide . . . diffamer les cuide*: It is not known whether Ovid—who humorously claimed to be the *praeceptor Amoris*, or Cupid's teacher, in *Ars Amatoria* (*The Art of Love and Other Poems*, Bk. 1, l. 17)—practiced what he wrote. No biography of Ovid was transmitted to the late Middle Ages from antiquity, but his popularity especially in the Middle French period prompted the confabulation of a "life" according to his literary works. See Fausto Ghisalberti, "Mediæval Biographies of Ovid," *Journal of the Warburg and Courtauld Institutes* 9 (1946):10–59. Christine elaborates on this accusation against Ovid in the *Cité* (Bk. 1, ch. 9) when she claims that Ovid was castrated and then blamed women for his impotence, an accusation similar to that made in the *Epistre* about old men; see vv. 337–38 and note.

328 **plunges** *se boute*: This verb can have a sexual connotation.

332 *ceulz*: This masculine plural demonstrative pronoun appears here where *celles* is to be expected.

337–38 *homs*, *raisons*: An approximate rhyme. See vv. 747–48 and Versification, p. 53.

337–38 **When, an old man, . . . argument** *vieilz homs . . . raisons:* A similar claim is made by Chaucer's Wife of Bath:

> The clerk, whan he is oold, and may noght do
> Of Venus werkes worth his olde sho,

> Thanne sit he doun, and writ in his dotage
> That wommen kan nat kepe hir mariage! (vv. 707–10)

See "The Wife of Bath's Prologue," in *The Riverside Chaucer*, ed. Larry D. Benson (Boston: Houghton Mifflin, 1987), 114.

339–45 **But if someone were to blame . . . all women in general** *Mais qui blasmast . . . toutes communement*: The idea also appears in *Leesce*, in which LeFèvre uses the example of Calpurnia to say that she alone should be blamed, not all women (*Leesce*, vv. 1113–17).

349–50 **She doesn't pursue him . . . seek out his dwelling** *Ne le va pas prier . . . en son hostel querir*: Christine repeats this idea in a letter to Jean de Montreuil in the Debate, asking: "Te vont elles en ton hostel querir, ne prier ou prendre a force?" (Do they pursue you at your home, beg you or take you by force?) See *DR* ed. Hicks, 18; *DR* trans. Hult, 58.

356 **to play** *se . . . deporter*: This verb can have a sexual connotation.

369–76 **He called it . . . *False Appearances*** *Si l'appella . . . faulse apparance*: Christine repeats this in her letter to Pierre Col of October 2, 1402 in the Debate of the *Rose*, calling Ovid's book the Art de faulse et malicieuse industrie de decepvoir fanmes (Art of Delusive and Malicious Efforts to Deceive Women). See *DR* ed. Hicks, 138–39; *DR* trans. Hult, 181.

370 **behaviors** *condicïons*: Christine employs the term to refer to both inborn and acquired characteristics, not unambiguously: cf. vv. 660, 678, 683, 695, and 715, and see the Introduction, pp. 23–26.

384 **castle** *chastel*: The castle, generally a metaphor for the lady to be conquered, is what must be breached in the *Roman de la Rose.*

386 **exiled** *en exil*: Christine implies here that Ovid was exiled because of what he wrote, an explanation that the poet himself gave in his *Tristia*. There were competing opinions about Ovid's banishment: that Ovid was exiled chiefly because of his many lovers, one of whom would have been the empress; that he accidentally discovered the Emperor Augustus committing an act that ought not to have been seen; and that he pursued a corrupting career. See Ghisalberti, "Mediæval Biographies of Ovid," 32). Pierre Col, in his *Rose* debate letter dated end of summer 1402, states that Ovid was forced to leave because he taught "assailants" how better to attack the "castle," and Roman husbands were jealous. But, he claims, Jean de Meun wrote in order to teach the defenders how to guard the castle: *DR* ed. Hicks, 104–5; *DR* trans. Hult, 149–50.

403 *ilz*: An alternative form of the feminine plural pronoun; see v. 162 and note.

403–4 **they aren't . . . changeable in their ways** *Qu'ilz ne soient . . . faiz si muables*: Blamires dubs this the "topos of sexual stability," and he argues that Christine has "subsume[d] the narrow traditional question of sexual steadfastness within a much larger category of rational stability" (*The Case for Women*, 144).

407–9 **books . . . habits** *livres . . . meurs*: Chaucer's Wife of Bath expresses the same idea by asking:

> Who peyntede the leon, tel me who?
> By God, if wommen hadde writen stories,
> As clerkes han withinne hire oratories,
> They wolde han writen of men moore wikkednesse
> Than al the mark of Adam may redresse. (vv. 692–96)

("The Wife of Bath's Prologue," in the *Riverside Chaucer,* 114.)
The reference is to Aesop's fable in which a man and a lion dispute who is stronger; the man shows the lion a picture of a lion being killed by a man as evidence of man's superiority. But the lion asks who painted the picture, and says that if a lion had painted it, it would depict a man being strangled by a lion. The lion then eats the man.

435–42 **how was Medea . . . went away** *Que fu jadis Medee . . . s'en party*: Christine frequently invoked Medea, Dido, and Penelope as examples of women loyal to men; of the three, only Penelope was not betrayed. Medea—who murdered her own children to punish her husband Jason—was an iconically defensible figure for other authors as well. Jean LeFèvre writes in her defense twice: as the person who made possible Jason's capture of the Golden Fleece (since he would never have succeeded without her help, vv. 2371–412), and as an unparalleled mistress of the Seven Arts (vv. 3636–45); he notes Matheolus's accusation that Medea was a sorceress who engaged in magic (vv. 3041–42). Jean de Meun's character Old Woman (La Vieille) talks with sympathy about Medea (vv. 13199–234; *RR*, trans. Horgan, 204). See also Ruth Morse, *The Medieval Medea* (Cambridge: D.S. Brewer, 1996), 94–102, 230–36, 214–19, and Christine Reno, "Feminist Aspects of Christine de Pizan's 'Epistre d'Othea a Hector,'" *Studi francesi* 71 (1980): 271–76, esp. 274–75. Christine writes again about Medea in the *Cité* (Bk. 2, ch. 56) and in the *Epistre Othea* (ed. Parussa, 275–76 and 281–82). Medea features very often in the *Mutacion* (see the Table des noms propres in Solente's edition, 4:151, and *Mutability* 15 and 167–72). See John Jay Thompson, "Medea in Christine de Pizan's *Mutacion de Fortune*, or How to Be a Better Mother," *Forum for Modern Language Studies* 35 (1999): 158–74.

436 *Tresloyal! Et lui fist la toison*: A nine-syllable line in L_1 and L_2, corrected in succeeding manuscripts by adding *e* to make *Tresloyale*; adjectives were not uniformly made to agree with feminine nouns in this period, and *Tresloyal* would also have been acceptable.

443–58 **And what about Dido . . . great pity** *Que fu Dydo . . . grant pitié*: Dido's story is found in Book 4 of Virgil's *Aeneid.* Aeneas and Dido fall in love, but Mercury, at the bidding of Jupiter, tells "pious Aeneas" to go on his way and conquer Italian lands. Dido is inconsolable and kills herself. Christine tells Dido's story in the *City of Ladies* (Bk. 1, ch. 46; Bk. 2, ch. 55), and in the *Mutacion*, vv. 18259–95, 20599–639. For the view that Christine, especially in the *City of Ladies*, "appears to figure her authorial self in the act of reading Dido," see Marilynn Desmond, "Christine de Pizan's Feminist Self-Fashioning," in *Reading Dido: Gender, Textuality, and the Medieval* Æneid (Minneapolis: University of Minnesota Press, 1994), 195–224, at 201. A different portrait of Dido is found in the *Roman*, where Old Woman says that Dido erred in having just one lover (*RR* ed. Lecoy, 13143–80, 13235–42; *RR*, trans. Horgan, 203). LeFèvre's comments in *Leesce* are a mixed bag: in one passage (vv. 2442–60), he is sympathetic, but in another (vv. 2563–76) he criticizes her as a suicide and claims she was pregnant at the time; in his final comment, he defends her (vv. 2743–52).

447 **knights** *chevaliers*: A common medieval anachronism.

459–64 **Penelope, Ulysses' wife . . . renowned** *Peneloppe, la femmë Ulixés . . . renommee*: While Ulysses was forced by the gods to wander for ten years, Penelope, besieged by men hoping to become her husband, never lost hope for his return. In the *Cité* Christine praises Penelope's chastity during Ulysses's absence (Bk. 2, ch. 41). Jehan LeFèvre tells her story in *Leesce*, saying she was above reproach (vv. 1474–86).

477–78 **If God . . . falseness** *Est ce doncques, se Dieux . . . fausseté*: The clause **if God should give you health** (*se Dieux vous doint santé*) can be understood as an aside, not tightly linked to its context. A similar formulation is used in the *Debat de deux amans* (v. 1645).

487–88 **At least . . . without a flaw** *Au mains . . . senz faille*: It is probably not surprising that Christine chose not to include these two lines in *D* and *R*, since they weaken the argument for women.

492 **If they're served up the same dish** *fait de tout autel pain soupe*: Literally, "make soup with the same bread," a Middle French idiomatic expression meaning to have done to you what you have inflicted on others.

521 *travaillent*: In *R*, the second *a* of *travaillent* is a correction on erasure, probably from an original *e*; the correction preparation *a* remains above the corrected letter.

539–40 **Troy . . . put to the torch** *Troye . . . en feu esprise*: See vv. 23–32 and note. Christine cites this argument once more in the Debate letters, in which she says that she has already asked, in the *God of Love's Letter*, "where are the countries or kingdoms that have been ravaged by women's great iniquities?" (*DR* ed. Hicks, 17–18; *DR* trans. Hult, 57).

543 **fine flattery** *beaux blandissemens:* See note to v. 35.

547–48 **a simple little thing / A simple little woman** *une chose simplete / Une ignorant petite femmelette* Tania van Hemelryck reads these verses as the debut of Christine's "authorial world"; no longer will Christine be the ignorant little woman who does not write ("*L'Epistre au dieu d'amours* ou 'l'origine du monde' auctorial," 241–54). Christine repeats this idea in the Debate of the Rose when she writes to Pierre Col, ironically stating that even she herself, a *simple fammellette* (a simple little woman) is capable of seeing the errors in Col's reasoning because she knows the doctrine of the Holy Church (*DR* ed. Hicks, 132; *DR* trans. Hult, 175). There were certainly precedents for this: Hildegard of Bingen's use of this modesty topos, common among monastic writers, is discussed by Barbara Newman in *Sister of Wisdom: St. Hildegard's Theology of the Feminine* (Berkeley and Los Angeles: University of California Press, 1987), 1–41.

566 **Perfect love** *Parfaite amour*: In courtly vocabulary, a variant of *fin'amor*, true love.

578 **worthy of bearing the Son of God** *du filz Dieu porter elle fut digne*: The privilege of woman called *e conceptione*. See the Introduction, pp. 9, 15, note to vv. 594–606, and Blamires, "Eve and the Privileges of Women," in *The Case for Women*, 96–125, with definitions at 96–97.

583–84 **form, formed** *fourme, fourma*: In Thomistic theology, form (*forma*) gives existence. See Herbert McCabe, *On Aquinas*, ed. Brian Davies (London and New York: Continuum, 2008), 42. By rhyming a noun and a verb from the same root, Christine once more deploys a *rime équivoque*; see note to vv. 39–40.

593 **image** *semblance*: Both *imago* (image) and *similitudo* (likeness) existed in clerical writing. In conceding *similitudo* to women, clerics asserted that woman was made not directly in God's image but in Adam's. Christine here asserts woman's right to *imago*, that is, the image of God, and in the *Cité* she explains that the term "image of God" refers not to a physical resemblance but to the soul (Bk.1, ch. 9). Rosemary Ruether observes that in "the classical Christian tradition found in Augustine and Aquinas, maleness and spirituality are equated. Women as women cannot be made in the image of God or represent Christ because God and Christ are male, and maleness represents rationality, spirituality, and the divine. So women can be included in the image of God restored in Christ only in a sex-neutered form." See *Women and Redemption*, 4–5. On further background to this debate see Kari Elisabeth Børresen, *Subordination and Equivalence: The*

Nature and Role of Women in Augustine and Thomas Aquinas, trans. Charles H. Talbot (Washington, DC: University Press of America, 1981), and *Image of God and Gender Models in Judaeo-Christian Tradition*, ed. Børresen (Oslo: Solum Vorlag, 1991).

594–95 **And gave her . . . understanding** *Et lui donna . . . entendement*: God's bestowing of intellectual gifts to women has a spiritual value that is linked to their salvation, a connection that derives from the Church's teaching of the seven gifts of the Holy Spirit. Four of these are intellectual: wisdom, understanding, counsel, and knowledge. (We are grateful to the Rev. Robert Imbelli for this explanation.)

594–606 **And gave her . . . Not man** *Et lui donna . . . Non pas l'omme*: Two of the privileges of women: *e materia* (that Eve was created from the bone of man, not from earth) and *e loco* (that woman was the first to be created in paradise, whereas Adam was made outside paradise). Christine does not mention two other arguments: *e nomine* (in Hebrew, Eve means life, Adam means earth) and *ex ordine* (Eve was the final created thing and therefore was God's masterpiece). See the Introduction, pp. 9, 15, and note to v. 578.

599–600 *omme, fourme*: An approximate rhyme. In *D* and *R*, *fourme* is changed to *somme* (see variant v. 600).

606–18 **And as for the deception . . . not really deceit** *Mais du decevement . . . n'est ce decevance voir*: In the Middle Ages Eve's culpability was at the center of discussions about woman's nature. Christine's argument, to which the words *simplece* (v. 615) and *simplement* (v. 610) are crucial, extracts positive value from patristic assertions of woman's weakness and intellectual lack of focus. It advances a view of woman as inherently trusting, not gullible, and resembling Jesus Christ.

620 **Isn't paradise their reward** *Par desservir n'ont elles paradis:* Christine answers this question at v. 772 (and see note), where she indicates that women who pursue honor will merit paradise.

638–39 **It's far better . . . hold my tongue** *Si se vault mieux . . . m'en tais*: it was important to Christine to point out the error of misspeaking about others, which could be construed as slander. See note 405–7 to the *Dit de la Rose*.

643–50 **Women don't kill . . . the worst** *N'occient gent . . . des pires*: It is sometimes asserted that Christine made a point of not engaging in tit for tat by blaming men. This is only partly true, for these charges, however indirect, clearly aim at men. In *Leesce*, LeFèvre has a very similar list (murder, robbery, larceny, arson, bearing false witness, adultery, magic, poisoning, falseness, and treason), which he calls the "maulx des hommes" (vv. 1187–95). Christine repeats this in the Debate of the *Rose*, in her letter to Jean de Montreuil of summer 1401, recalling that she has already made the point in the *Epistre au dieu d'Amours* (*DR* ed. Hicks, 17–18; *DR* trans. Hult, 57).

645 **disinherit** *desheritent*: Disinheritance would have been a personal matter for Christine, given the numerous lawsuits she was forced to bring against those who refused her her land and income after the death of her husband. See note to v. 647 and Charity Cannon Willard, *Christine de Pizan: Her Life and Works*, 39–40.

647 **inheritance** *eritage*: See note to v. 645.

671 **fearful, and timorous** *paoureuse et doubtable*: See note to v. 675.

675 **When angered, she quickly calms her ire** *en courroux tost appaise son yre*: The common medieval axiom held that women were good at soothing men's ire. When Thomas Hoccleve composed his own *Letter of Cupid* based on Christine's *God of Love's Letter,* he reverted to the more common version of the adage, "And wel they can a mannes ire asswage," (And women can restore man's angry mind), Hoccleve, *Letter of Cupid*, in *Poems of Cupid, God of Love*, v. 341. In the Middle Ages anger was a trait thought appropriate to the construction of manliness, whereas peacefulness, even meekness, purportedly characterized women. See, e.g., Felicity Riddy, "Women Talking about the Things of God: A Late Medieval Sub-culture," in *Women and Literature in Britain, 1150–1500*, ed. Carol M. Meale (Cambridge: Cambridge University Press, 1993), 104–27, at 116. In the *Trois Vertus*, in a chapter devoted to a good princess's obligation to bring peace between the prince and his barons if there is any discord, Christine explains that this task falls principally to women, for men are by nature more hot-blooded and their desire for vengeance doesn't allow them to see the perils or ills that might ensue from their actions. She says that "nature de femme est plus paoureuse et aussi de plus doulce condicion, et pour ce, se elle veult et elle est saige, estre puet le meilleur moyen a pacifier l'omme, qui soit" ("woman's nature is more fearful and of sweeter disposition, and for that reason, if she so desires and if she is wise, she can be the best means of pacifying man that exists"; *Livre des Trois Vertus*, 34–35). See also *Leesce*, vv. 1241–43. The context here, however, lacks any explicit or implicit indication that *men's* anger is in question, just as the surrounding lines concentrate on women only and never mention men. Christine has therefore created a different dictum.

683 *ilz*: See note to v. 162.

691 **Nor . . . penalty or blame** *në en peine n'en coulpe*: Roger Ellis has pointed out that *n'en peine në en coulpe* is a version of *a pena et culpa*, which distinguishes between the penalty for a fault and the fault itself: "Chaucer, Christine de Pizan, and Hoccleve: *The Letter of Cupid,*" in *Essays on Thomas Hoccleve*, ed. Catherine Batt (Turnhout: Brepols, 1996), 29–54, at 37.

694 **God . . . courtesy** *Dieu courtoisie*: Use of the word *courtoisie* to describe God's love for women goes beyond the modern understanding of the term as merely a polite act, for it calls up the language of *fin'amor* and hints at God as the *fin amant* of women. Barbara Newman has called this *la mystique courtoise*. See *From Virile Woman to WomanChrist: Studies in Medieval Religion and Literature* (Philadelphia: University of Pennsylvania Press, 1995), 137–67.

698 **souls** *armes*: The word *ame*, "soul," often appears spelled as *arme* in medieval French texts.

706–7 **Saint Nicholas . . . tempted** *Saint Nicolas . . . tempté*: Not yet associated with Christmas, Saint Nicholas was among the most popular saints of the Middle Ages, known widely from the tenth century and celebrated in plays and in iconography. Although little is known of his life, these lines allude to the belief that he showed an aptitude for religious piety even as a baby, for he is said to have refused his mother's breast Wednesdays and Fridays. See David Hugh Farmer, *The Oxford Dictionary of Saints* (Oxford: Oxford University Press, 2004).

717–18 **vices that damage** *vices, qui / Va dommagant*: The third person singular verb *va* is the predicate to the plural subject **vices**. Marchello-Nizia does not mention simple subjects in the plural with verbs in the singular, but she does note cases of compound subjects with verbs in the singular (*fortune et honneur . . . leur court sus*, fortune and honor came to them), and she provides one compound featuring a plural subject and a singular subject with a verb in the singular (*les poisons et le venin est mis au bon morcel*, the poisons and the venom was [were] put on the tasty morsel) (*La Langue française aux XIV*[e] *et XV*[e] *siècles*, 405). In those instances, the verb is seen to agree with the one subject immediately preceding the verb.

733 **equal, perfectly like** *per . . . semblable*: In this verse Christine doubly affirms the equality of the sexes. *Per*, normally used to describe the lover's lady, who is "without equal," here expresses the equality of the sexes; the primary meaning of *semblable* in Middle French is "identical." See *DMF*.

752–56 **If she is bad . . . sons resemble their mothers** *Se mauvaise est . . . aux meres bien ressemblent les fieulx*: This may be "a quasi-scientific claim for a decisive transmission of maternal influence to a son," over against the "tendency . . . to exalt the paternal influence" (Blamires, *The Case for Women*, 74n17). For relevant discussion of the Aristotelian one-seed theory and of Galen's competing two-seed theory, see Joan Cadden, *Meanings of Sex Difference in the Middle Ages*, 120.

753 **no good fruit comes from a bad tree** *nul bon fruit de mal arbre ne vient*: Cf. Matt. 7:17–18 and 12:33, and Luke 6:43. Medieval tree imagery frequently expresses a concern for bloodlines and genealogy.

772 **And paradise in the end** *Et paradis en la fin*: See v. 620 and note.

799–824 **From the mighty God of Love . . . cry out** *Par le dieu d'Amours . . . leurs clamours*: On the shift from decasyllables to heptasyllables, to octosyllables, then back to heptasyllables, see Versification, p. 49.

804 **Phaethon** *Phaethon*: son of Phoebus, god of the sun, Phaethon burned to death when he lost control of his father's chariot. See Ovid, *Metamorphoses*, trans. Frank Justus Miller, rev. G.P. Goold (Cambridge, MA: Harvard University Press, 1972): Bk. 2, ll. 1–400.

805 **Mercury, god of language** *Mercurïus, dieu de langaige*: Mercury was associated with the medieval language arts by Martianus Capella, a fifth-century writer in Latin who shaped the trivium and the quadrivium (the Seven Liberal Arts).

808 **Glaucus** *Glaucus*: A fisherman transformed into a sea-god. See Ovid, *Metamorphoses*, 13: ll. 898–968.

813–18 **Pallas . . . Diana** *Pallas . . . Dÿane*: The goddesses and heroines listed here have been chosen for their qualities as loving wives, sweethearts, or mothers, or as chaste women. In the *Aeneid*, it is said that Juno, the protector of marriage, planned for Dido and Aeneas to marry, but when that failed, the goddess took Dido's soul from her body to relieve her suffering. Latona (Leto) was the mother of Apollo and Diana, and she was worshipped for her children. Ceres, Roman goddess of the fruitful earth and mother to Persephone, suffered when Pluto took her daughter into the underworld; she had to settle for having Persephone with her only six months of the year. Vesta was a virgin goddess of the hearth and of its fire. Antigone, loyal daughter of Oedipus and sister of Polynices and Eteocles, defied King Creon and buried Polynices after the brothers died in single combat against each other. As for Aurora, Christine probably has in mind her devotion to her Trojan lover Tithonous and to their son Memnon, whose death caused Aurora to weep tears (dew) each morning ever after. See *Epistre Othea* (ed. Parussa), where Memnon is called Cygnus (chap. 44, ll. 9, 14, and 16), and *Othea's Letter to Hector*, ed. and trans. Renate Blumenfeld-Kosinski and Earl Jeffrey Richards (Toronto: Iter Press; Tempe: Arizona Center for Medieval and Renaissance Studies, 2017), 79. Thetis was a sea goddess and mother to Achilles in Greek mythology. Arethusa was a nymph, companion and follower of Diana, protector of chastity; like Diana, she too was a virgin huntress.

816 **Who accused the god Pluto** *le dieu Pluto encusa*: It was Ceres, not Arethusa, who demanded that Pluto send back her daughter. Christine is referring to the fact that Arethusa tells Ceres where to find Persephone. Pleading with the angry Ceres not to destroy the land of Sicily, from which Persephone has disappeared,

Arethusa reveals to her that she has seen Persephone with her "very eyes" as Pluto's reluctant consort: "She seemed sad indeed, and her face was still perturbed with fear; but yet she was a queen, the great queen of that world of darkness, the mighty consort of the tyrant of the underworld." See Ovid, *Metamorphoses*, 5: ll. 487–508.

817 **Minerva** *Minerve*: Pallas (Pallas Athena) and Minerva were names for the same goddess. In the *Mutacion*, Christine explains that Minerva is the name for the goddess of battle and Pallas the name for the goddess of wisdom, while she recognizes that the two are the same (*Mutacion*, vv. 11986–99, 12004–16). In manuscripts *D* and *R* the goddess also appears in the *Epistre Othea*, ch. 14, with a striking illustration. See <https://gallica.bnf.fr/ark:/12148/btv1b60007552/f25.image.r> and <www.pizan.lib.ed.ac.uk/gallery/pages/103r.htm>.

824 As noted in the variants, the signature "Creintis" (fearful, an anagram for Christine) appears in *D* after "Cui amans font leurs clamours." See also the *Livre du Dit de Poissy*, where the word *creintis* is the last word of the poem.

LE DIT DE LA ROSE

THE TALE OF THE ROSE

Le Dit de la Rose

[fol. 74a] *Cy commence le Dit de la Rose.*

A tous les princes amoureux
Et aux nobles chevalereux
Que vaillantise fait armer,
Et a ceulz qui seulent amer
Toute bonté pour avoir pris,
Et a tous amans bien apris
De ce royaume et autre part,
Par tout ou vaillance s'espart;
A toutes dames renommees
Et aux damoiselles amees,
A toutes femmes honnorables,
Saiges, courtoises, agreables:
Humble recommandacïon
De loyal vraye entencïon.
Si fais savoir a tous vaillans
Qui pour honneur sont travaillans
Unes nouvelles merveilleuses,
Gracïeuses, non perilleuses,
Qui avenuës de nouvel
Sont en beau lieu plain de revel;
Aussi est droiz que ceulz le sachent
Qui mauvaistié devers eulz sachent,
Afin qu'ilz amendent leurs fais
Pour estre avec les bons parfais.
Si fut voir qu'a Paris advint,
Present nobles gens plus de vint,
Joyeux et liez et senz esmois,
L'an quatre cens et un, ou mois
De janvier, plus de la moitié
—Ains la date de ce dittié—
Du mois passé, quant ceste chose
[fol. 74b] Advint en une maison close
Et assemblee de nobles gens
Riches d'onnour et beaulx et gens.
Chevaliers y ot de renom
Et escuiers de vaillant nom.

The Tale of the Rose

The Tale of the Rose begins here.

To all the courteous princes
And chivalrous nobles
Whom bravery inspires to arms,
And to those accustomed to love
All goodness to earn esteem,
And to all well-bred lovers
In this kingdom and elsewhere,
Wherever valor radiates;
To all renowned ladies
And beloved demoiselles,
To all honorable women,
Wise, courteous, and gracious:
Humble good wishes
In loyal and true intention.
I make known to all the valiant
Who strive for honor
Certain wondrous tidings,
Pleasing, not hurtful,
Which recently came
To a fine place filled with revelry.
It is right that those who mean them harm
Should know about this,
So they may mend their ways
And join the company of the good.
It happened indeed in Paris
Before more than twenty nobles,
Joyful, happy, and without a care,
In the year 140[2], in January,
The month before the date of this poem,
More than half that month had passed
When this event occurred
In a shuttered house
And a gathering of noble people
Rich in honor, handsome and genteel.
There were renowned knights
And squires known for bravery;

Ne m'estuet ja leurs noms nommer,
Mais chascun les seult bons clamer;
Notables sont et renommez,
Des plus prisiez et mieulx amez
Du tresnoble duc d'Orlïens
—Que Dieu gart de tous maulx lïens—;
Si sont de son hostel tous ceulx
Et n'y avoit pas un tout seulz
Qui n'aime, je croy, tous bons fais.
Lëans a assez de si fais;
Assemblez les ot celle part
Courtoisie, qui ne depart
De ceulz qui sont de gentil sorte.
La fu bien fermee la porte,
Car vouloient en ce lieu estre
Senz estranges gens, privez estre
Pour deviser a leur plaisir.
La fu apresté a loisir
Le soupper; si furent assis,
Joyeux et liez et non pensis.
Bien furent servis par les tables
De mez a leur gré delitables,
Car ne fu, j'en ose jugier,
Pas tout leur plaisir ou mangier,
Mais en la compaignie qui
De vraie et bonne amour nasqui.
Liez estoient et esbatans,
[fol. 74c] Gays et envoisiez et chantans
Tout au long de cellui souper,
Comme gent qui sont tout un per
Et amis vrais, sens estrangier.
La n'ot parlé a ce mengier
Fors de courtoisie et d'onnour,
Senz diffamer grant ne menour,
Et de beaulx livres et de dis
Et de balades plus de dix,
Qui mieulx mieulx chascun devisoit,
Ou d'amours qui s'en avisoit,
Ou de demandes gracïeuses.
Vïandes plus delicïeuses
N'y ot, com je croy, a leur goust,

I needn't state their names,
But everyone proclaims their worth.
They are illustrious and renowned,
Among the most esteemed and best loved
Of the very noble Duke of Orléans
—May God keep him from all evil associations.
All of them are of his household
And there was not a single one,
I believe, who doesn't love good deeds;
Many there are made that way.
They'd been assembled in that place
By Courtesy, who never leaves
Those who are the genteel kind.
The door was firmly closed,
For they wanted to be there
Privately, without others,
To talk as they pleased.
A leisurely meal was prepared for them
And so they took their seats,
With joy and good cheer and without a care.
At the tables they were served
Dishes to delight their taste,
Yet I dare to conjecture
That their pleasure was not all in the food
But in the company,
Which was born of good, true love.
They were happy and enjoying themselves
In high spirits and lively and singing
Throughout the supper,
Like people who are peers
And true friends, with no other company.
They talked at that dinner
Only of courtesy and honor,
Defaming neither great nor small,
And of fine books and poems,
And more than ten ballades,
Of which each vied to write the best,
Either on love, by whoever pondered it,
Or in writing gracious questions.
No food was more delicious
Or more suited to their taste, I believe,

Tout soyent d'assez petit coust,
Et de ris et de bonne chiere;
De ce n'orent ils pas enchiere.
¶Ainsi se firent longuement
En ce gracïeux parlement.
Mais Amours, ses loyaulx amis
Qui a valeur se sont soubzmis
Volt visiter droit en ce point;
Car alors seurvint tout a point,
Non obstant les portes barrees
Et les fenestres bien sarrees,
Une dame de grant noblesse
Qui s'appella dame et deesse
De Loyauté, et trop belle yere!
La descendi a grant lumiere
Si que tout en resplent la sale;
Toute autre beauté si fut pale
Vers la sienne: de corps, de vis
[fol. 74d] Et de beau maintien, a devis
Bien paree et bien attournee.
Si fu entour avironnee
De nymphes et de pucelletes
Atout chappellés de fleurettes,
Qui chantoyent par grant revel
Hault et cler un motet nouvel
Si doulcement, pour voir vous dis,
Que bien sembloit que paradis
Fut leur reduit et qu'el venissent
De ce lieu dont fors tous biens n'issent;
Celle deesse a tel maisgnie.
Devant la table acompaignie
Vint o les siennes bien parees;
Si tenoient couppes dorees,
Si comme pour faire en present
A celle gent nouvel present.
¶Adont fut la sale estourmie,
Il n'y ot personne endormie,
Tuit fuyent vëoir la merveille;
Il n'y ot cellui qui l'oreille
Ne tendist pour bien escouter
Que celle leur vouloit noter,
Chascun se tut pour y entendre.

Even had its cost been small;
Of laughter and good cheer,
Of these they had no shortage.
    And so, for a long while, they engaged
In that agreeable conversation.
But Love, to whom
They'd gallantly pledged themselves,
Desired just then to visit his loyal friends.
For there suddenly appeared,
In spite of the bolted doors
And the firmly fastened windows,
A lady of great nobility
Called lady and goddess
Of Loyalty, and she was so very beautiful!
She descended amidst a great light
So that the entire room was resplendent.
All other beauty paled
Compared with her form, her face,
And her fine bearing, pleasingly
Well-groomed and well dressed.
She was surrounded
By nymphs and maidens
Wearing chaplets of tiny blooms,
Who were merrily singing a new motet
Loudly and brightly,
And so sweetly, I tell you truly,
It seemed that paradise
Was their haven and that they came
From the place that sends only good things;
Such is the household of this goddess.
She came before the table accompanied
By her richly dressed ladies.
They carried golden bowls
As if to offer a gift
To the assembled company.
    At that the room was abuzz:
No one slumbered!
Everyone sought out the marvel;
There were none who did not strain
An ear to listen carefully
To what she wanted them to note,
Each kept silent to hear.

Quant les pucelles a cuer tendre
Orent leur chançon affinee,
Adont se prist la belle nee,
Qui d'elles dame et maistresse yere,
A dire par belle maniere
Ces parolles qui ci escriptes
Sont en ces balades, et dittes.
Ne plus ne moins les ennorta
[fol. 75a] Et les balades apporta:

Balade

Cil qui forma toute chose mondaine
Vueille tousdiz en santé maintenir
Et en bauldour de grant leesse plaine
Ceste belle compaignie, et tenir.
Deesse suis; si me doit souvenir
De trestous bons et des bonnes et belles.
Pour ce qu'ainsi il doit appartenir,
Venue suis vous apporter nouvelles.

De par le Dieu d'amours, qui puet la peine
Des fins amans desmettre et defenir,
Present nouvel gracïeux d'odeur saine
Je vous apport, et salus sens fenir;
Si m'escoutez et vueilliez retenir,
Car je vous di que de haultes querelles,
Dont il pourra assez de biens venir,
Venue suis vous apporter nouvelles.

De Loyauté, deesse souveraine,
On m'appellë, et a mon seurvenir
Je ne port pas de discorde la graine,
Com fist celle qui Troyes fist bannir;
Ains pour tousjours loyauté soustenir
Et pour oster les mauvaises favelles,
Et les mauvaiz desloyaulx escharnir,
Venue suis vous apporter nouvelles.

Balade

Le dieu d'Amours, par moy il vous presente
Ces roses ci de voulenté entiere;
Cueillies sont de tresloyal entente

When the tender-hearted maidens
Had finished their song,
At that point the nobly born woman,
Who was their mistress and lady,
In lovely cadences began to utter
The words recorded and recited
In these ballades.
No more or less did she exhort them
And she offered these ballades:

Ballade

He who fashioned each worldly thing,
May he always want to keep this fine company
In good health and good cheer
Replete with great happiness.
I am a goddess, so I must remember
All good men and the good and fair ladies.
For that's how matters should be,
I have come bearing you news.

On behalf of the God of Love, who can
Take away and end the pain of true lovers,
This gracious, wholesome news
I bring to you, with greetings unending;
Listen to me and please remember,
For I'm telling you about great deeds,
From which many good things can ensue,
I have come bearing you news.

Sovereign goddess of Loyalty
I am called; and in my coming here
I bring no seed of discord,
As did she who brought Troy down;
Rather, in order to sustain loyalty forever
And to eliminate evil slander,
And deride the wickedly disloyal,
I have come bearing you news.

Ballade

The God of Love through me presents
These roses to you wholeheartedly;
They were faithfully gathered

[fol. 75b] Es beaulx vergiers dont je suis courtilliere.
Si vous mande qu'a tres joyeuse chiere
Preigniez le don; mais c'est par couvenant
Que desormais en trestoute maniere
Yrez l'onneur des dames soustenant.

Si veult qu'ainçoiz que nullui se consente
A recevoir la rose belle et chiere;
Qu'il face veu que jamaiz il n'assente
Blasme ou mesdit en nesune maniere
De femme, qui son honneur tiengne chiere;
Et pour ce, a vous m'envoye maintenant;
Si vouez tous qu'a parolle pleniere
Yrez l'onneur des dames soustenant.

Chevaliers bons et tous de noble sente
Et tous amans, c'est bien droit qu'il affiere
Qu'a ce veu ci vo cuer se represente;
Amours le veult, si n'y mettez enchiere.
Mais ne soit pas de voulenté legiere,
Car a l'estat de vous appartenant;
Et si jurez que jusques a la biere
Yrez l'onneur des dames soustenant.

En disant ces balades cy,
La deesse, sienne mercy,
Assist les couppes sur les tables;
Dedens ot roses odorables,
Blanches, vermeilles, et trop belles,
Et cueillies furent nouvelles.
Et avecques ce presentoit,
En beaulx rolez qu'elle gettoit,
[fol. 75c] Ceste balade, qui recorde
Qu'Amours veult qu'ainçois qu'on accorde
A prendre la jolie rose,
Que l'en face veu de la chose
Qui est en l'ecript contenu,
Et qu'il soit juré et tenu.
Et qui tout ce vouldra vouer
Et celle promesse advouer,
Hardiëment preingne la rose

In the beautiful orchards where I'm the gardener.
He prays that you accept the gift
Cheerfully, but with the understanding
That from now on in every way,
You will uphold the honor of ladies.

He wants no one to consent
To receive the dear and lovely rose
Unless he vows first never to tolerate
Blame or any kind of slander
Of woman, whose honor he should hold dear.
That's why he sends me to you now;
So all of you vow unreservedly that
You will uphold the honor of ladies.

Good knights and all of noble stock,
And lovers all, it is rightly appropriate
That your hearts perform this vow.
Love wants it, so raise no opposition.
Do not be of fickle will,
For this befits people of your estate;
And swear that until you're in the ground
You will uphold the honor of ladies.

Reciting these ballades,
The goddess, may she be thanked,
Placed the bowls on the tables;
Inside were fragrant roses,
White, vermillion, and very beautiful,
And they had been freshly plucked.
And with that she offered,
In fine scrolls that she tossed,
This ballade, which records
That Love wishes, before one agrees
To accept the lovely rose,
That one vow to the terms
Contained in the written document,
And that it be sworn and upheld.
And whoever agrees to swear to all of this
And makes this promise,
Should boldly take the rose

Ou toute doulçour est enclose.
Si oyez lire la balade
Qu'apporta la deesse sade:

Balade

A bonne Amour je fais veu et promesse,
Et a la fleur qui est rose clamee,
A la vaillant de Loyauté deesse,
Par qui nous est ceste chose informee,
Qu'a tousjours mais, la bonne renommee
Je garderay de dame en toute chose,
Ne par moy ja femme n'yert diffamee;
Et pour ce prens je l'Ordre de la Rose.

Et si promet a toute gentillesse
Qu'en trestous lieux et prisee et amee
Dame sera de moy comme maistresse;
Et celle qui j'ay ma dame nommee
Souveraine, loyauté confermee
Je lui tendray jusques a la parclose;
Et de ce ay voulenté affermee;
Et pour ce prens je l'Ordre de la Rose.

Et si merci Amours en son humblesse,
[fol. 75d] Qui nous a cy tel semence semee,
Dont j'ay espoir que serons en l'adresse
De mieulx valoir; c'est bien chose informee
Que de lui vint honneur tresrenommee;
Si defendray, s'aucun est qui dire ose
Chose par quoy dame estre puist blasmee;
Et pour ce prens je l'Ordre de la Rose.

Princes haultains ou valeur est fermee,
Faites le veu—bonté y est enclose.
L'enseingne en vueil porter en mainte armee,
Et pour ce prens je l'Ordre de la Rose.

Adont furent en audiance
Levez, et senz contrariance
Firent tous le beau veu louable,
Qui est gentil et honnorable.
Quant nullui ne vit contredire,

In which all sweetness is enclosed.
So hear the ballade read
That the winsome goddess brought:

Ballade

To true love I vow and promise,
And to the flower called a rose,
And to the brave goddess Loyalty,
By whom we are told of this,
That forevermore a lady's good name
I will keep in all things,
Nor will woman be defamed by me;
And thus I take the Order of the Rose.

And so I promise to all gentle folk
That in all places a lady will be
Praised and loved as my sovereign;
And to the one I've selected to rule
Over me, my firmly pledged loyalty
I will extend to her until the end;
And in this I have affirmed my intention,
And thus I take the Order of the Rose.

I thank Love in his humility,
Who has sown such seed among us here,
From which I hope that we are headed
Toward greater worth; it's well established
That from him comes very great honor;
So I will forbid it, should someone dare to say
Anything by which a lady might be blamed.
And thus I take the Order of the Rose.

Lofty princes whose worth is certain,
Take the vow—in it goodness is enclosed.
I wish to bear its standard in many an army,
And thus I take the Order of the Rose.

At that they stood before one another,
And without disagreement
All recited the fine, commendable vow,
Which is noble and honorable.
When she saw that no one disagreed,

La deesse adont prist a dire
Ce rondelet, prenant congié;
Si n'y a pensé ne songié.

Rondel

Or m'en vois dire les nouvelles
Au dieu d'Amours, qui m'envoya.

De ses belles roses nouvelles
Or m'en vois dire les nouvelles.

Adieu vous dy, tous ceulz et celles
Que bonne amour cy avoya.
Or m'en vois dire les nouvelles
Au dieu d'Amours, qui m'envoya.

¶ Quant ce fut dit, lors s'envola
Celle deesse qui vint la.
[fol. 76a] Mais les nymphes, qui furent liez,
De leurs doulces voix delïez
Commencierent tel mellodie
—Ne cuidiez que mençonge die—
Quë il sembloit a leur doulz chant
Qu'angelz feussent ou droit enchant.

¶Ainsi parti de celle place
La deesse, qui de sa grace
Ot la compaignie esjoÿe,
Tel nouvelle leur ot gehie!
D'elle font feste et de ces choses
Et tous se parent de ses roses,
Par teste, par braz, par poitrine,
En promettant foy enterine,
Si comme ou veu est devisié
Qu'ilz orent moult bien avisié.
¶Quant assez selon leur loisir
Orent esté en ce plaisir,
Chantans, rians a chiere lie,
Senz dueil et sens merencolie,
Partis s'en sont, congié ont pris,
Emportant la rose de pris.
Et je, qui n'oz pas le cuer noir,

The goddess then began to recite
This rondeau, taking her leave.
She thought no further on the matter.

Rondeau

I'm leaving now to report the news
To the God of Love, who sent me.

About his beautiful fresh roses
I'm leaving now to report the news.

Adieu I say to you, all you men and women
Whom true love has guided here.
I'm leaving now to report the news
To the God of Love, who sent me.

When that had been said, away flew
The goddess who had come there.
But the nymphs, who were happy,
In their delicate and sweet voices
Began such a melody
(Don't think I'm lying)
That it seemed by their sweet song
They were angels or a true enchantment.

And thus she left that place,
The goddess who through her favor
Had cheered the company;
Such news had she revealed!
They celebrate her and her rulings,
And all bedeck themselves with her roses:
In their hair, over their arms and against their breasts,
While promising perfect faith,
As specified in the vow
That they had so well noted.
When, according to their likes, they'd
Spent enough time in those pleasures,
Singing, laughing happily,
Without grief or gloom,
They left, saying goodbye,
Carrying away the valued rose.
And I, who hadn't a heavy heart,

Demouray en cellui manoir
Ou ot esté celle assemblee
Ou je ne fus de riens troublee.
Tart fut ja et saison en l'eure
D'aller coucher, et bien fu heure.
Mais la deesse, qui m'ama
—Sienne merci—et me clama
Sa belle suer de cuer eslit,
M'ot apresté un trop beau lit:
[fol. 76b] Blanc comme noif, encourtiné,
Richement et bien ordonné,
En belle chambre toute blanche
Comme la noif qui chiet sur branche;
Pour ce l'ot fait, je n'en doubt mie,
Que je suis a Dÿane amie,
La deesse treshonnouree,
Qui toudis de blanc est paree.
¶La me couchay seulette et nue
Et m'endormy. Lors une nue
Si m'apparu en mon dormant,
Clere et luisant; de ce formant
Me merveillay que pouait estre.
De la nue, qui fu a destre
Costé du lit, luisant et clere
Comme en esté temps qui esclere.
Yssi une voix gracïeuse
Trop plaisant et trop amoureuse.
¶Adont ou que dormisse ou non,
La voix m'appella par mon nom.
Si me dist lors: "Amie chiere,
Qui m'as amez et tenu chiere
Toute ta vie, bien le sçay,
Car souvent t'ay mise a l'essay,
Je suis la deesse loyale
De la haulte ligne royale
De Dieu, qui me fist et fourma
Et de ses rigles m'enforma.
Or m'entens, m'amie certaine,
Et je te diray qui me maine.
¶"Tu scez comment en ta presence
Je vins presenter par plaisance
[fol. 76c] Nagueres les roses jolies,

Remained in that residence
Where the gathering had been,
Where nothing troubled me.
It was late and the time had come
To retire and go off to bed.
But the goddess, who loved me
—May she be thanked—and called me
Her fair sister of excellent heart,
Had prepared a very fine bed for me,
White as snow, draped around
Richly and carefully arranged,
In a beautiful chamber, perfectly white
Like the snow that lies upon the branch.
I don't doubt that she had done it
Because I am a friend to Diana,
The greatly honored goddess,
Who is always garbed in white.

Alone and unclad I went to bed
And fell asleep. Then a cloud
Appeared to me in my sleep,
Bright and shining. Greatly
Did I wonder what this might be.
From the cloud, which was at the right
Side of the bed, brilliant and bright
Like the light of a summer's day,
A gracious voice issued forth,
Very pleasant and very loving.

Then whether I was sleeping or not,
The voice called me by my name.
It said to me: "Dear friend,
You who have loved and cherished me
All your life, as I well know,
For I have often tested you;
I am the loyal goddess
Of the venerable royal line
Of God, who made and shaped me
And taught me his laws.
So hear me out, my steadfast friend,
And I will tell you what brings me here.

"You know how I came
Before you a while ago and was delighted
To present the pretty roses

Qui en nul temps ne sont palies,
De par vraie Amour, qui conduit
Ceulz qui de bien faire sont duit,
Qui encor devers toy m'envoye
—Messagiere de ceste voye
Lui plaist que soye par usage—
Et volontiers fais le message.
¶"Amours se plaint trop fort et duelt
D'une coustume qui trop suelt
Estre en mains lieux continuee;
Bien vouldroit qu'elle fust muee,
Car elle est male, laide, et vilz
Et vilaine, je te plevis,
Et par especïal en ceulx
Qui ne doivent estre pareceux
D'acquerir toutes bonnes meurs
Pour plus acroistre leurs honneurs:
C'est es nobles et es gentilz
Hommes qui doivent ententis
Estre a mieulx valoir qu'autre gent;
Bonté leur siet mieulx que or n'argent.
Mais des vilains ne fais je force,
Car ceulx ne font bien fors a force,
N'on ne les pourroit amender
Pour leur ennorter ne mander,
Car la condicïon vilaine,
Qui pis flaire que male alaine,
Si est trop fort a corigier;
Trop est fort cil vice a purgier.
J'appelle 'vilains' ceulz qui font
Villenies qui les deffont;
[fol. 76d] Je n'entens pas par baz lignaige
Le vilain, mais par vil courage.
¶"Mais cellui qui noble se fait
De lignie, trop se deffait
Se sa noblesse en villenie
Tourne. Dis je voir? Ne le nye.
Si font plus qu'autres a reprendre
S'on les puet en vilains faiz prendre.
Et pour ce dis, ce n'est pas bourde,
Qu'en lait fait n'en parolle lourde
Tout nobles homs, s'il aime pris,

That never fade
On behalf of true Love, who guides
Those instructed in doing good,
Who once again sends me to you
—He is pleased for me to be
The messenger on this route—
And I'm happy to bring this word.
    "Love laments and deeply grieves
About a habit that is all too commonly
Followed in many places.
He would very much like it altered,
For it is evil, ugly, base,
And vulgar, I promise you,
And especially in those
Who must not be lazy
About acquiring every good habit
In order to increase their honors.
This is for the noble and the well-born
Men who must aim
To be worthier than others;
Goodness suits them better than gold or silver.
But I make no issue of base people,
For they only do well in spite of themselves,
Nor could they be improved
By exhortation or command,
For the condition of baseness,
Which smells worse than bad breath,
Is too hard to correct;
This vice is too strong to purge.
I call those 'base' who commit
Vulgar acts that degrade them;
It is not by humble birth that I define
The base person, but rather by base disposition.
    "But he who is noble
By birth undoes himself greatly
If he turns his nobility into boorishness.
Do I speak the truth? Don't deny it.
They are more to reprove than others
If they're caught in vulgar deeds.
That's why I say, and it's no lie,
That each noble man, if he values esteem,
Should guard against being reproached

Se doit garder d'estre repris,
Car trop en vauldroit mains senz faille,
Tout fëust il preux en bataille.
Car la prouesse seulement
Ne gist pas ou grant hardement
D'assaillir, ne de soy defendre
Contre aucun qui le vueille offendre,
Car ce sont prouesses de corps.
Mais certes, mieulx valent encors
Les bontez qui viennent de l'ame;
Ce ne me puet nÿer nulle ame.
C'est vaillantise et grant prouesse
Quant un noble cuer si s'adresse
Qu'en vertus il soit bien propice
Et eschever et fuïr vice,
Ne qu'on ne puist trouver en lui
Riens dont puist mesdire nullui,
Se n'est a tort ou par envie;
Car n'est en ceste mortel vie
Homme qui soit de touz amez,
Ne de toutes gens bons clamez.
[fol. 77a] Ce fait Envie, qui s'efforce
D'abatre loz; n'y face force
Bon homme, ains face toudiz bien,
Car loz vaincra, je te di bien.
Et s'un tel homme ainsi apris
Peut aussi d'armes avoir pris,
Tant que Renommee tesmoingne
Qu'en tout bien faire s'embesoingne,
Et qu'en riens ne soit recrëant,
Un tel vassal, je te crëant,
Est bien digne de loz acquerre,
Se bon est en paix et en guerre,
Et juste et loyal en tout cas.
Et o lui ait pour advocas
Courtoisie, qui si l'enseingne
Que de gentil porte l'enseingne
En fait, en dit, et en parolle,
Senz orgueil, qui maint homme affolle.
Si ait hault cuer et haulte emprise;
Ce n'est pas l'orgueil qu'on desprise
Que d'avoir si haultain courage

For an ugly deed or vulgar word,
For he'd certainly be less worthy,
No matter his bravery in battle;
For prowess does not reside
Only in the great boldness
To make assaults or defend oneself
Against someone who might attack,
For those are the body's feats.
But surely, of yet greater worth
Are the good acts that come from the soul;
No one can tell me otherwise.
It is valor and great bravery
When a noble heart directs itself
Thus to favor virtue
And avoid and flee from vice,
So that no one finds in him
A reason for maligning him,
Unless it's wrong or in envy;
For in this mortal life,
No man is loved by everyone
Or called good by everyone.
That's what Envy does, who works
To destroy renown; a good man
Should pay no heed; rather, may he always do good,
For renown will win, I tell you.
And if such a well-bred man
Can also be praised for his feats of arms,
To the point where Renown shows
He's busy doing every good
And that he hangs back in nothing,
Such a vassal, I promise you,
Is indeed worthy of acquiring renown,
If he is good in peace and war,
And fair and faithful in everything.
Let him have Courtesy with him
As his counselor, to teach him
So that he bears the stamp of nobility
In deed, in opinion, and in word,
Without arrogance, which harms many a man.
May he be of noble heart and noble endeavor;
That's not the kind of pride one scorns—
That is, being so high-minded

Qu'on ne daingnast faire viltage,
Et que l'en aime les haultaines
Choses contraires aux vilaines.
Telz choses sont appartenans
Aux nobles, et que soustenans
Soient justice en tout endroit
Et toute bonté; c'est leur droit.
¶"Mais pour revenir au propos
Pour quoy vins ça sur ton repos
Par le commandement mon maistre,
Amours, qui au monde Dieu fist naistre,
[fol. 77b] Et de quoy se deult et complaint,
Et dont par moy a toy se plaint:
C'est de la coustume perverse,
Qui l'honneur de mainte gent verse,
De mesdire—que Dieux mauldie—,
Par qui mainte femme est laidie
A tort et a grant desraison,
Et maint bon homme senz raison,
Qui queurt ores plus qu'onques mais.
Ce fait Envie, qui tel mais
Apporte d'enfer pour donner
Aux gens et tout empoisonner
Et occire de double mort
Qui a si fait vice s'amort.
Mesdire, qui bien y regarde,
C'est tel glaive et si faite darde
Que meismes cil qui le balance
Occist, et cil sur qui le lance.
Mais aucunes fois plus blecié
Demeure cil qui l'a lancié
Que ne fait cil sur qui le rue,
Ou soit en maison ou en rue,
Et son ame plus griefment blece,
Et son honneur et sa noblesse,
Que ne fait souvent l'encusé.
Et tel s'est maintes foiz rusé
D'autre qui mieulx de soy valoit
Pour ce que son bien lui douloit.
Et tel diffame autrui souvent
Qui est plus seurpris, je m'en vent,
Du mesmes meffait et tachié

As not to stoop to vileness;
And may lofty things be loved,
Not the lowly ones.
Such things are befitting
To nobles, and may they
Uphold justice everywhere,
And every good act; it's their rightful task.
"But to return to my subject,
The reason I came here while you slept
At the command of my master
Love, whom God brought into the world,
And why he grieves and laments
And thus complains to you through me:
The cause is that corrupt habit
Of slandering, which undoes the honor
Of many—may God curse it—
By which many a woman is vilified
Wrongfully and senselessly,
And many a good man, unreasonably;
It is spreading unchecked more than ever before.
That's what Envy does, who delivers such food
From hell to give to people
And poison everything,
And kill, by double death,
Whoever destroys himself by such a vice.
Slander, if you examine it,
Is the type of sword or spear
That kills the very person
Who wields it and the one at whom it's hurled.
But sometimes the person who's launched it
Is left with a greater wound
Than the one he's launched it at,
Whether indoors or in the street,
And he damages his own soul more grievously,
As well as his honor and nobility,
Than he does the one he's accused.
Many a time a person like that rejects
Another, worthier one,
Because the other's wealth caused him pain.
And often such a man defames others
Who is himself more caught up, I declare,
In the same misdeed and stained by it

Qu'il dit que l'autre est entechié.
[fol. 77c] Si est faulte de congnoissance,
Et d'Envie vient la naissance,
Car nul ne vouldroit que tel verve
On deist de lui, quoy qu'il desserve.
Mais chascun puet estre certain
Qu'il est un Juge si certain
Qui tout congnoist et hors et ens,
Tout scet et tout est cler vëans;
Si rendra a chascun desserte
De bien ou de mal, chose est certe.

¶"Trop font mesdisans a haïr
Et leur compaignie a fuïr
Plus que de gent bataillereuse;
Plus male et trop plus perilleuse
Est compaignie, et plus nuysant
D'omme jangleur et mesdisant;
Qui male compaignie hante
Ne puet que du mal ne se sente,
Et avec les loups fault huler
Et de leur peau soy affuler.
Et quant je di 'homs,' j'entens famme
Aussi, s'elle jangle et diffame;
Car chose plus envenimee,
Ne qui doye estre moins amee,
N'est que langue de femme male
Qui, soit a certes ou par gale,
Mesdit d'autrui, moque ou ramposne.
Et se mal en vient, c'est aumosne
A celle qui s'i acoustume,
Car c'est laide et orde coustume.
N'a femmes n'affiert a mesdire;
Ainçois, quant elles oyent dire
[fol. 77d] Chose qui face autrui dommage,
Abaissier doivent le langaige
A leur pouoir, ou elles taire
S'autre chose ne peuent faire.
Car avoir doit, en verité,
Doulceur en femme, et charité;
S'autrement font, c'est leur contraire,
Car bien siet a femme a point taire.
Mais pour ce que ceste coustume

Than he says the other is.
The error is one of judgment,
And Envy gives it life.
For no one wants such fantasies
Said of himself, whatever he deserves.
But each of us may be assured
That there is a Judge so sure
Who knows everything, both inside and out;
He knows all and sees all clearly;
He'll render to each his just desserts
Of good or evil, that is certain.

"Gossipers fully deserve to be scorned
And their company shunned
Even more than the quarrelsome;
More evil and far more dangerous
And more harmful is the company
Of a gossiping and slanderous man.
Whoever frequents evil company
Cannot help but be touched by evil,
And he must howl with the wolves
And dress himself in their skin.
And when I say 'man,' I mean woman
Too, should she gossip and speak ill;
For nothing is more poisonous
Nor should be less loved
Than the tongue of an evil woman
Who, whether earnestly or in fun,
Speaks ill of others, or ridicules or derides them.
And if misfortune comes of it, that's a gift
To the woman who has the habit,
For it's an ugly, loathsome custom.
Nor does it suit women to slander;
Rather, when they hear something said
That damages another,
They must subdue such talk
As they are able, or else keep silent,
If there's nothing more they can do.
For in truth, there must be
Gentleness in woman, and charity;
If they act otherwise, it's not how they are,
For it suits a woman to be quiet at the right moment.
But because this practice

Court en mains lieux qu'Envie alume,
Vouldroit bien Amours errachier
D'entre ceulz qu'il aime et tient chier;
C'est des nobles a qui tel tache
Trop messiet s'elle s'i atache,
Car si preux n'est, je l'ose dire,
Que s'il a renom de mesdire,
Qu'il n'en soit par tout moins amé,
Moins prisié, et jangleur clamé.
Mais sur toutes autres diffames,
Het Amours qu'on parle des fammes
Laidement en les diffamant.
Ne veult que ceulz qui noblement
Se veulent mener pour acquerre
Pris et honneur en mainte terre
Soient de tel tache tachié,
Car c'est maufait et grant pechié.
Et pour estrapper tel verjus
M'envoya bonne Amour ça jus
Atout l'Ordre belle et nouvelle
De quoy j'apportay la nouvelle
Present toy n'a gueres de temps.
Mais encor veult, si com j'entens,
[fol. 78a] Amours que ceste chose soit
Publiee, comment qu'il soit,
Et qu'on le sache en maint paÿs
Afin que mesdit soit haÿs
En toutes pars ou noble gent
Sont d'acquerre loz diligent.
Si veult qu'ayes legacïon
De faire en toute nacïon
Procureresses qui pouoir
Ayent, s'elles veulent avoir,
De donner l'Ordre delittable
De la belle Rose agreable,
Avec le veu qui appartient.
Mais Amours veult, bien m'en souvient,
Que nulle ne soit establie
A donner l'Ordre gente et lie
S'elle n'est dame ou demoiselle
D'onnour, courtoise, franche et belle:
Toutes sont belles quant bonté

Abounds in many places Envy sets aflame,
Love would like to root it out
From among those he loves and cherishes:
It is nobles in whom such a blemish
Is deeply ill-suited, should it fasten onto them,
For there's none so fine, I dare say,
That, if he's known to slander
Will not be less loved everywhere,
Less prized, and called a gossipmonger.
But above all other kinds of defamation
Love hates for people to utter
Ugly talk about women that defames them.
He doesn't want those who nobly
Comport themselves in order to merit
Praise and honor in many a land
To be blemished by such a stain,
For that's a crime and a great sin.
So to draw out that bitter juice,
Good Love has sent me down here
With the lovely new Order
Whose proclamation I brought
Before you a short while ago.
As I understand, Love also wants
This matter to be
Made public in whatever way,
And for it be known in many countries
So that ugly talk be despised
In every place where noble people
Are diligent in earning praise.
Thus he wants you to have the mission
Of creating, among all peoples,
Lady deputies who have the power,
Should they accept it,
To bestow the delightful Order
Of the pleasing Rose,
With the relevant vow.
But Love wants, I remember well,
That no woman be ordained
To bestow the noble, joyful Order
Unless she's a lady or a maiden
Of honor, courteous, well-bred, and beautiful:
All are beautiful when goodness

A la beauté plus seurmonté.
¶"Ainsi auras par ce couvent
Ceste charge doresenavant.
Si l'envoye par toute terre
Ou noble gent poursuivent guerre
Aux dames, de qui renommee
Est de leur grant bonté semee.
A celles veult et te commande
Bonne Amour par moy, et te mande
Que tu commettes le bel Ordre
Ou nulz ne puet par droit remordre.
Et combien que j'aye apportees
Les roses qui seront portees
[fol. 78b] Des bons, a qui je les donnay
—Et de telles assez en ay,
Car en mon vergier sont cueillies—
Ne veult pas Amours que faillies
Els soient es autres contrees
Ou telles ne sont encontrees;
Car quiconques d'orfaverie
D'or, d'argent, ou de brouderie
De soye ou d'aucune autre chose,
Mais que soit en façon de rose,
Portera l'Ordre, qui donnee
Sera de la dame ordonnee
De par toy pour l'Ordre establir,
Il souffist. Et pour acomplir
Ceste chose, voy ci les bulles:
Ou monde n'a pareilles nulles,
Si tesmoing la commissïon.
Cil Dieu qui souffri Passïon
Te maintiengne toudiz en l'euvre
D'estude qui grant scïence euvre,
Et t'otroi son saint paradis—
Je m'en vois et adieu te dis."
¶Adont est elle esvanoÿe.
Je m'esveillay toute esbahye:
Ne vy ouvert huys ne fenestre!
Merveillay moy que ce pot estre,
Si me pensay que c'estoit songe.
Mais ne le tins pas a mençonge
Quant coste moy trouvay la lettre

Has risen above beauty.
“Thus through this covenant you will have
This charge from today forward.
Send it to every place
Where noble people are at war
Against ladies, whose renown
Has been sown by their great goodness.
To them good Love wants and commands you
Through me, and he mandates you
To deliver the fine Order
Where no one can rightfully challenge it.
And although I have brought
The roses that will be worn
By the good, to whom I gave them
—And I have enough of them,
For they are gathered from my garden—
Love does not want them to be lacking
In other lands
Where they are not found;
For whether worked in gold,
In silver, or in embroidered
Silk, or something else,
As long as it’s in the shape of a rose,
Whoever will wear the Order, given
By the lady ordained
By you to establish it,
That suffices. And to accomplish
That end, here is the bull;
It has no equal in all the world:
The mandate so testifies.
May God who suffered the Passion
Sustain you always in the work
Of studying, which builds great knowledge,
And grant you his holy paradise,
I now take my leave and bid you adieu.”
At that, she disappeared.
I awoke in great astonishment
And saw no door or window open!
I wondered what it could have been
And thought it was a dream.
But I saw it was no lie
When next to me I found the letter

De la deesse au royal sceptre
Qu'elle mist dessus mon chevet
Coste moy, puis volant s'en vet.
[fol. 78c] ¶Par grant entente prises ay
Les bulles, et moult y musay,
Car j'avoye lumiere d'oile.
Je me levay et la chandoile
Alumay adonc senz tarder
Pour mieulx la bule regarder.
Mais oncques ne vy en ma vie
Si de beauté lettre assouvie!
Merveilles os, je vous plevy,
De la grant beauté que g'i vy.
Estrange en est moult la maniere:
Le parchemin de fin or yere,
Et les lettres furent escriptes
De fin azur, non trop petites
Ne trop grans, mais si bien formees
Que mieulx ne peust. Non pas rimees
Ne furent, mais en belle prose;
La contint l'Ordre de la Rose.
Le laz en fu de soye azure,
Et le seel, de belle mesure,
Fut d'une pierre precïeuse
Resplandissant et gracïeuse.
Le dieu d'Amours fut d'une part:
Les piez ot sur un liëpart;
De l'autre part fut la deesse
De Loyauté, dame et princesse.
Les empraintes moult merveilleuses
En furent, et trop gracïeuses,
Et bien sembla de si belle estre
Que n'estoit pas chose terrestre.
Si leuz la lettre senz y point
Faillir, et notay chascun point.
[fol. 78d] ¶Lye fu de la visïon
Et d'avoir tel commissïon,
Car combien que je ne le vaille,
Ay je desir que nul ne faille.
Et pour ce, moy, qui suis commise
A ce, ne doy estre remise
De faire si bien mon devoir

From the goddess with the royal scepter,
Which she placed at the head of my bed
Next to me, and then flew off.
With great curiosity I took
The bull and stared at it intently,
For I had the light of an oil-lamp.
Then I got up and without delay
Lit the candle,
The better to look at the document;
But never in my life had I seen
A letter so beautifully prepared!
I marveled, I promise you,
At the great beauty I saw there.
Its fashioning was quite unusual:
The parchment was of fine gold,
And the letters were written
In a delicate azure blue, not too small
Or too large, but so well formed
That no better could be found. Not in rhyme
Were they, but in a lovely prose;
It held the Order of the Rose.
Its ties were of azure blue,
And its beautifully proportioned seal
Was, by means of a precious gem,
Made resplendent and lovely.
The God of Love was on one side,
His feet upon a leopard;
On the other side was the goddess,
The lady and princess of Loyalty.
Its imprint was most marvelous
And filled with charm,
And it seemed of so fine an essence
As not to be an earthly object.
So I read the letter and missed
Not a bit of it, noting each point.
I was delighted at the sight
And with having such a commission,
For although I don't merit it,
I'm eager that no one fall short.
And because I am the one charged
To do this, I must not be remiss
At fulfilling my duty so well

Que je n'en doye blasme avoir.
Et pour ce ay je fait ce dittié
Ou j'ay tout l'estat appointtié
Et mis la fourme et la maniere
Comme il avint et ou ce yere,
Afin qu'on le sache en tous lieux.
Si soient tous, jeunes et vieux,
Desireux d'estre retenus
En l'Ordre, maiz n'y entre nulz
S'il ne veult bien son devoir faire,
Car il se pourroit trop meffaire.
¶Aussi aux dames amoureuses,
Qui de tout bien sont desireuses,
J'entens de l'amour ou n'a vice,
Mal, vilennie, ne malice;
Car quiconques le die ou non,
En bonne amour n'a se bien non.
Et a celles generaulment
Qui aiment honneur bonnement,
Soit en ce regne ou autre part,
Qui ont les cuers de noble part:
De par la deesse je donne
Le plain pouoir et habandonne
De donner l'Ordre gracïeux
A tous nobles et en tous lieux
[fol. 79a] Ou bien employé le verront
A ceulz qui avoir le voulront.
Mais s'aucun le prent et le jure
Et puis aprés il s'en parjure,
Cellui soit tenu pour infame,
Haÿ de tout homme et de famme,
Car ainsi le veult la deesse
Qui ceste chose nous adresse.
¶Si feray fin—il en est temps—
Priant Dieu queë aux escoutans
Et a ceulz qui liront mes dis
Doint bonne vie et paradis.
Escript le jour saint Valentin
Ou mains amans tres le matin
Choisissent amours pour l'annee;
C'est le droit de celle journee.
¶De par celle qui ce dittié

That no blame can come to me.
And so I've composed this poem
In which I've entered all the facts
And described the form and the way
It happened, and where,
So that people everywhere may know of it.
And may all the young and old
Desire to be admitted
Into the Order; but let none enter
Unless he wants to do what's required,
For he could do himself much harm.

Thus for loving ladies
Desirous of every good,
I intend love that's free of vice,
Without evil, baseness, or spite;
For whoever says so or not,
In true love there is only good.
And to women generally
Who truly cherish honor,
Whether in this kingdom or elsewhere,
Who have noble hearts:
On behalf of the goddess, I give
And relinquish full power
To bestow the beneficent Order
Upon all nobles and in all places
Where they'll see it well used
By those who'll agree to accept it.
But if someone takes it and swears the vow
And then later perjures himself,
May he be considered disgraced,
Despised by every man and woman;
That is how the goddess wants it
Who has guided us in this.

And so I'll end—the time has come—
Praying God that to those who are listening
And to those who will read my poetry
He grant a good life and paradise.
Written on St. Valentine's Day
When many lovers, from break of dawn,
Choose their sweethearts for the year:
That's what's done on this day.

On behalf of the one who wrote

A fait par loyale amittié.
S'aucun en veult le nom savoir,
Je lui en dirai tout le voir:
Qui un tout seul *cry* crieroit
Et la fin d'aou*st* y mettroit,
Se il disoit avec une *yne*
Il sauroit le nom bel et digne.

Cy fine le *Dit de la Rose.*

This little poem in loyal friendship,
If someone wants to know her name,
I'll tell the whole truth of it:
Whoever would utter a single *cry*,
And then add on Augu*st*'s end,
And if he said it with an –*yne*,
He'd know the fine and worthy name.

The *Tale of the Rose* ends here.

Rejected Readings and Variants to the French Edition of the Dit de la Rose

Rejected Readings from Base Manuscript L_1 (Chantilly, Bibliothèque du Château, 492)

216	ceste chose i.
253	ses choses
534	veulz

Variants from L_2 (Paris, BnF, fr. 12779)

22	eulx *om.*
26	xx.
28	iiij.^{C} et j.
33	Ot assemble
105	elz v.
157	tres si j. ch.
179	sus
253	ses ch.
352	f. il bien preux
445	a ahir
651	Explicit

28 **the year 140[2]** *L'an quatre cens et un*: The French states that it is 1401. Under the Julian calendar then in force, the year began not January 1 but at the movable feast of Easter, which in 1401 (1402) was March 28, thus after the dinner party and after the writing of the poem. For us, however, January would be dated 1402.

32 **shuttered house** *maison close*: Christine evokes one of Louis d'Orléans's Parisian residences again at the beginning of the *Livre de Prodommie de l'homme*, a text dating from ca. 1406 and still unpublished. See the Vatican Library (Biblioteca Apostolica Vaticana) manuscript 1238, fols. 1r–2r. At v. 50, Christine adds that the door was *bien fermee* (firmly closed), and at vv. 87–88 that the house was *close* by means of its *portes barrees* (bolted doors) and *fenestres bien sarrees* (firmly fastened windows). Such repetitions emphasize the unembodied, otherworldly nature of Loyalty and her maidens, and they bespeak a power greater than any human one. Christine may be indicating her close relationship to the duke by suggesting that she alone among the guests remains in his residence overnight (see vv. 263–66).

43–44 *ceulx, seulz*: a rhyme for the eye, given that the *l* of *ceulx* is silent, whereas that of *seulz* is pronounced. See Versification, p. 53.

47–75 **They'd been assembled in that place . . . gracious questions** *Assemblez les ot celle part . . . demandes gracïeuses*: This gathering of nobles recalls the exclusionary character of Pleasure's (Deduit's) garden in the *Romance of the Rose*, where figures such as Hate, Avarice, Sorrow, Poverty, and Old Age are denied entrance, while Idleness, Courtesy, Joy, Pleasant Looks, and the God of Love himself are admitted (*RR* ed. Lecoy, vv. 139–956). The festive event that Christine paints, where good cheer and literary performance are on display, reflects the early fifteenth-century chivalric cultural norms that Guenée describes in *Un meurtre, une société: l'Assassinat du duc d'Orléans, 23 novembre 1407* (Paris: Gallimard, 1992), 148. In medieval literature, "true love" was the province of the privileged.

65–66 *souper, per*: Although in modern French *souper* rhymes with *soupé*, in the late Middle Ages final *–r* could still be pronounced, especially in poetry, and this pair of rhyme words is effective. Hesitation over the final *r* is captured in the differing views of two sixteenth-century grammarians. John Palsgrave (ca. 1485–1554), an English cleric tasked with teaching French to English-born Queen Mary, third wife of the French king Louis XII, maintained that *–r* in all positions was pronounced in correct French: *L'Eclaircissement de la langue française par Jean Palsgrave, suivi de la Grammaire de Giles du Guez*, ed. François Génin (Paris: Imprimerie Nationale, 1852), p. xix. The French printer and grammarian Henri Estienne (1528–1598), however, claimed that Parisians were dropping the final

–*r*, thus *papié* instead of *papier*, *plaisi* instead of *plaisir*, etc. See Mildred K. Pope, *From Latin to Modern French, with Especial Consideration of Anglo-Norman*, rev. ed. (Manchester: Manchester University Press, 1952), §400.

72 **ten** *dix*: "Ten" is perhaps not to be taken literally, as it may simply suggest a large number.

75 **gracious questions** *demandes gracïeuses*: The *demande d'amour* was a "love problem" posed for conversation. Christine makes it the very substance of her *Debat de deux amans*, in which a knight, a squire, and two ladies retreat to a garden to discuss love questions. The squire asks the knight to give his opinion of service to love (*l'amoureux servage*): whether it bestows bravery, joy, or honor on the lover, or whether it causes damage (vv. 403–6). The two men, the principal debaters, go on to discuss the question at length, using evidence not from their own experience (which is presumed), but from the stories of lovers of legend and history.

86–89 **For there suddenly appeared . . . A lady of great nobility** *Car alors seurvint tout a point . . . Une dame de grant noblesse*: This motif of heavenly figures coming to Christine as she sleeps recurs in the *Chemin*, where the Sibyl appears at Christine's bedside in vv. 451–61 (although she is not yet asleep), as well as in the *Cité* (Bk. 1, ch. 2), and again in the *Trois Vertus* (Bk. 1, ch. 1) when the ladies Reason, Rectitude, and Justice return to encourage Christine. See the note to vv. 548–51.

105 *qu'el*: *El* occasionally appears as an alternative to *elles* in this period; used here, it avoids a nine-syllable line.

118 **to note** *noter*: The French verb may also mean "to sing" (*DMF* s.v. *noter*).

129–76 **He who fashioned . . . uphold the honor of ladies** *Cil qui forma . . . l'onneur des dames soustenant*: Maureen Boulton observes that these "lyric insertions," frequent for depicting court life, serve to enliven scenes of celebration (Boulton, *The Song in the Story*), 80.

136, 139, 144, 152 **news** *nouvelles*: by phrasing the God of Love's message as "news" (in particular, in the refrain), Christine may have intended a parallel with biblical annunciation, that is, the "good news" angels bring to the shepherds in Luke 2:8–20 of Jesus's birth, and the similar announcement to Mary in Luke 1:26–38 that she would conceive a son through the intervention of the Holy Spirit. See also vv. 233, 236, 239, and note.

148 **she who brought Troy down** *celle qui Troyes fist bannir*: Using *bannir*, lit. "to banish," to describe Troy's loss to the Greeks gives pause. In Old and Middle

French the distinction between nominative *qui* and accusative *que* was not always observed, with the result that *qui* here can be read as "whom." Helen of Troy, married to King Menelaus of Sparta, was abducted by—or eloped with—Paris of Troy, which ignited the Trojan War. Helen is not among women Christine defends, as she does women of legend whom she believes maligned; cf. in the *Epistre* her defenses of Medea (v. 435) and Dido (v. 443), who reappear in the *Cité* as women wronged by their male partners (for Medea, Bk. 1, ch. 32 and Bk. 2, ch. 56; for Dido, Bk. 1, ch. 46 and Bk. 2, ch. 55). Helen's story was told and inflected differently by many authors, and some narratives note that as the war dragged on, the citizens of Troy became increasingly unhappy with Helen's presence among them.

172 **so raise no opposition** *si n'y mettez enchiere*: Lit., do not raise the bid.

184 **scrolls** *rolez*: Most likely, these are rolls of parchment.

233, 236, 239 **news** *nouvelles:* in a parallel but opposite move to Loyalty's bringing the "news" down from the God of Love, in this rondeau Loyalty carries the news of the company's vow back up to the God of Love. See vv. 136, 139, 144, 152, and note.

243–44 *liez, deliëz*: The pair *liez* and *deliëz* are feminine plurals, modifying *nymphes* and *voix*, respectively. Here, the pronunciation of *liez* is [li], one syllable, but *lïez* of *(de)lïez* is [lije], two syllables. These are rhymes for the eye. See Versification, p. 53.

283 **Alone** *seulette*: Christine's emphasis on her solitude recalls the famous Ballade XI of her *Cent Balades*, long considered a personal lament for the death of her husband (*Œuvres poétiques*, 1:12).

319–20 *vilz, plevis*: It is likely that *vilz* was pronounced [vil], while the second syllable of *plevis* would have been [-vi], making this an example of assonance.

322 *doivent . . . pareceux*: Eliding the third person plural *–ent* ending of *doivent* keeps this verse octosyllabic; although rare, such elision before a vowel does occur in this period (see Georges Lote, *Histoire du vers français,* 3 vols. [Paris: Boivin, 1949–55]), 3:102–6. In L_2 the *p* of *pareceux* has a bar across its downstroke, making an abbreviation that modern editors normally expand to *per* or *par*. Roy chose to assure the octosyllable, however, by transcribing this as *preceux* (v. 321, *Œuvres poétiques*, 2:39).

330 **in spite of themselves** *a force*: These lines contain a pun on *force*: the expression *a force* can mean "by force" or "forcibly," and the plural *forces* can refer to "shears." This may allude to a common proverb, *La force paist le pré* (shears mow the field). See *Li Proverbe au vilain*, ed. Adolf Tobler (Leipzig: S. Hirzel, 1895), and

Louise W. Stone, "Un proverbe du moyen âge: *Force paist le pré*," *Zeitschrift für romanische Philologie* 73, nos. 1–2 (2009): 145–59.

339 **humble birth** *baz lignaige*: In the *Mutacion* Christine expresses sympathy for the poor, describing their hardships and the material deprivation they suffer (vv. 3433–81), and she goes on to criticize the rich, saying that the wealthy, who believe that silver and gold are theirs by right, ought to take pity on the poor (vv. 3482–94). Brian Woledge has shown that Christine is one of the few medieval writers to have written on the subject of poverty at all. See Woledge, "Le thème de la pauvreté dans la *Mutacion de Fortune* de Christine de Pisan," in *Fin du Moyen Age et Renaissance*, 97–106. Susan J. Dudash has given full treatment to Christine's understanding of the *menu peuple* (little people). See Dudash, "Christinian Politics, the Tavern, and Urban Revolt in Late Medieval France," in Green and Mews, *Healing the Body Politic*, 35–59; and Dudash, "Christine de Pizan and the 'menu peuple,'" *Speculum* 78 (2003): 788–831.

368–69 **For in this mortal life, / No man is loved by everyone** *Car n'est . . . mortel vie / Homme qui soit de touz amez*: See Christine's *Advision* for the statement that no person, not even Jesus Christ, was perfect enough to avoid human criticism (*Advision*, Bk. 2, ch. 17).

402 *Amours, qui au monde Dieu fist naistre*: Although this has the appearance of a nine-syllable line, most probably the –*i* of *qui* was elided when reading aloud, giving *qu'au*, one syllable, instead of *qui au*, two syllables.

405–7 **that corrupt habit / Of slandering, . . . —may God curse it—** *la coustume perverse, . . . De mesdire—que Dieux mauldie—*: Slander was and is regarded as a sin; see "Detractio," in Casagrande and Vecchio, *Les Péchés de la langue*, 239–52. See also vv. 638–39 of the *God of Love's Letter* and accompanying note.

412 *mais*: Alternate spelling of *mets*, a dish (of food).

465 **slander** *mesdire*: See the note to vv. 405–7.

495 *Ordre belle et nouvelle*: The word *Ordre* is feminine here but masculine at v. 625 (*Ordre gracïeux*). The *DMF* attests to the word's flexible gender. We thank Angus Kennedy for this observation.

512–18 **But Love wants . . . risen above beauty** *Mais Amours veult . . . A la beauté plus seurmonté*: The emphasis here on honor, courtesy, sincerity, and goodness as necessary qualifications for those awarding the Order of the Rose has its parallel in the *Cité* (Bk. 3, ch. 19), which concludes with the statement that the *Cité* has been constructed to house all honorable women.

533 **garden** *vergier*: The garden as a *locus amoenus* congenial to love is a standard topos; in this case, it is probably also meant to recall the garden in the *Roman*.

545, 564 **bull** *bulles*: In these verses *bulles* is plural, but at v. 568 it is *bule*, singular (and with slightly altered spelling). The term *bulle*, normally a document issued by a pope, comes from its leaden seal, which was called a *bulla* and served to authenticate the document. See also the note to vv. 559, 570, 593.

548–51 **May God . . . holy paradise** *Cil Dieu . . . saint paradis*: Loyalty is an early example of Christine's use of allegorical figures who serve to validate the autobiographical narrator persona as an intelligent, studious woman worthy of special attention. Such validation also occurs through the figure of the Cumaean Sibyl in the *Chemin*; the allegories Reason, Rectitude, and Justice in the *Cité* and the *Trois Vertus*, and the figure of Philosophy/Theology in the *Advision*. See the note to vv. 86–89.

557–58 **dream, lie** *songe, mençonge*: A frequent rhyme in medieval French poetry, the pair is especially foregrounded in the two opening verses of the *Roman*.

559, 570, 593 **letter** *lettre*: An alternate way of referring to the bull. It was common procedure to have the statutes of a newly founded order sealed as letters patent, a written order issued by a sovereign ruler generally granting an office, right, monopoly, title, or status.

565–67 **light of an oil-lamp . . . Lit the candle** *lumiere d'oile . . . la chandoile / Alumay*: The oil lamp is not enough to read by, so Christine lights a candle, the better to read the document. *Chandoile* is an alternate spelling for *chandelle*.

568 **document** *bule*: See the note to vv. 545, 564.

574–92 **The parchment was of fine gold . . . earthly object** *Le parchemin de fin or yere . . . chose terrestre*: Letters patent were commonly written on parchment but not on gold leaf, which was too fragile to support writing. Inès Villela-Petit observes that Christine departs from describing a real bull. Instead of plain parchment and black ink, the letter appears on gold parchment with azure ink. Villela-Petit further points out that its seal is a precious stone rather than an impression in the more usual lead, which in itself testifies to an otherworldly level of wealth and refinement. She underscores that the kingly figure on the front of the seal, with his feet on a leopard, echoes representations of earthly kings and of the biblical King Solomon, who are depicted with lions at their feet. Brigitte Bedos Rezak comments that the fanciful pairing here of a gold writing surface and azure blue ink recalls the heraldic tinctures of the royal coat of arms, perhaps even more characteristic of the French royal coat than the *fleur-de-lys*. We are grateful to both scholars for their insights.

579 **prose** *prose*: Prose was usual for letters patent.

581 **ties** *laz*: The seal was attached to the document by means of braided silk strings which, like the ink, are of azure blue.

582 *seel*: Lucy M. Gay maintained that *seel* here is one syllable, assuring that the verse is octosyllabic: "On the Language of Christine de Pisan," *Modern Philology* 6 (1908–9): 70–96, at 85. On the other hand, both it and the form *seau* can still be given as two syllables in the sixteenth century. See *Dictionnaire de la langue française du seizième siècle*, ed. Edmond Huguet (Paris: Edouard Champion, 1965).

595 *Lye*: See the note to vv. 243–44.

625 *Ordre gracïeux*: In this instance, *Ordre* is masculine. See note to v. 495.

639–41 **St. Valentine's Day . . . their sweethearts for the year** *le jour saint Valentin . . . amours pour l'annee*: Christine mentions the medieval custom of choosing a sweetheart for the coming year in Virelay 10 (*Œuvres poétiques*, 1:111–12) and in ballades 72 and 73 in the *Cent Ballades d'amant et de dame*, ed. Jacqueline Cerquiglini (Paris: Union générale d'éditions, 1982), 103–4.

647–49 **a single cry . . . with an -*yne*** *un tout seul cry . . . avec une yne*: A puzzle signature, common in poetry of the period and frequently employed by Christine.

A POEM ON MAN AND WOMAN

Jean Gerson
A Poem on Man and Woman
Translated from the Latin by Thomas O'Donnell

Introduction

Jean Gerson (1363–1429) became a doctor of theology in 1395 and was made chancellor of the University of Paris in the same year, ultimately becoming one of the most influential men of his time. He left a large body of work in Latin, with some notable exceptions, such as his *Montagne de Contemplation* (Mountain of Contemplation), composed in French and intended for his own sisters and other women who wished to bring structure to their spiritual lives.[1] In addition to his treatise against the *Romance of the Rose* in the Debate of the Rose, he wrote about Joan of Arc in *Super facto puellae et credulitate sibi praestanda* (*About the Feat of the Maid, and the Faith that Should be Placed in Her*).[2] Christine's own poem about Joan of Arc, in French, *Le ditié de Jehanne d'Arc* (see the Bibliography to this volume), celebrates the Maid's accomplishment both for France and as a woman.

Unlike Christine's *God of Love's Letter* and *Tale of the Rose*, Gerson's poem is not a defense of women. It is translated here to show its clear outline of fifteenth-century belief about the relationship between women and men, authoritatively explained by a leader of the Church with whom Christine was thought to have had an "intellectual friendship."[3]

Gerson begins by speaking of the natures of man and woman, comparing them with the limbs of a body that need and cherish each other. He asserts that all "humans are of the same species," that God made men and women equal and of the same substance. He urges male and female to practice reason, where the expression "nobility's enjoyment" alludes to human exceptionalism, centered on a capacity for reason which is not shared with the other animals.

1. Gerson's writing is collected in *Œuvres complètes*, ed. Palémon Glorieux, 10 vols. (Paris: Desclée) 1960–73; his French works appear in vol. 7, parts 1 and 2. For the English translation of the *Montagne de Contemplation*, see Brian Patrick McGuire, trans., *Jean Gerson: Early Works* (New York: Paulist Press, 1988).

2. See Sean Field, "A New English Translation of Jean Gerson's Authentic Tract on Joan of Arc: *About the Feat of the Maid, and the Faith that Should be Placed in Her,*" *Magistra* 18 (2012): 36–54.

3. See Earl Jeffrey Richards, "Christine de Pizan and Jean Gerson: An Intellectual Friendship," in *Christine de Pizan 2000: Studies on Christine de Pizan in Honour of Angus J. Kennedy*, ed. John Campbell and Nadia Margolis (Amsterdam and Atlanta, GA: Rodopi, 2000), 197–208; and Richards, "Jean Gerson's Writings to His Sisters and Christine de Pizan's *Livre des Trois Vertus*: An Intellectual Dialogue Culminating in Friendship," in *Virtue Ethics for Women 1250–1500*, ed. Karen Green and Constant Mews (Dordrecht: Springer Netherlands, 2011), 81–98.

Beginning at verse 33, Gerson asks whether women can be saved, which suggests the topicality of the issue. In the next stanza, vv. 39–56, addressed to men, he states that woman is man's partner, but he does not say that man is woman's partner: this is not an oversight, since man is in fact not woman's partner, he is her superior. According to Thomas Aquinas, woman "is included in nature's intention as directed to the work of generation," and in that sense she is intended as man's helper; in other work, however, man is more efficiently helped by another man.[4] Because men's leadership is therefore said to have been given by God, it cannot be questioned: man is the head of woman, and she is required to submit to his will. And although woman is man's "helper," says Gerson, she can be fickle, vain, quarrelsome, and seductive; further, "if the female sex tends to excessive vanity, let our prudent masculine care set a limit." He advises men to "direct, advise, nurture, love, and keep her, as Christ does the Church."

In the next section, Gerson addresses women, counseling them to obey their husbands. Continuing the assumptions of the preceding sections, he anticipates possible bad behavior on women's part and admonishes them to conduct themselves with integrity. He concludes by saying, "Let there be between you a bond in virtuous love and one heart, as you are one species, and have a single end." As we have seen, Christine too believes that women have "modesty and heartfelt devotion," and perhaps that "weeping and . . . tenderness" are women's special gift, in an arrangement of complementarity in which leadership in some of the most important domains is granted to men.

Through the voice of an imagined interlocutor, the poem makes the claim that women, like Eve, can be inclined toward bad behavior, which they are urged to control. Gerson allows that women can display "excessive vanity," but he does not speculate on any masculine flaws (compare Christine's implications in the *Letter* that men start wars, destroy kingdoms, and bring about the ruin of women by their gossiping). Only women's alleged flaws are mentioned.

In the end, although Christine would have welcomed Gerson's direction to men to treat women kindly, certain of his views, such as his negative generalizations about women as a group, were of a kind she would not have embraced. Perhaps, although she enjoyed the chancellor's support, she also had to recognize the irreconcilables embedded in their association.

Translator's Note

Gerson's poetry reflects the kind of authoritative Latin writing that Christine de Pizan strove to imitate in the vernacular. Like medieval French, medieval Latin was a lively and varied medium with a diverse audience, and Gerson's poetry followed classical, scriptural, and contemporary medieval models. His style, however,

4. *ST* Ia. 92.1.

definitely reflects his male intellectual milieu. For example, he uses words like "species" and "vires" ("faculties," line 71) with senses drawn from Scholastic philosophy unfamiliar outside university precincts. The Greek-derived words in his poem, such as "scisma" ("schism," line 9), "microcosmus" and "macrocosmus" ("microcosm" and "macrocosm," lines 79–80), and "plasmator" ("shaper," line 13), can be compared with the use of academic jargon today. These words provide the structure for complex ideas (such as the ideal correspondence between celestial and human orders advocated by Gerson) as well as a certain élan, but their use can exclude those who have not received a formal education in the schools. Almost all medieval women would have found themselves in this latter group. Although a fair number of women were accomplished Latin scholars (for example, Heloise in France, the Nun of Barking in England, Hildegard of Bingen in the Holy Roman Empire, Isotta Nogarola in Italy and other Italian women of her time), none among them could have acquired that education in universities, from which women were barred.

The opposition between harmony and division, as nearly abstract concepts, organizes Gerson's discussion of the relation between the sexes. It is unfortunate that the English word "sex" does not hold the same associations as the Latin "sexus," which is more obviously related to the Latin verb "seco," to cut, to divide, or to injure, because this association lays the foundation for the poem's entire aesthetic. In explicating humanity's primary "division," Gerson makes the case not only for the underlying unity of humanity but also for the benefits that our diversity makes possible. He describes three traditional roles of man and woman in marriage—both can be servant, companion, and master—and gives them ethical and Trinitarian overtones. For Gerson, sexual division and harmony are of a piece with the divisions and harmonies of the individual person, human endeavor, the universe, and the Godhead itself. The spiritual equality and the friendship between women and men assumed by Gerson ignore the lived experience of inequality that dismayed a thinker like Christine de Pizan.

In turning Jean Gerson's poem into English prose from its original Latin poetic form, I have hoped to offer a version that is both readable and accurate. I have tried to preserve some of Gerson's donnish mannerism, described above, and his fondness for antitheses such as those in lines 7–16, 23–32, or 57–70, which are so typical of medieval Latin poetry and so closely related to his thematic oppositions. Inevitably, some special features of his Latin style, such as the absence of connecting words, evocative tense shifts, and rhythm, have had to be eliminated.

A Poem on Man and Woman
by Jean Gerson[5]

1–6: High glory to God; and to you, man and woman, [such] peace as will unite you forever in equal love. Let whoever desires to compare the ways of humankind, [and the ways] that either sex shows to be particularly its own, beware of causing offense, for such discussions usually breed ill-feeling. Let the bond of friendship be praised instead.

7–16: In a true body, the parts cherish one another: just so, let each sex of humankind please the other. The limbs harmonize with another; in the body there is no schism. The eye does not say to the hand, "You are not fit for me!" Humans are of the same species, whether female or male. Souls are alike which thrive on reason. One author, shaper, and creator—and an origin just as good—has granted them nobility's enjoyment. Finished by a like death, a similar substance has been granted to them, and an identical end has been established for them from the beginning.

17–22: Depend on it that no one cheerfully wishes to have his sins repeated, when all are used to being puffed up by praise of themselves. Therefore, you should say what might join both sexes together in a delightful union. Urge both sexes to cherish and to love one another, to anticipate one another in gratifying acts of obedience.

23–32: If you consider the life of humankind, and then the human character, [you will find that] no one is without fault, neither the young nor the old. You, the greater madman, spare the lesser at last! Let him who is bound by greater guilt not condemn others. Does not the same doom draw us all together? We are all one lost lump of sin. Whoever is saved is saved by grace alone; no glory is yours as a free gift.[6] The Lord made us, and he made us anew when we were in ruins, and before the Lord woman and man are equal.

33–38: Shall everlasting life bless males alone? Shall this salvation be given to the ranks of woman? He who blames the female or male sex blames you, merciful Virgin, along with your son, insults his own foremothers and forefathers, shamelessly spits on the saints, male and female.

39–56: Good man, remember that woman is to be your partner, and has been given to you as a helper to please you. You, man, who are stronger the more firmly your mind holds sway over your forceful will, if a woman has a mutable and

5. Translated from Antonius Placanica, ed., "Ioannis Gersonii, 'Carmen de viro et muliere,'" *Studi Medievali*, 3rd ser., 31 (1990): 435–53.

6. That is, every glory is transmitted by grace and belongs ultimately to God, not to you.

always changing heart, in your affection be more patient with her, pity her more. You are her leader, her guide, her head; direct, advise, nurture, love, and keep her, as Christ does the Church. "But," you will say, "woman throws stumbling blocks in my way one after the other, with her flatteries, her quarrels, her vanities, and her enticements." Take care not to give your consent [to such things], and I assure you, they shall harm you not at all, if her guilt, not yours, makes this danger.[7] What then? Though everything be a snare of guilt for the wicked, everything is not for all that to be hated by the good. If the female sex tends to excessive vanity, let our prudent masculine care set a limit: Adam should have restrained Eve, but when he consented, he was punished for his own fault.

57–70: Woman, be subject to man; he is your head; obey him. Let his praise be your praise, your glory, good name, and distinction. Know that, if you are good, reproaches uttered by the wicked are compliments to you. The honor of virtue is the shame of vice. The stinking libel of the guilty does not harm the blameless; before the Judge everyone will bear his own burden. Woman, as you have modesty and heartfelt devotion, make use of your dowry in weeping and in tenderness: Know that the Almighty has often shattered the mighty through your sex, bestowing [on you] martyrdom's prize. Therefore strive to imitate virtuous women; you strong men toil at works requiring strength; let the praise of one belong to both. Let there be between you a bond in virtuous love and one heart, as you are one species, and have a single end.

71–80: The spirit receives three faculties bound to him, as a bridegroom receives three things: a maidservant, a companion, and a mistress. The flesh is the maidservant, reason the freeborn, but the mind is the mistress; she conceives through the Lord alone. The servile arts are pursued by the swarthy, the liberal by the fair; only the demigoddess wishes to pass her time with God alone. The spirit is more or less a slave, a freeman, or a lord, to the degree that he submits to each of these of his free will. If in the microcosm this threefold tie were in harmony, you would see nothing more beautiful in the macrocosm.

7. This rendering accepts Placanica's suggested emendation of the edited text, which would otherwise read "if your guilt, not hers, makes this danger" ("Hoc tua si preceps, non sua culpa facit," line 50). See Placanica, 450n50.

Bibliography

Primary Sources

Manuscripts of the *Epistre au dieu d'Amours* and *Dit de la Rose*

Chantilly, Bibliothèque du Château, 492.

London, BL, Harley MS 4431, accessible online at <www.pizan.lib.ed.ac.uk>.

London, Westminster Abbey, MS 21.

Paris, Arsenal, 3295 accessible online at <https://gallica.bnf.fr/ark:/12148/btv1b8451477p.r=Arsenal%20ms%203295?rk=21459;2>.

Paris, BnF, fr. 604 accessible online at <https://gallica.bnf.fr/ark:/12148/btv1b8448964p>.

Paris, BnF, fr. 835, accessible online at <https://gallica.bnf.fr/ark:/12148/btv1b8449047c>.

Paris, BnF, fr. 12779, accessible online at <https://gallica.bnf.fr/ark:/12148/btv1b60001038>.

Paris, BnF, Moreau 1686, accessible online at <https://gallica.bnf.fr/ark:/12148/btv1b85311387>.

Christine de Pizan Digital Scriptorium, accessible online at <https://dlmm.library.jhu.edu/fr/christine-de-pizan-digital-scriptorium/>.

Editions and Translations of the *Epistre au dieu d'Amours* and *Dit de la Rose*

Brownlee, Kevin, trans. "The God of Love's Letter." In *The Selected Writings of Christine de Pizan: Translations, Criticism*, edited and translated by Renate Blumenfeld-Kosinski, 15–28. New York: W. W. Norton, 1997.

Fenster, Thelma, trans. *Letter of the God of Love* and *Tale of the Rose* (selections). In *The Writings of Christine de Pizan*, edited by Charity Cannon Willard, 145–50 and 162–70. New York: Persea, 1994.

Fenster, Thelma, and Mary Carpenter Erler, ed. and trans. *Poems of Cupid, God of Love: Christine de Pizan's* Epistre au dieu d'Amours *and* Dit de la Rose; *Thomas Hoccleve's* The Letter of Cupid; *with George Sewell's* The Proclamation of Cupid. Leiden and New York: Brill, 1990.

Heuckenkamp, Ferdinand, ed. *Le Dit de la Rose von Christine de Pisan*. Halle a.S.: Buchdruckerei des Waisenhauses, 1891.

McWebb, Christine, ed. *Debating the* Roman de la Rose: *A Critical Anthology*. New York and London: Routledge, 2007. [Reprints *Epistre au dieu d'Amours* from Fenster and Erler, eds., *Poems of Cupid* (above), 50–105.]

Pratt, Karen, trans. "From The Letter of the God of Love." In *Woman Defamed and Woman Defended: An Anthology of Medieval Texts*, edited by Alcuin

Blamires, with Karen Pratt and C. W. Marx, 279–86. Oxford: Clarendon Press; New York: Oxford University Press, 1992.

Roy, Maurice, ed. *Epistre au dieu d'Amours* and *Dit de la Rose*. In *Œuvres poétiques de Christine de Pisan* [hereafter *Œuvres poétiques*], 2:1–27 and 29–48. Paris: Firmin Didot, 1891. <https://archive.org/details/oeuvrespotique02chriuoft>.

Spence, Sarah, trans. *Epistre au dieu d'Amours. The Epistle to* [*sic*] *the God of Love*. In *The Defiant Muse: French Feminist Poems from the Middle Ages to the Present*, edited by Domna Stanton, 15–29. New York: Feminist Press, 1986.

Selected Works by Christine de Pizan

Autres Balades, in *Œuvres poétiques*, 1:207–69.

Cent Ballades d'amant et de dame

Cent Ballades d'amant et de dame. Edited by Jacqueline Cerquiglini. Paris: Union générale d'éditions, 1982.

Cent Ballades d'amant et de dame. Edited and translated [into modern French] by Jacqueline Cerquiglini-Toulet. Paris: Gallimard, 2019.

Christine de Pisan's Ballades, Rondeaux, and Virelais: An Anthology. Edited by Kenneth Varty. Leicester: Leicester University Press, 1965.

"Christine de Pizan's *Epistre à la Reine* (1405)." Edited by Angus J. Kennedy. *Revue des langues romanes* 92 (1988): 253–64.

Christine de Pizan's Epistre de la prison de vie humaine. Edited by Angus J. Kennedy. Glasgow: Dr A. J. Kennedy, 1984.

Le Débat sur le *Roman de la Rose*

Le Débat sur le Roman de la Rose. Edited by Eric Hicks. Paris: Honoré Champion, 1977; rpt. Geneva: Slatkine, 1996.

Le Débat sur le Roman de la Rose. Translated by Virginie Greene. Paris: Honoré Champion, 2006.

Debate of the "Romance of the Rose." Edited and translated by David F. Hult. Chicago and London: University of Chicago Press, 2010.

"The Epistles on the Romance of the Rose and Other Documents in the Debate." Edited by Charles Frederick Ward. PhD diss., University of Chicago, 1911.

Le Livre des Epistres du debat sus le Rommant de la Rose. Edited by Andrea Valentini. Paris: Classiques Garnier, 2014; rpt. 2016.

La Querelle de la Rose: Letters and Documents. Translated by Joseph L. Baird and John R. Kane. Chapel Hill: University of North Carolina Department of Romance Languages, 1978.

Le Dit de la pastoure. In *Œuvres poétiques*, 2:223–94.

Ditié de Jehanne d'Arc

Ditié de Jehanne d'Arc: Christine de Pisan. Edited and translated by Angus Kennedy and Kenneth Varty. Oxford: Society for the Study of

Mediæval Languages and Literature; *Medium Ævum* monographs, n.s., 9, 1977.

Ditié de Jehanne d'Arc. Translated by Margaret Switten. In *Voix de femmes au Moyen Age: Savoir, mystique, poésie, amour, sorcellerie, XIIe–XVe siècle* [hereafter *Voix de femmes*], edited by Danielle Régnier-Bohler, 699–723. Paris: Robert Laffont, 2006.

Les Enseignemens moraulx. In *Œuvres poétiques*, 3:27–44.

L'Epistre Othea

Epistre Othea. Edited by Gabriella Parussa. Geneva: Droz, 1999; rpt. 2008.

Christine de Pizan's Letter of Othea to Hector. Translated by Jane Chance. Newburyport, MA: Focus Information Group, 1997.

Othea's Letter to Hector. Edited and translated by Renate Blumenfeld-Kosinski and Earl Jeffrey Richards. Toronto: Iter Press; Tempe: Arizona Center for Medieval and Renaissance Studies, 2017.

[*Fais d'armes et de chevalerie*] *L'Arbre des batailles et fleur de chevalerie.* Paris: Philippe Le Noir, 1527. *The Book of Fayttes of Armes and of Chyualrye,* trans. and printed by William Caxton [in 1489] from the French original by Christine de Pisan. London: Published for the Early English Text Society by Humphrey Milford, Oxford University Press, 1932; reissued with corrections, 1937.

Les Heures de contemplacion sur la Passion de Nostre Seigneur Jhesucrist. Edited by Liliane Dulac and René Stuip, with Earl Jeffrey Richards. Paris: Honoré Champion, 2017.

Le Livre de la Cité des dames

The Book of the City of Ladies. Translated by Earl Jeffrey Richards. Rev. ed. New York: Persea, 1998.

The Book of the City of Ladies and Other Writings. Edited with an introduction by Sophie Bourgault and Rebecca Kingston. Translated by Ineke Hardy. Indianapolis and Cambridge: Hackett, 2018.

La Cité des dames. Translated by Thérèse Moreau and Eric Hicks. Paris: Stock, 1986.

La Città delle dame. Edited by Earl Jeffrey Richards. Translated [into Italian] by Patrizia Caraffi. 2nd ed. Milan: Luni, 1998.

The City of Ladies. Translated by Rosalind Brown-Grant. New York: Penguin, 1999.

"The Livre de la Cité des dames of Christine de Pisan: A Critical Edition." Edited by Maureen Cheney Curnow. PhD diss.,Vanderbilt University, 1975.

"*Livre de la Cité des dames*: Kritische Text-edition auf Grund der sieben überlieferten 'manuscrits originaux' des Textes." Edited by Monika Lange. Diss., University of Hamburg, 1974.

Le Livre de la Mutacion de Fortune

Le Livre de la Mutacion de Fortune. Edited by Suzanne Solente. 4 vols. Paris: Picard, 1959–66.

The Book of the Mutability of Fortune. Translated (with summaries of untranslated passages) by Geri L. Smith. Toronto: Iter Press; Tempe: Arizona Center for Medieval and Renaissance Studies, 2017.

Le Livre de Paix

The Book of Peace by Christine de Pizan. Edited and translated by Karen Green, Constant J. Mews, Janice Pinder, and Tania van Hemelryck, with the assistance of Alan Crosier. University Park: Pennsylvania State University Press, 2008.

The "Livre de la Paix" of Christine de Pisan: A Critical Edition with Introduction and Notes. Edited by Charity Cannon Willard. The Hague: Mouton, 1958.

Le Livre des Fais et bonnes meurs du sage roy Charles V

Le Livre des Fais et bonnes mœurs du sage roy Charles V. Edited by Suzanne Solente. 2 vols. Paris: Honoré Champion, 1936–40.

Le Livre des Faits et bonnes mœurs du sage roi Charles V. Translated by Joël Blanchard and Michel Quereuil. Paris: Pocket, 2013.

Le Livre des Faits et bonnes mœurs du roi Charles V le Sage. Translated by Eric Hicks and Thérèse Moreau. Paris: Stock, 1997.

Le Livre des Trois Vertus

Le Livre des Trois Vertus a l'enseignement des dames. Edited by Charity Cannon Willard and Eric Hicks. Paris: Honoré Champion, 1989.

Le Livre des Trois Vertus. Translated by Liliane Dulac. In *Voix de femmes*, 543–698.

A Medieval Woman's Mirror of Honor: The Treasury of the City of Ladies. Translated by Charity Cannon Willard. Edited by Madeleine Pelner Cosman. New York: Persea, 1989.

The Treasure of the City of Ladies, or The Book of the Three Virtues. Translated by Sarah Lawson. Rev. ed. New York: Penguin, 2003.

Le Livre du Chemin de longue étude. Edited and translated [into Modern French] by Andrea Tarnowski. Paris: Librairie générale française, 2000.

Le Livre du Corps de policie

Le Livre du Corps de policie. Edited by Angus J. Kennedy. Paris: Honoré Champion, 1998.

The Book of the Body Politic. Edited and translated by Kate Langdon Forhan. Cambridge and New York: Cambridge University Press, 1994.

Le Livre du Duc des vrais amants

Le Livre du Duc des vrais amants. Edited and translated by Dominique Demartini and Didier Lechat. Paris: Honoré Champion, 2013.

The Book of the Duke of True Lovers. Translated by Thelma Fenster and Nadia Margolis. New York: Persea, 1991.

Le Livre du Duc des vrais amans. Edited by Thelma Fenster. Binghamton, NY: Center for Medieval and Early Renaissance Texts and Studies, 1995.

The Love Debate Poems of Christine de Pizan: Le Livre du Debat de deux amans, Le Livre des Trois Jugemens, Le Livre du Dit de Poissy. Edited by Barbara K. Altmann. Gainesville: University Press of Florida, 1998.

Œuvres poétiques de Christine de Pisan. Edited by Maurice Roy. 3 vols. Paris: Firmin Didot, 1886–96; rpt. New York: Johnson Reprint, 1965.

Oraison Nostre Dame. In *Œuvres poétiques*, 3:1–9.

Oroison de la vie et passion de Nostre Seigneur. In *Œuvres poétiques*, 3:15–26.

Quinze Joyes de Nostre Dame rimees. In *Œuvres poétiques*, 3:11–14.

Les Sept Psaumes allegorisés. Edited by Bernard Ribémont and Christine Reno. Paris: Honoré Champion, 2017.

La Vision de Christine

Le Livre de l'Advision Cristine. Edited by Christine Reno and Liliane Dulac. Paris: Honoré Champion, 2001.

Christine's Vision. Translated by Glenda K. McLeod. New York and London: Garland, 1993.

Lavision-Christine: Introduction and Text. Edited by Sister Mary Louis Towner. Washington, DC: Catholic University of America, 1932; rpt. New York: AMS, 1969.

La Vision de Christine. Translated by Anne Paupert. In *Voix de femmes*, 407–542.

The Vision of Christine de Pizan. Translated by Glenda McLeod and Charity Cannon Willard. Cambridge: D. S. Brewer, 2005.

Voix de femmes au Moyen Age: Savoir, mystique, poésie, amour, sorcellerie, XIIe–XVe siècle. Edited by Danielle Régnier-Bohler. Paris: Robert Laffont, 2006.

Other Primary Works Cited

Augustine. *City of God*. Translated by Marcus Dods. In *St. Augustine's* City of God *and* Christian Doctrine, vol. 2 of *Nicene and Post-Nicene Fathers*, edited by Philip Schaff, 1–511. Buffalo, NY: Christian Literature Company, 1887. Revised and edited for New Advent by Kevin Knight. <http://www.newadvent.org/fathers/1201.htm>.

———. *The Literal Meaning of Genesis*. Translated by John Hammond Taylor. 2 vols. New York and Ramsey, NJ: Newman Press, 1982.

[Boucicaut.] Jean II le Maingre, dit Boucicaut. *The Chivalric Biography of Boucicaut, Jean II Le Meingre*. Translated by Craig Taylor and Jane H. M. Taylor. Woodbridge: Boydell and Brewer, 2016.

———. *Le Livre des Fais du bon messire Jehan le Maingre, dit Bouciquaut, Mareschal de France et gouverneur de Jennes.* Edited by Denis Lalande. Geneva: Droz, 1985.

Charles d'Orléans. *Poésies.* Edited by Pierre Champion. 2 vols. Paris: Honoré Champion, 1966–1971.

Chaucer, Geoffrey. "The Wife of Bath's Prologue and Tale." In *The Riverside Chaucer*, edited by Larry D. Benson, 105–22. Boston: Houghton Mifflin, 2008.

Chrétien de Troyes. *Cligès.* Edited by Charles Méla, Olivier Collet, and Marie-Claire Gérard-Zai. Paris: Librairie générale française, 1994.

Cicero. *De natura deorum.* Edited and translated by Harris Rackham. London: William Heinemann, 1933.

Guillaume de Lorris and Jean de Meun. *Le Roman de la Rose.* Edited by Félix Lecoy. 3 vols. Paris: Honoré Champion, 1965–70.

———. *The Romance of the Rose.* Translated by Frances Horgan. Oxford: Oxford University Press, 1994.

Hoccleve, Thomas. *The Letter of Cupid.* See Fenster and Erler, eds., *Poems of Cupid* [cited above].

Jacques Legrand. *Archiloge Sophie. Livre de bonnes meurs.* Edited by Evencio Beltran. Geneva: Slatkine; Paris: Honoré Champion, 1986.

Jean Gerson. "Ioannis Gersonii, 'Carmen de viro et muliere.'" Edited by Antonius Placanica. *Studi Medievali*, 3rd ser., 31 (1990): 435–53.

———. *Jean Gerson: Early Works.* Translated by Brian Patrick McGuire. New York: Paulist Press, 1998.

———. *The Mountain of Contemplation.* In *Jean Gerson: Early Works* [cited above], 75–127.

———. *Œuvres complètes.* 10 vols. Edited by Palémon Glorieux. Paris: Desclée, 1960–73.

———. *Traité contre le Roman de la Rose.* In *Le Débat sur le Roman de la Rose*, ed. Hicks [cited above], 59–87.

———. *Treatise against the* Romance of the Rose. In *Debate of the "Romance of the Rose,"* ed. and trans. Hult [cited above], 106–30.

———. *Treatise against* The Romance of the Rose. In *Jean Gerson: Early Works* [cited above], 378–98.

Jean LeFèvre. *The Book of Gladness / Le Livre de Leesce: A 14th Century Defense of Women, in English and French.* Translated by Linda Burke. Jefferson, NC, and London: McFarland, 2013. [Reprints van Hamel's edition of *Leesce* with minor changes; see *Les Lamentations de Matheolus*, below.]

Jean le Sénéschal. *Les Cent Ballades: Poème du XIVe siècle composé par Jean le Seneschal avec la collaboration de Philippe d'Artois, comte d'Eu, de Boucicaut le jeune et de Jean de Crésecque.* Edited by Gaston Raynaud. Paris: Firmin Didot, 1905.

Marie de France. *Lais de Marie de France.* Edited by Karl Warnke. Translated [into modern French] by Laurence Harf-Lancner. Paris: Librairie générale française, 1990.

———. *The Lais of Marie de France.* Translated by Glyn Burgess and Keith Busby. 2nd ed. London: Penguin, 1999.

Matheolus [Matheus von Boulogne]. *Lamentationes Matheoluli.* Edited by Thomas Klein, with Thomas Rubel and Alfred Schmitt. Stuttgart: Anton Hiersemann, 2014.

———. *Les Lamentations de Matheolus et le Livre de Leesce de Jehan le Fèvre de Resson: Poèmes français du XIVe siècle.* Edited by A. G. van Hamel. 2 vols. Paris: Emile Bouillon, 1892–1905.

Nicole Oresme. *Livre de divinacions.* In G. W. Coopland, *Nicole Oresme and the Astrologers: A Study of His* Livre de divinacions, 50–121. Cambridge, MA: Harvard University Press, 1952.

———. *Le Livre de Ethiques d'Aristote.* Edited by Albert D. Menut. New York: Stechert, 1940.

Ovid. *Ars Amatoria* and *Remedia Amoris.* In *Ovid: The Art of Love and Other Poems.* Translated by J. H. Mozley. Revised by G. P. Goold. Cambridge, MA: Harvard University Press; London: William Heinemann, 1979.

———. *Metamorphoses.* Translated by Frank Justus Miller. Revised by G. P. Goold. Cambridge, MA: Harvard University Press, 1977.

Thomas Aquinas. *Summa Theologica.* Translated by the Fathers of the English Dominican Province. 3 vols. New York: Benziger Bros., 1947–48.

Secondary Sources

Studies of the *Epistre au dieu d'Amours* and the *Dit de la Rose*

Batt, Catherine. "The *Epistre au dieu d'amours* and *The Letter of Cupid*: Christine de Pizan, Thomas Hoccleve, and Vernacular Poetics." In *Booldly bot meekly: Essays on the Theory and Practice of Translation in the Middle Ages in Honour of Roger Ellis*, edited by Catherine Batt and René Tixier, 427–41. Turnhout: Brepols, 2018.

Ellis, Roger. "Chaucer, Christine de Pizan, and Hoccleve: *The Letter of Cupid*." In *Essays on Thomas Hoccleve*, edited by Catherine Batt, 29–54. Turnhout: Brepols, 1996.

Fenster, Thelma S. "On the *condicions* and *nature de femme* in Christine de Pizan's *Epistre au dieu d'Amours.*" In *Christine de Pizan: La scrittrice e la città / L'écrivaine et la ville / The Woman Writer and the City*: Acts of the Seventh International Conference on Christine de Pizan (Bologna, September 22–26, 2009), edited by Patrizia Caraffi, 39–49. Florence: Alinea, 2013.

———. "Strong Voices, Weak Minds? The Defenses of Eve by Isotta Nogarola and Christine de Pizan, Who Found Themselves in Simone de Beauvoir's Situation." In *Strong Voices, Weak History: Early Women Writers and Canons in England, France and Italy*, edited by Pamela Benson and Victoria Kirkham, 58–77. Philadelphia: University of Pennsylvania Press, 2005.

———. "*Simplece* et sagesse: Christine de Pizan et Isotta Nogarola sur la culpabilité d'Eve." In *Une femme de lettres au Moyen Age: Etudes autour de Christine de Pizan*, edited by Liliane Dulac and Bernard Ribémont, 481–93. Orleans: Paradigme, 1995.

———."Did Christine Have a Sense of Humor? The *Evidence of the Epistre au dieu d'Amours*." In Richards et al., *Reinterpreting Christine* [cited below], 23–36.

Kong, Katherine. "Rhetorical Teaching in the *Epistre au dieu d'Amours.*" *Dalhousie French Studies* 78 (2007): 3–15.

Kooper, Erik. "Christine de Pizan en Thomas Hoccleves *Letter to* [*sic*] *Cupid*." In *Christine de Pizan, een bijzondere vrouw*, edited by R. E. Stuip, 75–88. Hilversum: Verloren, 2004.

Massé, B. "Les Champs sémantiques de *L'Epistre au dieu d'Amours* de Christine de Pisan." *Cahiers des Utilisations de Machines à des Fins d'Information et de Documentation* (UFR, Lettres et Sciences Humaines, Nice) 10 (1976): 69–77.

McLeod, Glenda K. "A Case of Faulx Semblans: *L'Epistre au Dieu d'Amours* and *The Letter of Cupid*." In *The Reception of Christine de Pizan from the Fifteenth through the Nineteenth Centuries: Visitors to the City*, 11–24. Lewiston, NY: Edwin Mellen Press, 1991.

Van Hemelryck, Tania. "*L'Epistre au dieu d'amours* ou 'l'origine du monde' auctorial de Christine de Pizan." *Le Moyen français* 78–79 (2016): 241–54.

Waller, M.S. "Christine de Pisan's *Epistle of the God of Love* and the Medieval Image of Women." *Christianity and Literature* 27 (1978): 41–52.

Walters, Lori. "Fathers and Daughters: Christine de Pizan as Reader of the Male Tradition of *Clergie* in the *Dit de la Rose.*" In Richards et al., *Reinterpreting Christine* [cited below], 63–76.

———. "The Woman Writer and Literary History: Christine de Pizan's Redefinition of the Poetic *Translatio* in the *Epistre au dieu d'Amours.*" *French Literature Series* 16 (1989): 1–16.

Willard, Charity Cannon. "A New Look at Christine de Pizan's *Epistre au dieu d'Amours*." In Beck, Mombello, and Simone, *Seconda Miscellanea* [cited below], 73–92.

———. "Christine de Pizan and the Order of the Rose." In *Ideals for Women in the Works of Christine de Pizan*, edited by Diane Bornstein, 51–67. Detroit: Michigan Consortium for Medieval and Early Modern Studies, 1981.

Other Secondary Studies

Adams, Tracy. *The Life and Afterlife of Isabeau of Bavaria*. Baltimore: Johns Hopkins University Press, 2010.

———. "The Political Significance of Christine de Pizan's Love Poetry." *Cahiers de recherches médiévales et humanistes/Journal of Medieval and Humanistic Studies* (*CRMH*) 17 (2009): 353–71. <https://journals.openedition.org/crm/11539>.

Allen, Peter L. *The Art of Love: Amatory Fiction from Ovid to the Romance of the Rose*. Philadelphia: University of Pennsylvania Press, 1992.

Allen, Prudence. *The Concept of Woman: The Aristotelian Revolution, 750 BC–AD 1250*. Vol. 1. Montreal: Eden, 1985.

Altmann, Barbara K., and Deborah L. McGrady, eds. *Christine de Pizan: A Casebook*. New York and London: Routledge, 2003.

Andrei, Filippo. *Boccaccio the Philosopher: An Epistemology of the Decameron*. Cham, Switzerland: Palgrave Macmillan, 2017.

Arden, Heather. "Othon de Grandson and Christine de Pizan: Love's Martyrs." In Kosta-Théfaine, *Othon de Grandson* [cited below], 103–21.

Armstrong, Adrian, and Sarah Kay. "The *Roman de la Rose*." In Armstrong and Kay, *Knowing Poetry* [cited immediately below], 73–80.

———, with the participation of Rebecca Dixon, Miranda Griffin, Sylvia Huot, Francesca Nicholson, and Finn Sinclair. *Knowing Poetry: Verse in Medieval France from the Rose to the* Rhétoriqueurs. Ithaca, NY: Cornell University Press, 2011.

Astell, Ann W. *Eating Beauty: The Eucharist and the Spiritual Arts of the Middle Ages*. Ithaca, NY, and London: Cornell University Press, 2006.

Autrand, Françoise. *Christine de Pizan: Une femme en politique*. Paris: Fayard, 2009.

———. *Charles V le sage*. Paris: Fayard, 1994.

———. *Charles VI: La folie du roi*. Paris: Fayard, 1986.

Babbit, Susan M. "Oresme's '*Livre de politiques*' and the France of Charles V." *Transactions of the American Philosophical Society* 75 (1985): 1–158.

Badel, Pierre-Yves. *Le Roman de la Rose au XIVe siècle: Etude de la réception de l'œuvre*. Geneva: Droz, 1980.

Bagoly, Suzanne. "Christine de Pizan et l'art de 'dictier' ballades." *Le Moyen Age* 92 (1986): 41–67.

Baird, Joseph L., and John R. Kane. "*La Querelle de la Rose*: In Defense of the Opponents." *French Review* 48 (1974–75): 298–307.

Beck, Jonathan, Gianni Mombello, and Franco Simone, eds. *Seconda Miscellanea di Studi e Ricerche sul Quattrocento Francese*. Chambéry-Turin: Centre d'études franco-italien, 1981.

Berguerand, Claude. *Le duel d'Othon de Grandson (1397): Mort d'un chevalier-poète vaudois à la fin du Moyen Age*. Lausanne: Université de Lausanne, Section d'histoire, Faculté des Lettres, 2008.

Blamires, Alcuin. "Individuality." In The *Oxford Handbook of Medieval Literature in English*, edited by Elaine Treharne and Greg Walker, with the assistance of William Green, 478–95. Oxford, UK; New York: Oxford University Press, 2010.

———. *The Case for Women in Medieval Culture*. Oxford: Clarendon Press; New York: Oxford University Press, 1997.

———, with Karen Pratt and C. W. Marx. *Woman Defamed and Woman Defended: An Anthology of Medieval Texts*. Oxford: Clarendon Press; New York: Oxford University Press, 1992.

Blumenfeld-Kosinski, Renate. "Jean Gerson and the Debate on the *Romance of the Rose*." In *A Companion to Jean Gerson*, edited by Brian Patrick McGuire, 317–56. Leiden and Boston: Brill, 2006.

Børresen, Kari Elisabeth. "God's Image, Man's Image? Patristic Interpretation of Gen. 1:27 and I Cor. 11:7," and "God's Image: Is Woman Excluded? Medieval Interpretation of Gen. 1:27 and I Cor. 11:7." In *Image of God and Gender Models*, edited by Kari Elisabeth Børresen, 188–207 and 208–27. Oslo: Solum Vorlag, 1991.

———. *Subordination and Equivalence: The Nature and Role of Women in Augustine and Thomas Aquinas*. Translated by Charles H. Talbot. Washington, DC: University Press of America, 1981.

Boulton, Maureen Barry McCann. *The Song in the Story: Lyric Insertions in French Narrative Fiction, 1200–1400*. Philadelphia: University of Pennsylvania Press, 1993.

Bozzolo, Carla, and Hélène Loyau. *La Cour amoureuse, dite de Charles VI*. 3 vols. Paris: Le Léopard d'Or, 1982–92.

Brock, Stephen L. "Natural Inclination and the Intelligibility of the Good in Thomistic Natural Law." *Vera Lex*, n.s. 6 (2005): 57–78.

Brown-Grant, Rosalind. *Christine de Pizan and the Moral Defence of Women: Reading Beyond Gender*. Cambridge: Cambridge University Press, 1999.

———. "Christine de Pizan as a Defender of Women." In Altmann and McGrady, *A Casebook* [cited above], 81–100.

Brownlee, Kevin. "Discourses of the Self: Christine de Pizan and the *Romance of the Rose*." *Romanic Review* 79 (1988): 199–221.

———, and Sylvia Huot, eds. *Rethinking the Romance of the Rose: Text, Image, Reception*. Philadelphia: University of Pennsylvania Press, 1992.

Brucker, Charles, ed. *Traduction et adaptation en France à la fin du Moyen Age et à la Renaissance*. Actes du colloque organisé par l'Université de Nancy II (23–25 mars 1995). Paris: Honoré Champion, 1997.

Bruins, Jan G. *Observations sur la langue d'Eustache Deschamps et de Christine de Pisan*. Dordrecht: De Dordrechtsche drukkerij en uitgevers maatschappij, 1925.

Cadden, Joan. "Charles V, Nicole Oresme, and Christine de Pizan: Unities and Uses of Knowledge in Fourteenth-Century France." In *Texts and Contexts in Ancient and Medieval Science: Studies on the Occasion of John E. Murdoch's Seventieth Birthday*, edited by Edith Sylla and Michael R. McVaugh, 208–44. Leiden, New York, and Cologne: Brill, 1997.

———. *Meanings of Sex Difference in the Middle Ages: Medicine, Science, and Culture*. Cambridge and New York: Cambridge University Press, 1993.

Campbell, John, and Nadia Margolis, eds. *Christine de Pizan 2000: Studies on Christine de Pizan in Honour of Angus J. Kennedy*. Amsterdam and Atlanta, GA: Rodopi, 2000.

Casagrande, Carla, and Silvana Vecchio. *Les péchés de la langue: Discipline et éthique de la parole dans la culture médiévale* [translation of *I peccati della lingua: Disciplina ed etica della parola nella cultura medievale* (Rome: Istituto della Enciclopedia Italiana, 1987)]. Translated by Philippe Baillet. Paris: Cerf, 1991.

Cayley, Emma. *Debate and Dialogue: Alain Chartier in His Cultural Context*. Oxford: Clarendon Press; New York: Oxford University Press, 2006.

Cerquiglini, Jacqueline. "Le dit." In Poirion, *Grundriss der romanischen Literaturen des Mittelalters* [cited below], 86–94.

———. "Le rondeau." In Poirion, *Grundriss der romanischen Literaturen des Mittelalters* [cited below], 45–58.

Cerquiglini-Toulet, Jacqueline. "Christine de Pizan et le pouvoir du nom." *Le Moyen français* 75 (2014): 3–18.

———. "Introduction. L'Amour de Sophie: Poésie et savoir du *Roman de la Rose* à Christine de Pizan." In Dixon and Sinclair, *Poetry, Knowledge, and Community* [cited below], 1–15.

Chance, Jane, ed. *Gender and Text in the Later Middle Ages*. Gainesville: University Press of Florida, 1996.

Chaubet, Daniel. "Le duel Othon de Grandson – Gérard d'Estavayer du 7 août 1397: Une conséquence des événements qui agitèrent la Savoie dans les dernières années du XIVe siècle." In Kosta-Théfaine, *Othon de Grandson* [cited below], 11–42.

Clark, James G., Frank T. Coulson, and Kathryn L. McKinley, eds. *Ovid in the Middle Ages*. Cambridge and New York: Cambridge University Press, 2011.

Collett, Barry. "The Three Mirrors of Christine de Pizan." In Green and Mews, *Healing the Body Politic* [cited below], 1–18.

Collette, Carolyn P. *Performing Polity: Women and Agency in the Anglo-French Tradition, 1385–1620*. Turnhout: Brepols, 2006.

Combes, André. *Jean de Montreuil et le chancelier Gerson: Contribution à l'histoire des rapports de l'humanisme et de la théologie en France au début du XVe siècle.* Paris: J. Vrin, 1942.

Curnow, Maureen C. "'La Pioche d'Inquisicion': Legal-Judicial Content and Style in Christine de Pizan's *Livre de la Cité des Dames*." In Richards et al., *Reinterpreting Christine* [cited below], 157–72.

Davies, Brian, and Eleonore Stump, eds. *The Oxford Handbook of Aquinas*. Oxford and New York: Oxford University Press, 2012.

Davies, Peter V. "La rime chez Christine de Pizan: Quelques cas particuliers." In Hicks et al., *Au champ des escriptures* [cited below], 819–32.

———. "Si bas suis qu'a peine / Releveray: Christine de Pizan's Use of Enjambement." In Campbell and Margolis, *Christine de Pizan 2000* [cited above], 77–90.

D'Alverny Marie-Thérèse. "Comment les théologiens et les philosophes voient la femme." *Cahiers de Civilisation Médiévale: X^e^–XIIe Siècles* 20 (1977): 105–29.

Delany, Sheila. *Medieval Literary Politics: Shapes of Ideology*. Manchester and New York: Manchester University Press, 1990.

———. "'Mothers to Think Back Through': Who Are They? The Ambiguous Example of Christine de Pizan." In *Medieval Texts and Contemporary Readers*, edited by Laurie A. Finke and Martin B. Schichtman, 177–97. Ithaca, NY: Cornell University Press, 1987; rpt. in Delany, *Medieval Literary Politics* [cited above], 88–103.

———. "Rewriting Woman Good: Gender and the Anxiety of Influence in Two Medieval Texts." In *Chaucer in the Eighties,* edited by Julian N. Wasserman and Robert J. Blanch, 75–92. Syracuse, NY: Syracuse University Press, 1986; rpt. in Delany, *Medieval Literary Politics* [cited above], 74–87.

Delisle, Léopold. *Le Cabinet des manuscrits de la Bibliothèque impériale/nationale.* 4 vols. Paris: Imprimerie Impériale/Nationale, 1868–81.

———. *Recherches sur la librairie de Charles V, roi de France, 1337–1380.* Paris: Honoré Champion, 1907.

———, ed. *Mandements et actes divers de Charles V (1364–1380).* Paris: Imprimerie Nationale, 1874.

Delsaux, Olivier, Gilbert Ouy, Christine Reno, and Inès Villela-Petit. "Le premier recueil de la reine." *Médiévales* 53 (2012): 46–55.

Desmond, Marilynn. "Christine de Pizan." In Gaunt and Kay, *Medieval French Literature* [cited below], 123–36.

———. "Christine de Pizan's Feminist Self-Fashioning." In *Reading Dido: Gender, Textuality, and the Medieval Æneid*, 195–224. Minneapolis: University of Minnesota Press, 1994.

———. "The *Querelle de la Rose* and the Ethics of Reading." In Altmann and McGrady, *A Casebook* [cited above], 167–80.

———, ed. *Christine de Pizan and the Categories of Difference.* Minneapolis: University of Minnesota Press, 1998.

———, and Pamela Sheingorn. *Myth, Montage, and Visuality in Late Medieval Manuscript Culture: Christine de Pizan's Epistre Othea.* Ann Arbor: University of Michigan Press, 2003.

Dinshaw, Carolyn, and David Wallace, eds. *The Cambridge Companion to Medieval Women's Writing.* Cambridge: Cambridge University Press, 2003.

Dixon, Rebecca, and Finn E. Sinclair, eds. *Poetry, Knowledge and Community in Late Medieval France.* Cambridge: Boydell and Brewer, 2008.

Ducos, Joëlle. "Néologie lexicale et culture savante: Transmettre les savoirs." In *Lexiques scientifiques et techniques: Constitution et approche historique*, edited by Olivier Bertrand, Hiltrud Gerner, and Béatrice Stumpf, 249–54. Palaiseau: Editions de l'Ecole Polytechnique, 2007.

———. "Goût des sciences et écriture du savoir à la cour de Charles V." In *Le goût du lecteur à la fin du Moyen Age*, edited by Danielle Bohler, 225–43. Paris: Le Léopard d'Or, 2006.

Dudash, Susan J. "Christine de Pizan and the 'menu peuple.'" *Speculum* 78 (2003): 788–831.

———. "Christinian Politics, the Tavern, and Urban Revolt in Late Medieval France." In Green and Mews, *Healing the Body Politic* [cited below], 35–59.

Dulac, Liliane, and Christine Reno. "Rhétorique, critique et politique dans *Le Livre de Prudence* de Christine de Pizan: quelques aperçus." In *La Vertu de prudence entre Moyen Age et l'âge classique*, edited by Evelyne Berriot-Salvadore, Catherine Pascal, François Roudaut and Trung Tran, 193–22. Paris: Classiques Garnier, 2012.

———."L'humanisme vers 1400. Essai d'exploration à partir d'un cas marginal: Christine de Pizan, lectrice de Thomas d'Aquin." In *Pratiques de la culture écrite en France au XVe siècle.* Actes du colloque du CNRS (Paris, 16–18 mai 1992), organisé en l'honneur de Gilbert Ouy, edited by Monique Ornato and Nicole Pons, 161–78. Turnhout: Brepols, 1995.

———, and Christine Reno. "Traduction et adaptation dans *L'Advision-Cristine* de Christine de Pizan." In Brucker, *Traduction et adaptation* [cited above], 121–31.

———, and Bernard Ribémont, eds. *Une femme de lettres au Moyen Age: Etudes autour de Christine de Pizan.* Orleans: Paradigme, 1995.

———, Anne Paupert, Christine Reno and Bernard Ribémont, eds. *"Desireuse de plus avant enquerre."* Actes du VIe colloque international sur Christine de Pizan (Paris, 20–24 juillet 2006), en hommage à James Laidlaw. Paris: Honoré Champion, 2008.

Economou, George. *The Goddess Natura in Medieval Literature.* Cambridge, MA: Harvard University Press, 1972; rpt. Notre Dame, IN: Notre Dame University Press, 2002.

Enders, Jody. "The Feminist Mnemonics of Christine de Pizan." *Modern Language Quarterly* 55 (1994): 231–49.

Famiglietti, R. C. *Royal Intrigue: Crisis at the Court of Charles VI, 1392–1420.* New York: AMS Press, 1986.

Farquhar, James Douglas, and Eric C. Hicks, "Christine de Pizan's *Dit de la Pastoure*: Membra disjecta." *Scriptorium* 30 (1976): 192–200.

Fenster, Thelma, and Daniel Lord Smail, eds. *Fama: The Politics of Talk and Reputation in Medieval Europe*. Ithaca, NY: Cornell University Press, 2003.

Field, Sean L. "A New English Translation of Jean Gerson's Authentic Tract on Joan of Arc: *About the Feat of the Maid, and the Faith that Should be Placed in Her.*" *Magistra* 18 (2012): 36–54.

Fin du Moyen Age et Renaissance: Mélanges de philologie française offerts à Robert Guiette. Antwerp: Nederlandsche Boekhandel, 1961.

Fleming, John V. *The* Roman de la Rose: *A Study in Allegory and Iconography.* Princeton, NJ: Princeton University Press, 1969.

———. "The Moral Reputation of the *Roman de la Rose* before 1400." *Romance Philology* 18 (1965): 430–35.

Forhan, Kate Langdon. *The Political Theory of Christine de Pizan*. Aldershot, UK, and Burlington, VT: Ashgate, 2002.

———. "Reading Backward: Aristotelianism in the Political Thought of Christine de Pizan." In Hicks et al., *Au champ des escriptures* [cited below], 359–81.

Fox, John. *The Lyric Poetry of Charles d'Orléans*. Oxford: Clarendon Press, 1969.

Furr, Grover C. "The Quarrel of the *Roman de la Rose* and Fourteenth-Century Humanism." PhD diss., Princeton University, 1979.

Fuss, Diana. *Essentially Speaking: Feminism, Nature and Difference*. New York and London: Routledge, 1989.

Gaunt, Simon, and Sarah Kay, eds. T*he Cambridge Companion to Medieval French Literature*. Cambridge: Cambridge University Press, 2008.

Gay, Lucy M. "On the Language of Christine de Pisan." *Modern Philology* 6 (1908–9): 70–96.

Ghisalberti, Fausto. "Mediæval Biographies of Ovid." *Journal of the Warburg and Courtauld Institutes* 9 (1946): 10–59.

Gibbons [Landor], Mary Weitzel. "The Bath of the Muses and Visual Allegory in the *Chemin de long estude*." In Desmond, *Categories of Difference* [cited above], 128–45.

Green, Karen. "On Translating Christine de Pizan as a Philosopher." In Green and Mews, *Healing the Body Politic* [cited below], 117–37.

———, and Constant J. Mews, eds. *Healing the Body Politic: The Political Thought of Christine de Pizan*. Turnhout: Brepols, 2005.

Greene, Virginie. "Le débat sur le *Roman de la Rose* comme document d'histoire littéraire et morale." *Cahiers de recherches médiévales et humanistes/Journal of Medieval and Humanistic Studies* (*CRMH*), 14 Spécial (2007): 297–311. <https://journals.openedition.org/crm/2586?file=1>.

Guenée, Bernard. *Un Meurtre, une société: l'Assassinat du duc d'Orléans, 23 novembre 1407*. Paris: Gallimard, 1992.

———. *L'Opinion publique à la fin du Moyen Age d'après la chronique de Charles VI du Religieux de St. Denis*. Paris: Perrin, 2002.

Guynn, Noah D. "Authorship and Sexual/Allegorical Violence in Jean de Meun's *Roman de la Rose*." In *Allegory and Sexual Ethics in the High Middle Ages*, 137–70. New York: Palgrave Macmillan, 2007.

———. "*Le Roman de la Rose*." In Gaunt and Kay, *Medieval French Literature* [cited above], 48–62.

Hans-Collas, Ilona, and Pascal Schandel, with Hanno Wisjman. *Manuscrits enluminés des anciens Pays-Bas méridionaux*. Vol. 1: *Manuscrits de Louis de Bruges*. Paris: Bibliothèque nationale de France, 2009.

Heck, Christian. "De la mystique à la raison: La spéculation et le chemin du ciel dans le *Livre du Chemin de long estude*." In Hicks et al., *Au champ des escriptures* [cited below], 709–22.

Hexter, Ralph J. *Ovid and Medieval Schooling: Studies in Medieval School Commentaries on Ovid's* Ars Amatoria, Epistulæ ex Ponto, *and* Epistulæ Heroidum. Munich: Arbeo Gesellschaft, 1986.

Hicks, Eric. "De l'histoire littéraire comme cosmogonie: La Querelle du *Roman de la Rose*." *Critique* 32 (1976): 510–19.

———. "The 'Querelle de la Rose' in the *Roman de la Rose*." *Les Bonnes Feuilles* 3 (1974): 152–69.

———. "Sous les pavés, le sens: Le dire et le décorum allégoriques dans *Le Roman de la Rose* de Jean de Meun." *Etudes de Lettres* 2–3 (1987): 113–32.

———, ed., with Diego Gonzalez and Philippe Simon. *Au champ des escriptures*. Actes du IIIe colloque international sur Christine de Pizan (Lausanne, 18–22 juillet 1998). Paris: Honoré Champion, 2000.

———, and Ezio Ornato. "Jean de Montreuil et le débat sur le *Roman de la Rose*." *Romania* 98 (1977): 34–64, 186–219.

Hill, Jillian M. L. *The Medieval Debate on Jean de Meung's Roman de la Rose: Morality versus Art*. Lewiston, NY, Queenston, ON, and Lampeter, Wales: Edwin Mellen Press, 1991.

Hindman, Sandra. "The Composition of the Manuscript of Christine de Pizan's Collected Works in the British Library: A Reassessment." *British Library Journal* 9 (1983): 93–123.

———. "With Ink and Mortar: Christine de Pizan's 'Cité des Dames.'" *Feminist Studies* 10 (1984): 457–83.

———, and Stephen Perkinson. "Insurgent Voices: Illustrated Versions of Christine de Pizan's *Le Livre du duc des vrais amans*." In Zimmerman and De Rentiis, *City of Scholars* [cited below], 221–31.

Hult, David. "Poetry and the Translation of Knowledge in Jean de Meun." In Dixon and Sinclair, *Poetry, Knowledge and Community* [cited above], 187–201.

———. "The *Roman de la Rose*, Christine de Pizan, and the Querelle des Femmes." In Dinshaw and Wallace, *Medieval Women's Writing* [cited above], 184–94.

Huot, Sylvia. "Confronting Misogyny: Christine de Pizan and the *Roman de la Rose*." In *Translatio studii: Essays by his Students in Honor of Karl D. Uitti for his Sixty-fifth Birthday*, edited by Renate Blumenfeld-Kosinski, Kevin Brownlee, Mary B. Speer, and Lori J. Walters, 169–87. Amsterdam: Rodopi, 2000.

———. *Dreams of Lovers and Lies of Poets: Poetry, Knowledge, and Desire in the* Roman de la Rose. London: Legenda, 2010.

———. *The* Romance of the Rose *and its Medieval Readers: Interpretation, Reception, Manuscript Transmission.* Cambridge and New York: Cambridge University Press, 1993.

———. "Seduction and Sublimation: Christine de Pizan, Jean de Meun, and Dante." *Romance Notes* 25 (1985): 361–73.

Kay, Sarah. *The Romance of the Rose.* London: Grant and Cutler, 1995.

Kelly, Douglas. *Christine de Pizan's Changing Opinion: A Quest for Certainty in the Midst of Chaos.* Cambridge: D. S. Brewer, 2007.

Kennedy, Angus J., ed., with Rosalind Brown-Grant, James C. Laidlaw, and Catherine M. Müller. *Contexts and Continuities*: Proceedings of the IVth International Colloquium on Christine de Pizan (Glasgow, July 21–27, 2000). Published in honour of Liliane Dulac. 3 vols. Glasgow: University of Glasgow Press, 2002.

Kent, Bonnie. "Virtue Theory." In *The Cambridge History of Medieval Philosophy*, edited by Robert Pasnau and Christina van Dyke, 1:493–505. Cambridge: Cambridge University Press, 2010.

King, Margaret L. *Women of the Renaissance.* Chicago: University of Chicago Press, 1991.

Kobayashi, Noriko. "La dernière étape de l'enluminure des oeuvres de Christine de Pizan." *Art de l'enluminure* 18 (Sept.–Nov. 2006): 2–65.

Kosta-Théfaine, Jean-François, ed. *Othon de Grandson: Chevalier et poète.* Orleans: Paradigme, 2007.

Krueger, Roberta L. *Women Readers and the Ideology of Gender in Old French Verse Romance.* Cambridge and New York: Cambridge University Press, 1993.

Laidlaw, James C. "Christine and the Manuscript Tradition." In Altmann and McGrady, *A Casebook* [cited above], 231–49.

———. "Christine de Pizan: An Author's Progress." *Modern Language Review* 78 (1983): 532–50.

———. "Christine de Pizan: A Publisher's Progress." *Modern Language Review* 82 (1987): 35–75.

———. "Christine de Pizan: The Making of the Queen's Manuscript (London, British Library, Harley 4431)." In *Patrons, Authors and Workshops: Books and Book Production in Paris around 1400*, edited by Godfried Croenen and Peter Ainsworth, 297–310. Louvain, Paris, and Dudley, MA: Peeters, 2006.

———. "Christine de Pizan, the Earl of Salisbury and Henry IV." *French Studies* 36 (1982): 129–43.

———. "Christine's Lays: Does Practice Make Perfect?" In Kennedy et al., *Contexts and Continuities* [cited above], 2:467–81.

———. "The Date of the Queen's MS (London, British Library, Harley MS 4431)." Edinburgh: Edinburgh University Library, 2005. <http://www.pizan.lib.ed.ac.uk/harley4431date.pdf>.

Laird, Edgar. "Astrology in the Court of Charles V of France, as Reflected in Oxford, St. John's College MS 164." *Manuscripta* 34 (1990): 167–76.

———. "Christine de Pizan and the Controversy Concerning Star-Study in the Court of Charles V." *Allegorica* 18 (1997): 21–30.

Laird, Judith. "Good Women and *bonnes dames*: Virtuous Females in Chaucer and Christine de Pizan." *Chaucer Review* 30 (1995): 58–70.

Langlois, Charles V. "Les Lamentations de Mathieu." In *La Vie en France au Moyen Age*, 2:241–90. Paris: Hachette, 1925.

Lechat, Didier. "Discorde ou concorde des langages masculins et féminins dans *Le Livre du duc des vrais amans* de Christine de Pizan?" In *La discorde des deux langages: Représentations des discours masculins et féminins du Moyen Age à l'Age classique*, edited by Chantal Liaroutzos and Anne Paupert, 53–71. Paris: Université Paris 7-Denis Diderot, 2006.

Lecoy, Félix. "Pain bourgeois. Pain faitiz. Pain de retrait." In *Mélanges de philologie offerts à Alf Lombard à l'occasion de son soixante-cinquième anniversaire par ses collègues et ses amis* [no ed.], 101–7. Lund: C. W. K. Gleerup, 1969.

Lefèvre, Sylvie. "Christine de Pizan et l'Aristote oresmien." In Hicks et al., *Au champ des escriptures* [cited above], 231–50.

Léonard, Monique. "Le dit de la femme." In *Ecrire pour dire: Etudes sur le dit médiéval*, edited by Bernard Ribémont, 29–47. Paris: Klincksieck, 1990.

Lote, Georges. *Histoire du vers français.* 3 vols. Paris: Boivin, 1949–55.

Lugt, Maaike van der. "L'autorité morale et normative de la nature au Moyen Age." In *La nature comme source de la morale au Moyen Age*, edited by Maaike van der Lugt, 3–40. Florence: SISMEL, Edizioni del Galluzzo, 2014.

Luscombe, D. E. "Natural Morality and Natural Law." In *The Cambridge History of Later Medieval Philosophy*, edited by Norman Kretzmann, Anthony Kenny, and Jan Pinborg, 705–19. Cambridge: Cambridge University Press, 1982.

Lusignan, Serge. "Le Latin était la langue maternelle des Romains: La fortune d'un argument à la fin du Moyen Age." In *Préludes à la Renaissance:Aspects de la vie intellectuelle en France au XVe siècle*, edited by Carla Bozzolo and Ezio Ornato, 265–82. Paris: CNRS, 1992.

———. "Nicole Oresme, traducteur, et la pensée de la langue française savante." In *Nicolas Oresme: Tradition et innovation chez un intellectuel du XIVe siècle*, edited by Pierre Souffrin and Alain-Philippe Segonds, 93–104. Paris: Les Belles Lettres, 1988.

———. *Parler vulgairement: Les intellectuels et la langue française aux XIIIe et XIVe siècles.* Paris: J. Vrin; Montreal: Presses de l'Université de Montréal, 1987.

———. "La topique de la *translatio studii* et les traductions françaises de textes savants au XIVe siècle." In *Traduction et traducteurs au Moyen Age*: Actes du colloque international du CNRS (Paris, Institut de recherche et d'histoire des textes, 26–28 mai 1986), edited by Geneviève Contamine, 303–15. Paris: CNRS, 1989.

———. "*Translatio studii* and the Emergence of French as a Language of Letters in the Middle Ages." *New Medieval Literatures* 14 (2012): 1–19.

Marchello-Nizia, Christiane. *Histoire de la langue française aux XIVe et XVe siècles.* Paris: Bordas, 1979.

———. *La langue française aux XIVe et XVe siècles.* 2nd ed. Paris: Armand Colin, 2005.

Margolis, Nadia. "Christine de Pizan, mangeuse de savoir." In *L'Offrande du cœur: Medieval and Early Modern Studies in Honour of Glynnis Cropp*, edited by Margaret Burrell and Judith Grant, 45–60. Christchurch, NZ: Canterbury University Press with Massey University, 2004.

———. "Elegant Closures: The Use of the Diminutive in Christine de Pizan and Jean de Meun." In Richards et al., *Reinterpreting Christine* [cited below], 111–23.

———. *An Introduction to Christine de Pizan.* Gainesville: University Press of Florida, 2011.

———. "Les terminaisons dangereuses: Lyrisme, féminisme et humanisme néologiques chez Christine de Pizan." *Le Moyen français* 39–41 (1996–97): 381–404.

Martin, Robert, and Marc Wilmet, *Manuel du français du moyen âge,* 2 vols., Vol. 2: *Syntaxe du moyen français.* Bordeaux: Société bordelaise de diffusion des travaux de lettres et sciences humaines, 1980.

McCabe, Herbert. *On Aquinas.* Edited by Brian Davies. London and New York: Continuum, 2008.

McGrady, Deborah. "What is a Patron? Benefactors and Authorship in Harley 4431, Christine de Pizan's Collected Works." In Desmond, *Categories of Difference* [cited above], 195–214.

McLeod, Glenda. "Poetics and Antimisogynist Polemics in Christine de Pizan's *Le Livre de la Cité des Dames.*" In Richards et al., *Reinterpreting Christine* [cited below], 37–47.

McWebb, Christine, and Lori J. Walters. "Introduction: The *Roman de la Rose* and Christine de Pizan in the Digital Age." *Digital Philology: A Journal of Medieval Cultures* 6 (2017): 1–14.

Meiss, Millard. *French Painting in the Time of Jean de Berry: The Late Fourteenth Century and the Patronage of the Duke*. 2 vols. London and New York: Phaidon, 1967.

———, with Sharon Off Dunlap Smith and Elizabeth Home Beatson. *French Painting in the Time of Jean de Berry: The Limbourgs and their Contemporaries*. 2 vols. New York: Pierpont Morgan Library / George Braziller, 1974.

Meyer, Paul. "Notice d'un recueil manuscrit de poésies françaises du XIIIe au XVe siècle, appartenant à Westminster Abbey." *Bulletin de la Société des Anciens Textes Français* 1 (1875): 25–36.

Minnis, Alastair J. *Magister Amoris: The* Roman de la Rose *and Vernacular Hermeneutics*. Oxford and New York: Oxford University Press, 2001.

———. *Medieval Theory of Authorship: Scholastic Literary Attitudes in the Later Middle Ages*. 2nd ed. Philadelphia: University of Pennsylvania Press, 1988.

Mölk, Ulrich. *Le Roman de la Rose: über den Rosenroman*. Steinfurth: Rosenmuseum, 1993.

Mombello, Gianni. *La Tradizione manoscritta dell' "Epistre Othea" di Christine de Pizan: Prolegomeni all'edizione del testo*. Turin: Academia delle Scienze, 1967.

Monagle, Clare. *The Scholastic Project*. Kalamazoo and Bradford: Arc Humanities Press, 2017.

Morse, Ruth. *The Medieval Medea*. Cambridge: D.S. Brewer, 1996.

Morton, Jonathan. "Etat présent: *Le Roman de la Rose*." *French Studies* 69 (2015): 79–86.

Mühlethaler, Jean-Claude. "Désir et étonnement: de l'auteur au lecteur. Emotion, écriture et lecture au temps de Christine de Pizan." *Le Moyen français* 75 (2014): 19–42.

———, and Denis Billotte, eds., with Alain Corbellari, Marie-Thérèse Bonadonna, and Barbara Wahlen. *"Riens ne m'est seur que la chose incertaine": Etudes sur l'art d'écrire au Moyen Âge offertes à Eric Hicks par ses élèves, collègues, amies et amis*. Geneva: Slatkine, 2001.

Newman, Barbara. *From Virile Woman to WomanChrist: Studies in Medieval Religion and Literature*. Philadelphia: University of Pennsylvania Press, 1995.

———. *Sister of Wisdom: St. Hildegard's Theology of the Feminine*. Berkeley and Los Angeles: University of California Press, 1987.

Noakes, Susan. "From Boccaccio to Christine de Pizan." In *Timely Reading: Between Exegesis and Interpretation*, 98–134. Ithaca, NY, and London: Cornell University Press, 1988.

Nouvet, Claire. "Writing (in) Fear." In Chance, *Gender and Text* [cited above], 279–305.

Ornato, Ezio. *Jean Muret et ses amis Nicolas de Clamanges et Jean de Montreuil: Contribution à l'étude des rapports entre les humanistes de Paris et ceux d'Avignon (1394–1420)*. Geneva and Paris: Droz, 1969.

Ouy, Gilbert. "Une énigme codicologique: Les signatures des cahiers dans les manuscrits autographes de Christine de Pizan." In *Calames et Cahiers: Mélanges de codicologie et de paléographie offerts à Léon Gilissen*, edited by Jacques Lemaire and Emile van Balberghe, 119–31. Brussels: Centre d'Etude des Manuscrits, 1985.

———. "Paris, l'un des principaux foyers de l'humanisme en Europe au début du XVe siècle." *Bulletin de la Société de l'Histoire de Paris et de l'Ile de France* 94–95 (1967–68): 71–98.

———, and Christine Reno. "Les hésitations de Christine: Etude des variantes de graphies dans trois manuscrits autographes de Christine de Pizan." *Revue des Langues Romanes* 92 (1988): 265–86.

———, and Christine Reno. "Identification des Autographes de Christine de Pizan." *Scriptorium* 34 (1980): 221–38.

Paakinen, Ilse. "Gender and the Defense of Women in Christine de Pizan's Thought." PhD diss., University of Helsinki, 2016.

Parussa, Gabriella. "Christine de Pizan: Une lectrice avide et une vulgarisatrice fidèle des *Rumigacions du latin et des parleures des belles sciences*." In Brucker, *Traduction et adaptation* [cited above], 161–75.

———. "Veoir, oïr, et entendre: *L'Epistre Othea* et le cycle iconographique de deux manuscrits." In *Favola, mito ed altri saggi di letteratura e filologia in onore di Gianni Mombello*, edited by Antonella Amatuzzi and Paola Cifarelli, 335–57. Alessandria: Edizioni dell'Orso, 2004.

———, and Richard Trachsler. "*Or sus, alons ou champ des escriptures*. Encore sur l'orthographe de Christine de Pizan: l'intérêt des grands corpus." In Kennedy et al., *Contexts and Continuities* [cited above], 3:621–43.

Pasnau, Robert. *Thomas Aquinas on Human Nature*. Cambridge: Cambridge University Press, 2002.

Paupert, Anne. "'Te donrai preuve par exemples': Statut et fonction des exemples dans *Le Livre de la Cité des Dames* de Christine de Pizan." In *L'exemple historique: Norme et pédagogie de l'exemplarité du Moyen Age au XVIe siècle*, edited by Danièle Duport and Didier Lechat. *Elseneur* 31 (2016): 27–41.

Pellegrin, Elisabeth. "Les 'Remedia Amoris' d'Ovide: Texte scolaire médiéval." *Bibliothèque de l'Ecole des Chartes* 115 (1957): 172–79.

Phillips, John A. *Eve: The History of An Idea*. San Francisco: Harper and Row, 1984.

Piaget, Arthur. *Oton de Grandson: Sa vie et ses poésies*. Lausanne: Payot, 1941.

Planche, Alice. "La table comme signe de la classe: Le témoignage du *Roman du comte d'Anjou* (1316)." In *Manger et boire au Moyen Age: Actes du colloque de Nice*, Publications de la Faculté des Lettres et Sciences Humaines de Nice, edited by Denis Menjot, 2 vols., I:239–60. Paris: Belles Lettres, 1984.

Poirion, Daniel. *Le poète et le prince: L'évolution du lyrisme courtois de Guillaume de Machaut à Charles d'Orléans.* Grenoble: Allier, 1965; rpt. Geneva: Slatkine, 1978.

———, dir. *Grundriss der romanischen Literaturen des Mittelalters.* Vol. 8.1: *La littérature française aux XIV*[e] *et XV*[e] *siècles.* Edited by Armin Biermann and Dagmar Tillmann-Bartylla. Heidelberg: Carl Winter Universitätsverlag, 1988.

Quilligan, Maureen. *The Allegory of Female Authority: Christine de Pizan's* Cité des Dames. Ithaca, NY, and London: Cornell University Press, 1991.

Renck, Anneliese Pollock. *Female Authorship, Patronage, and Translation in Late Medieval France: From Christine de Pizan to Louise Labé.* Turnhout: Brepols, 2018.

Reno, Christine. "Christine de Pizan: 'At Best a Contradictory Figure'?" In *Politics, Gender and Genre: The Political Thought of Christine de Pizan*, edited by Margaret Brabant, 171–91. Boulder, CO: Westview, 1992.

———. "Christine de Pizan: Feminism and Irony." In Beck, Mombello, and Simone, *Seconda Miscellanea* [cited above], 125–33.

———. "Encore des néologismes de Christine de Pizan." In *De Christine de Pizan à Hans Robert Jauss: Etudes offertes à Earl Jeffrey Richards par ses collègues et amis*, edited by Danièle Buschinger and Roy Rosenstein. *Médiévales* 63 (2017): 135–44.

———. "Feminist Aspects of Christine de Pizan's 'Epistre d'Othea a Hector.'" *Studi francesi* 71 (1980): 271–76.

Ribémont, Bernard, ed. *Ecrire pour dire: Etudes sur le dit médiéval.* Paris: Klincksieck, 1990.

Richards, Earl Jeffrey. "Christine de Pizan and Jean Gerson: An Intellectual Friendship." In Campbell and Margolis, *Christine de Pizan 2000* [cited above], 197–208.

———. "Introduction: Returning to a 'Gracious Debate': The Intellectual Context of the Epistolary Exchange of the Debate about the *Roman de la Rose*." In McWebb, *Debating the* Roman de la Rose [cited above], xxi–xxxvi.

———. "Jean Gerson's Writings to His Sisters and Christine de Pizan's *Livre des Trois Vertus*: An Intellectual Dialogue Culminating in Friendship." In *Virtue Ethics for Women 1250–1500,* edited by Karen Green and Constant Mews, 81–98. Dordrecht: Springer, 2011.

———. "Justice in the *Summa* of St. Thomas Aquinas, in Late Medieval Marian Devotional Writings and in the Works of Christine de Pizan." In *Christine de Pizan: Une femme de science, une femme de lettres*, edited by Juliette Dor, Marie-Elisabeth Henneau, and Bernard Ribémont, 95–114. Paris: Honoré Champion, 2008.

———. "Rejecting Essentialism and Gendered Writing: The Case of Christine de Pizan." In Chance, *Gender and Text* [cited above], 96–131.

———. "*Seulette a part*'—The 'Little Woman on the Sidelines' Takes Up Her Pen: The Letters of Christine de Pizan." In *Dear Sister: Medieval Women and the Epistolary Genre*, edited by Karen Cherewatuk and Ulrike Wiethaus, 139–70. Philadelphia: University of Pennsylvania Press, 1993.

———, ed. *Christine de Pizan and Medieval French Lyric*. Gainesville: University Press of Florida, 1988.

———, ed., with Joan Williamson, Nadia Margolis, and Christine Reno. *Reinterpreting Christine de Pizan: Essays in Honor of Charity Cannon Willard*. Athens, GA: University of Georgia Press, 1992.

———, Liliane Dulac, and Delphine Reix. "Creating New Political and Allegorical Forms of Discourse and the Meaning of the Word 'Moral' in the Works of Christine de Pizan." In *"Ton nom sera reluisant aprés toy par longue memoire": Etudes sur Christine de Pizan*, edited by Anna Loba, 85–103. Poznan: Uniwersytet im. Adama Mickiewicza, 2017.

Riddy, Felicity. "Women Talking about the Things of God: A Late Medieval Subculture." In *Women and Literature in Britain, 1150–1500*, edited by Carol M. Meale, 104–27. Cambridge: Cambridge University Press, 1993.

Ruether, Rosemary Radford. *Women and Redemption: A Theological History*. 2nd ed. Minneapolis: Fortress Press, 2012.

Schaefer, Lucie. "Die Illustrationen zu den Handschriften der Christine de Pizan." *Marburger Jahrbuch für Kunstwissenschaft* 10 (1937): 119–208.

Schertz, Claire-Marie. "Autour de Christine de Pizan: Entre lyrisme courtois et engagement politique." *COnTEXTES* 13 (2013). <https://journals.openedition.org/contextes/5798>.

Semple, Benjamin M. "Christine de Pizan's Phenomenology of Beauty in the Lyric and the Dream Vision." In Richards, *Medieval French Lyric* [cited above], 187–205.

———. "The Critique of Knowledge as Power: The Limits of Philosophy and Theology in Christine de Pizan." In Desmond, *Categories of Difference* [cited above], 108–27.

Solente, Suzanne. "Christine de Pisan." In *Histoire littéraire de la France*, 40:335–422. Paris: Imprimerie Nationale, 1974. Also released as a pre-print, Paris: Imprimerie Nationale and Klincksieck, 1969.

Solterer, Helen. "Fiction versus Defamation: The Quarrel over the *Romance of the Rose*." *Medieval History Journal* 2 (1999): 111–41.

———. *The Master and Minerva: Disputing Women in French Medieval Culture*. Berkeley: University of California Press, 1995.

Sterling, Charles. *La peinture médiévale à Paris 1300–1500*. 2 vols. Paris: Bibliothèque des Arts / Fondation Wildenstein, 1987–90.

Stone, Louise W. "Un proverbe du moyen âge: Force paist le pré." *Zeitschrift für romanische Philologie* 73, nos. 1–2 (2009): 145–59.

Strubel, Armand. "Roman de la Rose." In *Dictionnaire du Moyen Age* [cited below], 1243–44.

Summit, Jennifer. "Women and Authorship." In Dinshaw and Wallace, *Medieval Women's Writing*, 91–108.

Swift, Helen J. *Gender, Writing, and Performance: Men Defending Women in Late Medieval France, 1440–1538*. Oxford: Oxford University Press, 2008.

Taylor, Jane H. M. "Lyric Poetry of the Later Middle Ages." In Gaunt and Kay, *Medieval French Literature* [cited above], 153–66.

Thompson, John Jay. "Medea in Christine de Pizan's *Mutacion de Fortune*, or How to Be a Better Mother." *Forum for Modern Language Studies* 35 (1999): 158–74.

Three Medieval Views of Women: "La Contenance des Fames," "Le Bien des Fames," "Le Blasme de Fames." Translated and edited by Gloria K. Fiero, Wendy Pfeffer, and Mathé Allain. New Haven, CT, and London: Yale University Press, 1989.

Tobler, Adolf, ed. *Li Proverbe au vilain*. Leipzig: S. Hirzel, 1895.

Tuve, Rosemond. *Allegorical Imagery: Some Mediæval Books and their Posterity.* Princeton, NJ: Princeton University Press, 1966.

Van Hemelryck, Tania, and Christine Reno. "Dans l'atelier de Christine de Pizan. Le manuscrit Harley 4431." In *Du scriptorium à l'atelier: Copistes et enlumineurs dans la conception du livre manuscrit au Moyen Age*, *Pecia* 13 (2010): 267–86.]

Vergne, Frédéric. *La Bibliothèque du Prince. Château de Chantilly. Les Manuscrits.* Paris: Editerra, 1995.

Videt-Reix, Delphine. "Christine de Pizan et la poétique de la justice." Diss., Aix-Marseille Université, 2011. <www.theses.fr/2011AIX10006.pdf>.

Villela-Petit, Inès. "La France et le gothique international (1360–1430)." In *L'Art du Moyen Age en France*, edited by Philippe Plagnieux, 382–441. Paris: Citadelles et Mazenod, 2010.

———. *Le Gothique international: L'art en France au temps de Charles VI*. Paris: Hazan / Musée du Louvre, 2004.

Walters, Lori. "The Figure of the *Seulette* in the Works of Christine de Pizan and Jean Gerson." In Dulac et al., "*Desireuse de plus avant enquerre*" [cited above], 119–39.

———. "*Translatio Studii*: Christine de Pizan's Self-portrayal in Two Lyric Poems and in the *Livre de la mutacion de Fortune*." In Richards, *Medieval French Lyric* [cited above], 155–67.

White, Hugh. *Nature, Sex, and Goodness in a Medieval Literary Tradition.* Oxford and New York: Oxford University Press, 2000.

Willard, Charity Cannon. *Christine de Pizan: Her Life and Works.* New York: Persea, 1984.

———. "Christine de Pizan's *Cent Ballades d'Amant et de Dame*: Criticism of Courtly Love." In *Court and Poet: Selected Proceedings of the Third Congress of the International Courtly Literature Society*, edited by Glyn S. Burgess, 357–64. Liverpool: Francis Cairns, 1981.

———. " Christine de Pizan's Clock of Temperance." *L'Esprit créateur* 2 (1962): 149–54.

Woledge, Brian. "Le thème de la pauvrété dans la *Mutacion de Fortune* de Christine de Pisan." In *Fin du Moyen Age et Renaissance* [cited above], 97–106.

Wolfthal, Diane. *Images of Rape: The "Heroic" Tradition and Its Alternatives.* New York: Cambridge University Press, 1999.

———. "'Douleur sur toutes autres': Revisualizing the Rape Script in the *Epistre Othea* and the *Cité des dames*." In Desmond, *Categories of Difference* [cited above], 41–70.

Zimmerman, Margarete. "Christine de Pizan et les féminismes autour de 1900." In *Sur le chemin de longue étude. . . .* Actes du colloque d'Orléans (juillet 1995), edited by Bernard Ribémont, 183–204. Paris: Honoré Champion, 1998.

———. "The *Querelle des Femmes* as a Cultural Studies Paradigm." In *Time, Space and Women's Lives in Early Modern Europe*, edited by Anne Jacobson Schutte, Thomas Kuehn, and Silvana Seidel Menchi, 17–28. Kirksville, MO: Truman State University Press, 2001.

———, and Dina De Rentiis, eds. *The City of Scholars: New Approaches to Christine de Pizan*. Berlin and New York: Walter De Gruyter, 1994.

Reference Works

Arden, Heather M., ed. *The Roman de la Rose: An Annotated Bibliography.* New York and London: Garland, 1993.

Bel, Catherine, and Herman Braet, eds. *De la Rose: Texte, image, fortune.* Louvain, Paris, and Dudley, MA: Peeters, 2006.

Blanchard, Joël, and Michel Quereuil, *Lexique de Christine de Pizan: Matériaux pour le Dictionnaire du Moyen Français.* Paris: Klincksieck, 1999.

Braet, Herman. *Nouvelle bibliographie du* Roman de la Rose. Louvain, Paris, and Bristol, CT: Peeters, 2017.

Brucker, Charles. *Lexique de Nicole Oresme.* Part of the *Dictionnaire du Moyen Français* [*DMF*] *(1330–1500).* Nancy, France: ATILF [Analyse et traitement informatique de la langue française], Université de Lorraine. <http://www.atilf.fr/dmf/Oresme/>.

Bulletin mensuel de la librairie Damascène Morgand, vol. 4, no. 23 (November 1888), 721–876.

Chantilly. Le Cabinet des Livres. Manuscrits. 3 vols. Paris: Plon-Nourrit, 1900.

Deferrari, Roy J. *A Latin-English Dictionary of St. Thomas Aquinas, based on the* Summa Theologica *and Selected Passages of His Other Works.* Boston: St. Paul Editions, 1960.

———, and M. Inviolata Barry, ed., with the technical collaboration of Ignatius McGuiness. *A Lexicon of St. Thomas Aquinas.* Washington, DC: Catholic University of America Press, 1948–49.

Dictionnaire de la langue française du seizième siècle. Edited by Edmond Huguet. 7 vols. Paris: Edouard Champion, 1925–67; rpt. Paris: Garnier, 2004.

Dictionnaire du Moyen Age. Edited by Claude Gauvard, Alain de Libéra, and Michel Zink. Paris: Presses universitaires de France, 2002.

Dictionnaire du Moyen Français (1330–1500) (*DMF*). <http://www.atilf.fr/dmf/>.

Dictionnaire étymologique de l'ancien français (*DEAF*). Edited by Kurt Baldinger, with Jean-Denis Gendron and Georges Straka. Quebec: Presses de l'Université Laval; Tübingen: Niemeyer; Paris: Klincksieck, 1974–2012.

Dictionnaire étymologique de l'ancien français. Complément bibliographique 2016. Edited by Frankwalt Möhren. Berlin and Boston: De Gruyter Akademie Forschung, 2016.

Farmer, David Hugh. *The Oxford Dictionary of Saints.* Oxford: Oxford University Press, 2004.

Französisches etymologisches Wörterbuch (*FEW*). Edited by Walther von Wartburg. Bonn: Klopp, 1922–2003.

Hassell, James Woodrow, Jr. *Middle French Proverbs, Sentences, and Proverbial Phrases.* Toronto: Pontifical Institute of Mediaeval Studies, 1982.

Kennedy, Angus J. *Christine de Pizan: A Bibliographical Guide.* London: Grant and Cutler, 1984.

———. *Christine de Pizan: A Bibliographical Guide.* Supplement. London: Grant and Cutler, 1994.

———. *Christine de Pizan: A Bibliographical Guide. Supplement 2.* Woodbridge, UK, and Rochester, NY: Tamesis, 2004.

Murphy, James J. *Medieval Rhetoric: A Select Bibliography.* 2nd edition. Toronto: University of Toronto Press, 1989.

The New Briquet, Jubilee Edition. A Facsimile of the 1907 edition with supplementary material contributed by a number of scholars. Edited by Allan Stevenson. 4 vols. Amsterdam: The Paper Publications Society, 1968.

Ouy, Gilbert, Christine Reno, and Inès Villela-Petit, with Olivier Delsaux and Tania van Hemelryck, editors and collaborators, and with the advice of James Laidlaw and Marie-Thérèse Gousset. *Album Christine de Pizan.* Turnhout: Brepols, 2012.

Palsgrave, John. *L'Eclaircissement de la langue française par Jean Palsgrave, suivi de la Grammaire de Giles du Guez.* Edited by François Génin. Paris: Imprimerie Nationale, 1852.

Paris, BnF, Moreau 1655. Sainte-Palaye, Jean Baptiste de La Curne. *Suite des notices de Manuscrits de France.* Vol. 3, Notices 401–600.

Paris 1400: Les arts sous Charles VI. Edited by Elisabeth Taburet-Delahaye, François Avril et al. Paris: Arthème Fayard / Réunion des musées nationaux, 2004.

Piccard, Gerhard. *Wasserzeichen: Blatt, Blume, Baum.* Stuttgart: W. Kohlhammer, 1982.

Pope, Mildred K. *From Latin to Modern French, with Especial Consideration of Anglo-Norman: Phonology and Morphology.* Rev. ed., Manchester: Manchester University Press, 1952.

Répertoire général et méthodique de la librairie Morgand et Fatout. Paris: Damascène Morgand and Charles Fatout, 1882.

Robinson, J. Armitage, and M. R. James. *The Manuscripts of Westminster Abbey.* Cambridge: Cambridge University Press, 1909.

Roman de la Rose Digital Library. Part of the Digital Library of Medieval Manuscripts. Johns Hopkins University Sheridan Libraries and Bibliothèque nationale de France. <http://dlmm.library.jhu.edu/en/romandelarose/>.

Schütz, Ludwig. *Thomas-Lexikon.* <http://www.corpusthomisticum.org/tl.html>.

Yenal, Edith. *Christine de Pisan: A Bibliography of Writings by Her and about Her.* Metuchen, NJ, and London: Scarecrow Press, 1982.

———. *Christine de Pizan: A Bibliography.* 2nd ed. Metuchen, NJ, and London: Scarecrow Press, 1989.

Index of Proper Nouns and Selected Topics in The God of Love's Letter

Numbers following entries refer to verses in the English translation.

Index of Proper Nouns and Selected Topics in The Tale of the Rose

Numbers following entries refer to verses in the English translation.

The Other Voice in Early Modern Europe: The Toronto Series

FOUNDING EDITORS Margaret L. King *and* Albert Rabil, Jr.

SERIES EDITOR Margaret L. King

SERIES EDITOR, ENGLISH TEXTS Elizabeth H. Hageman

Series Titles

MADRE MARÍA ROSA
Journey of Five Capuchin Nuns
Edited and translated by Sarah E. Owens
Volume 1, 2009

GIOVAN BATTISTA ANDREINI
Love in the Mirror: *A Bilingual Edition*
Edited and translated by Jon R. Snyder
Volume 2, 2009

RAYMOND DE SABANAC AND SIMONE ZANACCHI
Two Women of the Great Schism: The Revelations *of Constance de Rabastens by Raymond de Sabanac and* Life of the Blessed Ursulina of Parma *by Simone Zanacchi*
Edited and translated by Renate Blumenfeld-Kosinski and Bruce L. Venarde
Volume 3, 2010

OLIVA SABUCO DE NANTES BARRERA
The True Medicine
Edited and translated by Gianna Pomata
Volume 4, 2010

LOUISE-GENEVIÈVE GILLOT DE SAINCTONGE
Dramatizing Dido, Circe, and Griselda
Edited and translated by Janet Levarie Smarr
Volume 5, 2010

PERNETTE DU GUILLET
Complete Poems: A Bilingual Edition
Edited with introduction and notes by Karen Simroth James
Poems translated by Marta Rijn Finch
Volume 6, 2010

ANTONIA PULCI
Saints' Lives and Bible Stories for the Stage: A Bilingual Edition
Edited by Elissa B. Weaver
Translated by James Wyatt Cook
Volume 7, 2010

VALERIA MIANI
Celinda, A Tragedy: *A Bilingual Edition*
Edited with an introduction by Valeria Finucci
Translated by Julia Kisacky
Annotated by Valeria Finucci and Julia Kisacky
Volume 8, 2010

Enchanted Eloquence: Fairy Tales by Seventeenth-Century French Women Writers
Edited and translated by Lewis C. Seifert and Domna C. Stanton
Volume 9, 2010

Gottfried Wilhelm Leibniz, Sophie, Electress of Hanover and Queen Sophie Charlotte of Prussia
Leibniz and the Two Sophies: The Philosophical Correspondence
Edited and translated by Lloyd Strickland
Volume 10, 2011

In Dialogue with the Other Voice in Sixteenth-Century Italy: Literary and Social Contexts for Women's Writing
Edited by Julie D. Campbell and Maria Galli Stampino
Volume 11, 2011

Sister Giustina Niccolini
The Chronicle of Le Murate
Edited and translated by Saundra Weddle
Volume 12, 2011

Liubov Krichevskaya
No Good without Reward: Selected Writings: A Bilingual Edition
Edited and translated by Brian James Baer
Volume 13, 2011

Elizabeth Cooke Hoby Russell
The Writings of an English Sappho
Edited by Patricia Phillippy
With translations from Greek and Latin by Jaime Goodrich
Volume 14, 2011

Lucrezia Marinella
Exhortations to Women and to Others If They Please
Edited and translated by Laura Benedetti
Volume 15, 2012

Margherita Datini
Letters to Francesco Datini
Translated by Carolyn James and Antonio Pagliaro
Volume 16, 2012

Delarivier Manley and Mary Pix
English Women Staging Islam, 1696–1707
Edited and introduced by Bernadette Andrea
Volume 17, 2012

Cecilia del Nacimiento
Journeys of a Mystic Soul in Poetry and Prose
Introduction and prose translations by Kevin Donnelly
Poetry translations by Sandra Sider
Volume 18, 2012

Lady Margaret Douglas and Others
The Devonshire Manuscript: A Women's Book of Courtly Poetry
Edited and introduced by Elizabeth Heale
Volume 19, 2012

Arcangela Tarabotti
Letters Familiar and Formal
Edited and translated by Meredith K. Ray and Lynn Lara Westwater
Volume 20, 2012

Pere Torrellas and Juan de Flores
Three Spanish Querelle *Texts:* Grisel and Mirabella, The Slander against Women, *and* The Defense of Ladies against Slanderers*: A Bilingual Edition and Study*
Edited and translated by Emily C. Francomano
Volume 21, 2013

Barbara Torelli Benedetti
Partenia, a Pastoral Play*: A Bilingual Edition*
Edited and translated by Lisa Sampson and Barbara Burgess-Van Aken
Volume 22, 2013

François Rousset, Jean Liebault, Jacques Guillemeau, Jacques Duval and Louis de Serres
Pregnancy and Birth in Early Modern France: Treatises by Caring Physicians and Surgeons (1581–1625)
Edited and translated by Valerie Worth-Stylianou
Volume 23, 2013

Mary Astell
The Christian Religion, as Professed by a Daughter of the Church of England
Edited by Jacqueline Broad
Volume 24, 2013

Sophia of Hanover
Memoirs (1630–1680)
Edited and translated by Sean Ward
Volume 25, 2013

Katherine Austen
Book M: *A London Widow's Life Writings*
Edited by Pamela S. Hammons
Volume 26, 2013

Anne Killigrew
"My Rare Wit Killing Sin": Poems of a Restoration Courtier
Edited by Margaret J. M. Ezell
Volume 27, 2013

Tullia d'Aragona and Others
The Poems and Letters of Tullia d'Aragona and Others: A Bilingual Edition
Edited and translated by Julia L. Hairston
Volume 28, 2014

Luisa de Carvajal y Mendoza
The Life and Writings of Luisa de Carvajal y Mendoza
Edited and translated by Anne J. Cruz
Volume 29, 2014

Russian Women Poets of the Eighteenth and Early Nineteenth Centuries: A Bilingual Edition
Edited and translated by Amanda Ewington
Volume 30, 2014

Jacques Du Bosc
L'Honnête Femme: The Respectable Woman in Society *and the* New Collection of Letters and Responses by Contemporary Women
Edited and translated by Sharon Diane Nell and Aurora Wolfgang
Volume 31, 2014

Lady Hester Pulter
Poems, Emblems, *and* The Unfortunate Florinda
Edited by Alice Eardley
Volume 32, 2014

Jeanne Flore
Tales and Trials of Love, Concerning Venus's Punishment of Those Who Scorn True Love and Denounce Cupid's Sovereignity: *A Bilingual Edition and Study*
Edited and translated by Kelly Digby Peebles
Poems translated by Marta Rijn Finch
Volume 33, 2014

Veronica Gambara
Complete Poems: A Bilingual Edition
Critical introduction by Molly M. Martin
Edited and translated by Molly M. Martin and Paola Ugolini
Volume 34, 2014

Catherine de Médicis and Others
Portraits of the Queen Mother: Polemics, Panegyrics, Letters
Translation and study by Leah L. Chang and Katherine Kong
Volume 35, 2014

Françoise Pascal, Marie-Catherine Desjardins, Antoinette Deshoulières, and Catherine Durand
Challenges to Traditional Authority: Plays by French Women Authors, 1650–1700
Edited and translated by Perry Gethner
Volume 36, 2015

Franciszka Urszula Radziwiłłowa
Selected Drama and Verse
Edited by Patrick John Corness and Barbara Judkowiak
Translated by Patrick John Corness
Translation Editor Aldona Zwierzyńska-Coldicott
Introduction by Barbara Judkowiak
Volume 37, 2015

Diodata Malvasia
Writings on the Sisters of San Luca and Their Miraculous Madonna
Edited and translated by Danielle Callegari and Shannon McHugh
Volume 38, 2015

Margaret Van Noort
Spiritual Writings of Sister Margaret of the Mother of God (1635–1643)
Edited by Cordula van Wyhe
Translated by Susan M. Smith
Volume 39, 2015

Giovan Francesco Straparola
The Pleasant Nights
Edited and translated by Suzanne Magnanini
Volume 40, 2015

Angélique de Saint-Jean Arnauld d'Andilly
Writings of Resistance
Edited and translated by John J. Conley, S.J.
Volume 41, 2015

Francesco Barbaro
The Wealth of Wives: A Fifteenth-Century Marriage Manual
Edited and translated by Margaret L. King
Volume 42, 2015

Jeanne d'Albret
Letters from the Queen of Navarre with an Ample Declaration
Edited and translated by Kathleen M. Llewellyn, Emily E. Thompson, and Colette H. Winn
Volume 43, 2016

Bathsua Makin and Mary More with a reply to More by Robert Whitehall
Educating English Daughters: Late Seventeenth-Century Debates
Edited by Frances Teague and Margaret J. M. Ezell
Associate Editor Jessica Walker
Volume 44, 2016

Anna Stanisławska
Orphan Girl: A Transaction, or an Account of the Entire Life of an Orphan Girl by way of Plaintful Threnodies in the Year 1685: *The Aesop Episode*
Verse translation, introduction, and commentary by Barry Keane
Volume 45, 2016

Alessandra Macinghi Strozzi
Letters to Her Sons, 1447–1470
Edited and translated by Judith Bryce
Volume 46, 2016

Mother Juana de la Cruz
Mother Juana de la Cruz, 1481–1534: Visionary Sermons
Edited by Jessica A. Boon and Ronald E. Surtz
Introductory material and notes by Jessica A. Boon
Translated by Ronald E. Surtz and Nora Weinerth
Volume 47, 2016

Claudine-Alexandrine Guérin de Tencin
Memoirs of the Count of Comminge *and* The Misfortunes of Love
Edited and translated by Jonathan Walsh
Foreword by Michel Delon
Volume 48, 2016

Feliciana Enríquez de Guzmán, Ana Caro Mallén, and Sor Marcela de San Félix
Women Playwrights of Early Modern Spain
Edited by Nieves Romero-Díaz and Lisa Vollendorf
Translated and annotated by Harley Erdman
Volume 49, 2016

Anna Trapnel
Anna Trapnel's Report and Plea; or, A Narrative of Her Journey from London into Cornwall
Edited by Hilary Hinds
Volume 50, 2016

María Vela y Cueto
Autobiography and Letters of a Spanish Nun
Edited by Susan Diane Laningham
Translated by Jane Tar
Volume 51, 2016

Christine de Pizan
The Book of the Mutability of Fortune
Edited and translated by Geri L. Smith
Volume 52, 2017

Marguerite d'Auge, Renée Burlamacchi, and Jeanne du Laurens
Sin and Salvation in Early Modern France: Three Women's Stories
Edited, and with an introduction by Colette H. Winn
Translated by Nicholas Van Handel and Colette H. Winn
Volume 53, 2017

Isabella d'Este
Selected Letters
Edited and translated by Deanna Shemek
Volume 54, 2017

Ippolita Maria Sforza
Duchess and Hostage in Renaissance Naples: Letters and Orations
Edited and translated by Diana Robin and Lynn Lara Westwater
Volume 55, 2017

Louise Bourgeois
Midwife to the Queen of France: Diverse Observations
Translated by Stephanie O'Hara
Edited by Alison Klairmont Lingo
Volume 56, 2017

Christine de Pizan
Othea's Letter to Hector
Edited and translated by Renate Blumenfeld-Kosinski and Earl Jeffrey Richards
Volume 57, 2017

Marie-Geneviève-Charlotte Thiroux d'Arconville
Selected Philosophical, Scientific, and Autobiographical Writings
Edited and translated by Julie Candler Hayes
Volume 58, 2018

Lady Mary Wroth
Pamphilia to Amphilanthus *in Manuscript and Print*
Edited by Ilona Bell
Texts by Steven W. May and Ilona Bell
Volume 59, 2017

Witness, Warning, and Prophecy: Quaker Women's Writing, 1655–1700
Edited by Teresa Feroli and Margaret Olofson Thickstun
Volume 60, 2018

Symphorien Champier
The Ship of Virtuous Ladies
Edited and translated by Todd W. Reeser
Volume 61, 2018

Isabella Andreini
Mirtilla, A Pastoral: *A Bilingual Edition*
Edited by Valeria Finucci
Translated by Julia Kisacky
Volume 62, 2018

Margherita Costa
The Buffoons, A Ridiculous Comedy: *A Bilingual Edition*
Edited and translated by Sara E. Díaz and Jessica Goethals
Volume 63, 2018

Margaret Cavendish, Duchess of Newcastle
Poems and Fancies *with* The Animal Parliament
Edited by Brandie R. Siegfried
Volume 64, 2018

Margaret Fell
Women's Speaking Justified *and Other Pamphlets*
Edited by Jane Donawerth and Rebecca M. Lush
Volume 65, 2018

Mary Wroth, Jane Cavendish, and Elizabeth Brackley
Women's Household Drama: Loves Victorie, A Pastorall, *and* The concealed Fansyes
Edited by Marta Straznicky and Sara Mueller
Volume 66, 2018

Eleonora Fonseca Pimentel
From Arcadia to Revolution: The Neapolitan Monitor *and Other Writings*
Edited and translated by Verina R. Jones
Volume 67, 2019

Charlotte Arbaleste Duplessis-Mornay, Anne de Chaufepié, and Anne Marguerite Petit Du Noyer
The Huguenot Experience of Persecution and Exile: Three Women's Stories
Edited by Colette H. Winn
Translated by Lauren King and Colette H. Winn
Volume 68, 2019

Anne Bradstreet
Poems and Meditations
Edited by Margaret Olofson Thickstun
Volume 69, 2019

Arcangela Tarabotti
Antisatire: *In Defense of Women, against Francesco Buoninsegni*
Edited and translated by Elissa B. Weaver
Volume 70, 2020

Mary Franklin and Hannah Burton
She Being Dead Yet Speaketh: The Franklin Family Papers
Edited by Vera J. Camden
Volume 71, 2020

Lucrezia Marinella
Love Enamored and Driven Mad
Edited and translated by Janet E. Gomez and Maria Galli Stampino
Volume 72, 2020

Arcangela Tarabotti
Convent Paradise
Edited and translated by Meredith K. Ray and Lynn Lara Westwater
Volume 73, 2020

Gabrielle-Suzanne Barbot de Villeneuve
Beauty and the Beast: *The Original Story*
Edited and translated by Aurora Wolfgang
Volume 74, 2020

Flaminio Scala
The Fake Husband, A Comedy
Edited and translated by Rosalind Kerr
Volume 75, 2020

Anne Vaughan Lock
Selected Poetry, Prose, and Translations, with Contextual Materials
Edited by Susan M. Felch
Volume 76, 2021

Camilla Erculiani
Letters on Natural Philosophy: *The Scientific Correspondence of a Sixteenth-Century Pharmacist, with Related Texts*
Edited by Eleonora Carinci
Translated by Hannah Marcus
Foreword by Paula Findlen
Volume 77, 2021

Regina Salomea Pilsztynowa
My Life's Travels and Adventures: *An Eighteenth-Century Oculist in the Ottoman Empire and the European Hinterland*
Edited and translated by Władysław Roczniak
Volume 78, 2021